THE LAW'S STRANGEST CASES

THE LAW'S STRANGEST CASES

Extraordinary but true incidents from over
five centuries of legal history

Peter Seddon

Robson Books

First published in Great Britain in 2001 by Robson Books,
10 Blenheim Court, Brewery Road, London N7 9NT

A member of the Chrysalis Group plc

British Library Cataloguing in Publication Data
A catalogue record for this title is available from the British Library.

ISBN 1 86105 463 7

Typeset by SX Composing DTP, Rayleigh, Essex
Printed and bound in Great Britain by Creative Print and
Design, (Ebbw Vale), Wales.

Contents

Introduction

Few laymen would claim to be fascinated by accountancy or banking, exciting and rivetingly interesting though those professions undoubtedly are. Yet legal matters are altogether different, for equally few laymen would claim *not* to be seduced by the stories of murder, intrigue, crime, punishment and the pursuit of justice that have made 'The Law' such a perennially popular subject, more on a par with sport and the entertainment industry than its close relations in the other professions. With that in mind I put it to you that the law is 'theatre' – with a cast of thousands, a multitude of heroes and villains, improvised scripts and cliffhanger endings never revealed until the very last second of the final act.

It is for reasons of entertainment, therefore, that I offer the curious accounts in *The Law's Strangest Cases*, a collection of true stories that illustrate the idiosyncrasies of legal (and illegal) doings throughout centuries of history.

The choice at my disposal was mind-boggling. It would have been an easy task simply to fill the book with celebrated murder trials, but I set out instead to track down a much broader range of cases that would illustrate the many different facets of the law and the larger-than-life characters who seek either to make it or break it.

The result is by definition a purely personal selection in which humour, oddity and the macabre loom large. There are medieval tales such as the mass trial of moles for vandalism ('The Accused Have Gone to Ground') and the most outlandish admission of guilt of all time ('An Imaginative Confession'). There are astonishing survivals of the death penalty ('Well, I'll Be Hanged!'), the 'corpse' who gave spoken evidence at his own inquest ('The Eleventh Witness') and the heartening story of Capstick, the most diligent police officer of all time ('Capstick Makes an Impression').

Murder inevitably rears its ugly but strangely irresistible head in a number of my selections. 'Trust Me, I'm a Doctor' would be much too far-fetched a story even for Victorian melodrama, yet, thanks to Harold Shipman, the doctor with the worst bedside manner of all time, that all-too-true account comes almost at the end of the book at the very dawn of the 'civilised' twentieth century.

Were Shipman's evil crimes even worse than Carl Panzram's? You must be the judge of that, but only if you can first brave reading the stomach-churning evidence ('The Worst Criminal of All Time').

Other murder cases display a more light-hearted touch. Consider the murderess who collected rent from her mummified victim for 21 years ('A Very Quiet Tenant') or the wishful thinker who gave himself away by describing himself in a job application as 'a widower' *before* he'd bumped off his wife ('A Man Ahead of His Time').

I had imagined that judges might add a sober balance to such ridiculous tales as the serial cutlery-swallower ('A Knife-and-Fork Job') but how wrong I was, for time and again throughout my research the men and women on the bench simply demanded inclusion for reasons every bit as bizarre. I could no more leave out the inimitable lawmaking of the US judge Roy Bean ('Way Out West') than I could omit the English judge whose penchant for whisky and cigarettes landed him with a smuggling conviction ('One Case Too Many'). Nor could the Welsh judge who had his wig stolen in court ('A Symbolic Crime') and the judge who took forty winks during a murder trial ('A Sound (Asleep?) Verdict') escape inclusion. Barristers and solicitors, too, have had their moments. 'Cusack's Law' is the uniquely triumphant tale of the man who both prosecuted and defended at the same trial, and rather less triumphant were the solicitor arrested in court ('A Bad Day at the Office') and the American barrister who appealed for a verdict to be reversed because the opposition had broken wind throughout his closing speech ('The Most Desperate Appeal Ever').

Other cases were inspired by the peculiar characteristics of linguistic interpretation ('When Is a Beach Not a Beach?') and legal jargon ('Straight Talk At Last') and there are those in which words provoked celebrated libel cases ('No Half-Measures') or led to abject humiliation ('A Self-Inflicted Wound').

A number of animals get a look-in, too. 'Not So Dumb Witness' recalls the story of Tetter the dog, who gave winning evidence at an industrial tribunal, and the most famous snail in legal history is honoured in a celebrated case from the 1920s, which blazed a trail to the compensation culture we know today ('Once Pickled, Forever Toasted').

Some court proceedings took a distinctly odd turn because the defendants just couldn't take the consequences: striptease ('The Full Monty'), attempted suicide ('An Uncommonly Violent Protest') and serial absenteeism ('Heartily Sick of the Law') all provided unexpected entertainment, as too did the most irritating juror of all time ('Eleven Just Men and Wilson') and the evil desperado who failed to appear in court because he simply didn't exist ('Call Brendan Michael Forrester').

Most of the hundred or so cases are from Britain, with the Old Bailey inevitably figuring prominently, but I found it impossible to exclude a number of cases from the United States and elsewhere, as my research quickly revealed that strangeness is as likely to strike in Sydney and New York, or at the nether regions of Carlisle and Colchester, as at the very heart of the English legal system itself.

My sources were many and I am particularly indebted to the

anonymous scribes who compiled *The All England Law Reports* and the many accomplished, more 'popular' writers whose published works alerted me to cases I might have otherwise overlooked and provided leads and ideas to follow up.

Although I studied law as a module at university, I did not enter the profession, nor, thankfully, have I ever been in the dock, so I have approached the subject as an experienced practitioner of 'strangeology', but through the eyes of a legal layman, as it was my declared intention never to make *The Law's Strangest Cases* a dry legal textbook.

I would like to thank friends and members of the legal profession for suggesting subject matter. Julie Bunyan and Ian Methven were particularly helpful in their prompting and the specialist knowledge of solicitor Terry Birch, notably regarding 'A Question of Entry', was invaluable, as too was Kate Ibbitson's assistance in reading the manuscript and making useful suggestions.

Finally I would like to thank Jeremy Robson and his editorial team at Robson Books for embracing the idea of *The Law's Strangest Cases* so enthusiastically and guiding it through to completion.

THE STRANGEST CASE
OF ALL TIME?

JERUSALEM, CIRCA AD 33

The accused apparently died at 3 p.m. on Friday, 3 April, AD 33, although strangely some say it was three years earlier. Others assert that he didn't die at all. The records are inconclusive. The method of execution was barbaric and there had been no proper trial, only a hastily convened mock court presided over by officials of varying degrees of corruption. That 'trial', moreover, was conducted under Jewish law within which the empowerment to pass a death sentence was questionable. The Jewish authorities overcame this trifling difficulty by trumping up suitably embellished charges and handing the prisoner over to the Roman authorities, who operated under a completely different legal code by which powers of execution were unlimited.

Yet the Roman Governor of Judea was sceptical of the charges against his newly delivered prisoner. Yes, he had entered Jerusalem during the week preceding the great festival of Passover. Yes, he had aroused great fervour among many of the 300,000 pilgrims gathered in the city. Yes, he had preached at the temple and overturned the stalls of merchants trying to conduct business around it. He was a dissident of sorts, it was true. Perhaps even a prophet, as his disciples were to claim. But was he really 'King of the Jews', a direct threat to Roman authority? And was he truly 'the son of God' or just a harmless traveller with ideas beyond his station, skilled at making capital from a gullible public?

The Roman Governor was tempted to release his charge, for it was his custom to grant freedom to one prisoner during the Passover festivities. He was, too, rather afraid of the reaction of the prisoner's followers if the death sentence was confirmed. He decided to pursue a novel judicial procedure, putting the vote to the gathered crowd of Jews.

He announced to the unruly throng that he found no fault with the man in his custody; but, despite his charismatic appeal in some quarters, the prisoner got the thumbs-down from the majority and was therefore sent to execution on nothing more than a public show of hands. To compound the treachery of this flagrant miscarriage of justice, another prisoner, Barabbas, a known murderer, was freed instead.

Before his execution the condemned man was humiliated, verbally taunted and beaten by guards. And, after being subjected to that brutality at the hands of authority, he was forced to walk at daybreak, heavily burdened, to the place of execution, where he was nailed to a wooden cross. It took six lingering hours for the death by crucifixion to run its course.

We might add other curious oddities to this astonishing account. For starters, the condemned man had been betrayed by a 'supergrass' who was one of his own gang. And, by way of further sensationalism, some reports confirmed that the crucified man, after he had been taken from the cross by his friends, came back to life three days later.

It is the sort of story with which 21st-century tabloid newspapers would have a field day. Was Pontius Pilate, the Roman Governor of Judea, really the villain of the piece? Or did that dubious honour fall to the Jewish high priest, Caiaphas, head of the 'kangaroo court' that contrived the prisoner's demise? Could someone dish the dirt on Barabbas, the reprieved murderer? We need an exclusive interview with the 'grass', Judas Iscariot – headline the piece THE KISS OF DEATH and offer him thirty shekels. Has anyone tracked down the 'dead' man, Jesus of Nazareth? Is he really still alive, or was it the 'resurrection men', the body snatchers, who left the rock-cut tomb devoid of a corpse? There have been reported sightings, but could there be an impostor on the loose? Just get that story!

All these questions and many more related to the case have assailed the troubled minds of every generation for nearly 2,000 years. Yet the accounts of the events in Jerusalem are tantalisingly at odds with each other. Even those written a few decades later based on eyewitness evidence offer disparate solutions. Should we believe St Luke or should we favour other chroniclers of the biblical age? What, after all, really *is* the Gospel truth?

Scholars have argued the case since time immemorial. Bitter wars have been fought over the principles involved. Followers of the Christian religion believe passionately that the accused *was* cruelly wronged and that he *did* rise again. Sceptics say it's all a load of bunkum, just a heavily embroidered folk tapestry with far too many loose ends showing.

The Temple Authorities v. Jesus of Nazareth is arguably the strangest legal case of all time, so enshrouded in mystique that the whole truth seems likely to remain undiscovered for eternity. As we go to press the jury is still out and seems set to deliberate for some time.

LADY MARION'S ORDEAL

HEREFORD ASSIZES, 1207

But for the legacy of King Alfred the Great (849–99), the ardent Lady Marion of Hereford might have been able to indulge in a spot of panky of the hanky variety without getting her fingers burnt. As it was, she was caught well and truly red-handed.

That Alfred burnt the cakes may merely be the stuff of legend. Of far greater certainty was the tireless effort of this most celebrated of Saxon kings in bringing a degree of much-needed unity to the disparate Saxon kingdoms he presided over when he became King of Wessex in 871.

And nowhere was his intelligent approach more influential than in the field of English law. No sooner had the 22-year-old taken the throne than his *Book of Laws* made its appearance, combining the best long-held but primitive legal customs of Kent and Mercia with those of Wessex, throwing in some good solid biblical guidelines for good measure and adding a hint of Germanic and Roman legislation to the eclectic mix.

The resulting Saxon Law, which was still going strong over 300 years later, was by no means the complex and much-lauded English legal system that came to be a watchword for 'justice' the world over, but it was a start, and Alfred's advice in what was known as his Golden Rule sounds pretty sensible over a millennium later: 'What ye will that other men should not do to you, do ye not to other men.'

It may be a basic reworking of a more famous biblical

guideline, but if Alfred's good citizens had followed his advice then all sorts of dastardly deeds might never have got beyond the cunning plan stage.

Alas 'boys will be boys' and a system of compensatory fines or atonements proved necessary to help control the behaviour of a populace that seemingly couldn't help itself. Killed any common labourers lately? A 200-shilling fine was sure to follow. What about poking out a serf's eye? A mere 50 shillings. And anyone prepared to cough up 3,600 shillings could really go for broke and bump off an archbishop (or eighteen labourers). Then there was adultery, which in Lady Marion's case seems to have been of the multiple variety. Combining it with murder wasn't a good idea, and the Hereford Assizes court papers for 1207 record that she was accused of 'procuring her husband's murder, because she had committed adultery with a great many men, and after his death all his goods went missing from the house'.

A number of Marion's suspected lovers fled the area once the hue and cry started and things didn't look good for the lady, whose rampant sexual appetite was about to give her a spot of bother.

'What an ordeal!' How many times do we hear that throwaway line these days? But in Saxon times the phrase had an all too real ring to it, for trial by ordeal was a standard way of establishing guilt or innocence in the days before trial by jury became the norm.

Ordeal was the Saxons' way of 'letting God decide', the *judicium Dei*. There were a number of options of varying unpleasantness and Lady Marion was duly called upon to face ordeal by iron.

Naturally enough the 'court' was a church. Present would be a sheriff of the shire, representing the peacekeeping force of the land, and a bishop, representing the celestial judge on high. The trial took place during Mass but the large chalice of hot coals burning near the altar wasn't to keep the congregation warm, nor did it signal the annual fundraising 'sausage sizzle'.

A rod of iron was thrust into the fire, made red hot and

planted firmly into Lady Marion's outstretched hand. Three marks had been made on the floor and the accused was ordered to walk a distance of nine paces, which she was allowed to complete in three large strides before dropping the iron and stumbling to the altar, probably screaming, to be bandaged. Part two of the trial took place three days later, when the parties reassembled for the ceremonious removal of the bandages. If the hand was cleanly healing the culprit was pronounced innocent by a cry of 'God be praised!' If it proved to be uncleanly festering then guilt was the verdict.

A variation on the theme was the ordeal by hot water, in which the hand was plunged into a boiling vat to retrieve a ring or coin. On other occasions the hands were spared and walking the distance on hot ploughshares was implemented instead. By comparison, the ordeal by cold water, reserved for the lowly, was a doddle. In this the accused was bound and suspended from a rope, then lowered gently into the village pond. The idea was that God accepted the innocent fully into the waters, so incongruously it was the sinkers who were pardoned and the floaters who were guilty.

As for Lady Marion, the records state merely that she was 'given the iron' so her fate must be presumed, but whatever the outcome she would have been well advised to control her amorous instincts.

At least for the next twelve years, that is, for trial by ordeal was abolished by Henry III in 1219. Maybe he had sympathies in the illicit-dalliance camp. Or, more likely, his advisers did. Henry was only twelve at the time, surely too young even for Lady Marion.

A CHAMPION'S UNSEEMLY END

TYNEMOUTH PRIORY, 1220

The ancient practice of trial by battle (see 'So Whose Ox Is It, Anyway?', page 9) was all very well if the parties were sound in body and mind but not awfully effective in the case of weaklings, cowards or the mentally feeble.

Priests and the rich were particularly noted for shying away from judgment by fisticuffs, and therein lies the origin of the practice of hiring a 'champion' to fight their battles for them. Champions with good track records were naturally keenly sought.

One such was William Pygun, a monk at St Albans known to provide a half-decent service to the spiritually inclined, a sort of 'Champions-U-Like' for the monastery community of the Middle Ages.

But alas, even champions have to lose sometimes, and the wretched William Pygun met his end in most unusual and undignified circumstances.

Pygun was no ordinary monk. Medieval monasteries provided sanctuary for all sorts of villains and he was described by a contemporary chronicler as 'not so much a monk as a twisting fiend'. An odious fellow and therefore an ideal champion. But his luck started to run out when he was caught forging land deeds and using the St Albans Abbey seal to authenticate them. His punishment was a severe one, not quite as bad as breaking on the wheel, being buried alive, sawn in half or impaled on a stake, but pretty horrific all the same.

Pygun was put on the transfer list and sent north to Tynemouth Priory.

It was farewell to the Arcadian delights of St Albans. Gone were the carefree walks through verdant meadows. And those lazy afternoons in the hazy calm of the Abbey herb garden were but a distant memory. In their place were dank draughty corridors, vermin-infested dormitories and severe northeast weather, for Tynemouth was very much nonleague in the monastery standings. Pygun was soon pressed into action as champion to the prior in a monetary dispute with one Simon of Tynemouth, but his boxing skills deserted him. He survived the trial by battle, but was deemed the loser and shunned by his fellow monks. He turned not to God for solace but to drink and overindulgence.

His sorry end swiftly followed and was later chronicled in the *Deeds of the Abbots of St Albans*:

> It happened one night that William was sitting on the lavatory and he forgot the early service and went on sitting there, drunk and bloated after gorging himself. He began to sleep and his snores were loud and disgusting and soon that sleep turned into death which may have been from the cold but more likely the vengeance of God, for when the snoring stopped a voice from the privy was clearly heard bellowing 'Get him, Satan, get him' and in this disgraceful way this wretch lost his life whilst using the lavatory.

Many men have suffered extended lavatorial trials after a night of overindulgence (the torture following nine pints of real ale and a vindaloo is known to be particularly severe) but only William Pygun has *been* tried in such buttock-clenching circumstances.

The monks reluctantly granted Pygun a Christian burial without due ceremony. The story of his undignified trial and death sentence in mid-bowel-evacuation mode is perfectly true but, regrettably, that attaching to his appropriate epitaph is purely apocryphal: 'Taken at the Almighty's convenience. So much still to do'.

SO WHOSE OX IS IT, ANYWAY?

CARLISLE, 1292

'I am not guilty and this I am ready to defend with my body.' The likelihood of such a staunch defence being offered today, except as pure bravado, is slim indeed. Doubtless individuals still meet occasionally on a darkened night to thrash out some private grievance with the gloves off, but there is no part in the modern legal system for such barbarous ways of delivering justice.

Not so in the Middle Ages, when the so-called trial by battle was all the rage. Indeed, having a rage was quite useful if the suspect threw down the gauntlet to his accusers. Believing passionately in one's innocence was as good a way to get one's dander up as any.

It was the battling Normans who popularised the practice in England after a little skirmish on Senlac Hill, near Hastings, on 14 October 1066. On that occasion, as every school pupil used to know, William, Duke of Normandy, put one over on Harold II, King of England, to become King William I, 'the Conqueror'. Harold lost both an eye and his life during the confrontation on the field now adjacent the East Sussex town of Battle.

The Normans carried this penchant for battling into the legal system by formalising combat into a means of deciding guilt or innocence. Like trial by ordeal, it was seen as a religious rite, and the accused swore on the Bible that he was not guilty of the offence before submitting the decision to the

9

will of God. Men were prepared to risk their lives over what seem in retrospect to be trivial offences, but, as the punishment for being found guilty might be losing a foot or a hand, having an eye gouged out or being put to death by a variety of horrific means, many were prepared to take a chance.

Hugh Bolare was one such. Having just acquired a new ox, he wasn't averse to cruising around with it in a rather ostentatious fashion so that the neighbours got the message. No doubt he gave it a wash-down every Sunday morning. This seems to have got up the nose of one 'Gilbert the Goose', who accused the boastful Hugh of stealing it from him at the court of Robert le Brus. 'Leave it out,' quoth Hugh – or in medieval words to that effect – much put out by Gilbert's bare-faced cheek: 'I bought the ox honestly from William the Long.'

Perhaps it's best not even to conjecture on how said Willie got his name, but suffice to say he created a major impasse by denying the ox had ever been his.

There was nothing for it but trial by battle, so at Carlisle in 1292 the court ordered that Hugh should fight William to establish the truth.

Dispense with noble visions of knights in shining armour, white steeds, lances and battle-axes. That was showcase stuff. Trial by battle generally entailed the combatants in being dressed in ordinary drab civvies, often unarmed, or at best given a wooden club or a sandbag to swing.

The rules were simple. They fought to the death or nightfall, whichever came first. If both men still stood as the stars came out, then the accuser was said to have lost and was labelled a perjurer. The only other option was for either party to give up by crying 'craven', but, as this amounted to losing the battle and accepting the resulting punishment, it was scarcely a popular choice.

Hugh Bolare didn't crave mercy, but nor did he perish during the fight. He saw the stars over Carlisle that night but so too did William the Long. Both men survived the conflict. Perhaps it was no more than 'codpieces at ten paces'.

But, as it was Hugh who had brought the case by falsely accusing William of selling him the ox, the court was bound to brand Hugh the perjurer and he was duly hanged. So was it 'Gilbert the Goose's' ox? Only the ox knew the truth – but he wasn't talking.

There is a curious postscript to this case. Although trial by battle fell largely into disuse by the end of the thirteenth century, the practice was, like many 'laws', never formally wiped from the statute books.

Thus it was that a judge in Warwickshire shifted uneasily in his chair in 1818 when a defendant found not guilty of murdering a girl was confronted, on the pronouncement of the verdict, by the fair maiden's brother noisily accusing him afresh. As a consequence, the defendant entered a legal time warp and cried, 'I am not guilty and this I am ready to defend with my body!'

The judge manfully managed to avert such an anachronistic spectacle and a year later in 1819 Lord Chancellor Eldon moved in the House of Lords that trial by battle be abolished. The bill was agreed to without a word of opposition and indeed witnesses have written that 'the Lords were dumb-struck with astonishment' that such a supposedly obsolete matter should be the subject of debate at all.

So now it is much safer to be a two-ox family, although, strangely enough, lawyers about to face each other in court can still sometimes be heard to talk of 'doing battle'.

THE ACCUSED HAVE GONE TO GROUND

STELVIO, ITALY, 1519

Five centuries ago it was a far less secure life being part of the animal kingdom than it is now. No *Vets in Practice*, *Pet Rescue* or bearded antipodeans named Rolf to promote the cuddly image of God's creatures. Just a society that saw animals as equally capable of committing crime as humans and a legal system fully equipped to try them and hang them if the need arose.

It may seem like making mountains out of molehills, and that was certainly the case at Stelvio in northern Italy in 1519, when the authorities decided that damage done to crops in the vicinity of the town was an act of pure wanton destruction.

The identity of the culprits was obvious and a warrant was promptly issued to summon a number of moles, which the court desired 'should show cause for their conduct by pleading their exigencies and distress'.

The moles, while quite evidently vandals of the lowest order, must have had a modicum of intelligence because they cunningly failed to turn up at their trial on the appointed day.

The court passed judgment in their absence and the moles were sentenced to exile, although as an act of mercy they were promised safe conduct on their journey 'and an additional respite of 14 days to all those who are with young'.

But, even as the sentence was read, the pesky burrowers were already shovelling like blazes, making their great escape, ready to pop up in some other poor devil's field to create the same havoc all over again. Little varmints!

Nor is this by any means an isolated case. In May 1545 the residents of St Julien in France held a mass trial of vine weevils when their precious wine crop was destroyed. The beetles had their own lawyer, Pierre Falcon, but he failed to bring home their case.

It seems pigs were the real delinquents of the animal kingdom. Records show that 34 were executed for the murder of children, and the porcine culprits were often dressed in human clothing for their court appearances before being publicly hanged or burnt at the stake.

Astonishingly, the notion of animals as criminals survived until the end of the nineteenth century, and the last known such trial was in Switzerland in 1906, when two men and a dog were tried for robbing and killing a man. The men got life but the dog was condemned to death.

One supposes we have moved on. Now we may prosecute the owners of troublesome beasts and order that the worst offending creatures be 'put down', but the idea of animals or birds being 'tried' as such seems ludicrous.

Nonetheless, that doesn't stop the animal kingdom occasionally making legal headlines even in our more enlightened times. Take the case heard at Oxford Crown Court on 9 October 1992. Mark Leach, the accused, had suffered neighbour trouble going right back to 1988, when Susan and Paddy Williams moved in next door – with two parrots.

The incessant squawking drove Leach to distraction and he responded first in kind by using a football rattle to create a rival racket. Still the parrots squawked and relations reached an all-time low in March 1992, when Leach and his wife Dolores decided enough was enough.

They kicked down the garden fence and marched on the aviary. Then, amid a flurry of feathers and spine-chilling screeching, Leach strangled one of the birds. Not content merely with parroticide, he bit Williams on the thigh as he tried to intervene. It was too late, though, for the poor feathered wretch had been dispatched to meet his maker.

In court, Leach admitted the strangling and to damaging property, for which he was fined £600 and ordered to pay £350 costs, but not before his defence, David Osborne, had played a thirty-second tape to the court in which the squawking of the inconsiderate but now sadly dead parrot had been registered in his prime at nearly ninety decibels.

This is believed to be the only case of an ex-parrot (not a Norwegian Blue, as far as I'm aware) being called to give evidence in a court of law. Maybe we're not as far removed from the sixteenth-century Italians as we like to think.

AN IMAGINATIVE CONFESSION

NORTH BERWICK, SCOTLAND, 1590

It was Queen Elizabeth I (1533–1603) who first highlighted witchcraft as an official crime in 1563, but it was James VI of Scotland, later James I of England (1566–1625), whose hatred of 'these detestable slaves of the Devil' soared to such heights that scores of innocent women were put to horrific death during his reign.

The witch-hunt at North Berwick in 1590 is one of the most famous of his culls and gave rise to what must be a candidate for the most outlandish confession of all time.

Accused of being a witch, Agnes Sampson was brought before King James himself for interrogation. He had a particular downer on these 'instruments of Satan' at that time because he was convinced that witches were to blame for saddling him with the wedding arrangements from hell.

Twice in November 1589, his bride-to-be, sixteen-year-old Princess Anne of Denmark, had set sail across the North Sea to join him for the nuptials in Scotland, but twice she was forced back by violent storms. Naturally, James, being a red-blooded 23-year-old, became a tad frustrated. It was obviously the work of witches. So James decided to sail for Denmark himself, hand-picking several ladies-in-waiting to present to his bride. One drowned crossing the River Leith. The 'evil enchanters' had struck yet again before the wedding party was even under way.

His voyage across the North Sea was a rough one (damn

witches!) and when he finally landed at Uppsala and clapped his lustful eyes on the Princess his initial amorous overtures were rejected. No prizes for guessing who was to blame.

Eventually, after 'a few words privily spoken', James and Anne hit it off, were married, and settled in Scotland, but only after his ship had almost foundered on the journey home. If there'd been a wedding video it would certainly have turned out blank. Why wouldn't the old hags leave him be?

By now James had become obsessed with the evil ways of witches, making a deep personal study of the subject and vowing 'to prove that such diveelish artes have been and still are in existence and to exact the trial and severe punishment they merite'.

Poor Agnes Sampson was one of the first to be rounded up. James was determined she would confess to witchcraft. A rope was twisted around her forehead and progressively tightened as an aide-mémoire.

'It was me who called the maelstrom to your ship after your marriage,' she confessed. 'I cast a cat into the sea with parts of a dead body to raise a storm.'

That was mere junior witchcraft as far as James was concerned. The rope was twisted afresh. Agnes needed inspiration: 'One All Hallows' Eve myself and two hundred other witches went to sea.' Mere standard fodder: 'We sailed up the Firth from North Berwick to Leith in a magic sieve,' she added with a gleam in her eye. James seemed to warm to this one but still wanted more: 'Then we landed back here at North Berwick and danced in this manner.' (Pause for manic contortions of Club Ibiza variety.)

But the royal torturer remained sceptical. Agnes went for the big one: 'We went to North Berwick Church and there met the Devil. He made us kiss his buttocks and swear hostility to the King of Scotland and he declared Your Majesty to be the greatest enemy he had in the world.'

It was good. Too good for James. He wasn't keen on the last bit: 'You witches are all extreame lyars,' he is reported to have said according to transcripts from the *Newes of Scotland*. Another twist of the rope was applied.

Having thus overegged the pudding Agnes, described by a witness as 'no common or sordid hag, but a grave and douce matron who gave serious and discreet answers', took a more cerebral approach.

She took the King aside and whispered in his ear what she claimed to be the very words that had privily passed between him and his wife on their wedding night. It must have been an inspired guess, for we are told that at last 'the King wondered greatly and swore by the living God that he believed all the devils in hell could not have discovered the same, for the words were most true'.

Agnes's confession had at last passed muster. She had triumphed. As a reward for this the rope around her forehead was blessedly loosened. But, as a reward for now being a proven witch, she was soundly thrashed and burnt at the stake at Haddington in 1591!

Being a suspected witch in the reign of James VI was no joke. He spent much of his time thereafter looking for the signs and wrote a treatise, *The Daemonologie*, on the subject in 1597. His Witchcraft Act of 1603 was responsible for many more deaths and being a witch remained a capital offence until the Witchcraft Act of 1735. It is no longer possible in law to 'be a witch' in the old sense, for that act was repealed in 1961.

But beware all ye who seek to dabble in 'matters occult' for it was replaced in that year by the Fraudulent Mediums Act. Even in these enlightened post-James days both 'susceptibility to' and 'suspicion of' supposedly supernatural powers are alive and well. You have been warned.

A DELAYED DECISION

LONDON, 1613

'An incompetent attorney can delay a trial for years or months. A competent attorney can delay one even longer.'

When the Attorney General of California, Evelle J Younger, delivered that somewhat cynical line in the *Los Angeles Times* in March 1971 he was, it has to be said, merely echoing what those who earn a living from the legal profession have known since time immemorial. There's little to be gained from hurrying.

It follows that legal history is replete with long, drawn-out cases but this one from 1613 was the slow-burner of all time.

It was James I (1566–1625), that 'wisest fool in Christendom', who started it. Such were his absurdly high views of the royal prerogative that he was prepared to go to great lengths to secure for the Crown by legal action what he felt rightly ought to be his. In 1613 the particular object of his desire was the ancient site of Smithfield market. But, ever since he succeeded Elizabeth I to the English throne in 1603, people had been telling him the market wasn't his. There were pretty solid rumours that it had been granted by charter to the citizens of the City of London back in the fifteenth century. James wasn't having that.

The subsequent court action brought by the Crown was intended to establish their ownership once and for all, but hopes of a quickie were soon dispelled. While the Crown Commissioners brought forth evidence that the site was part of

18

the royal demesne way back in the fourteenth century, the opposition would keep banging on about later charters granted by Henry VI and Henry VII, which ceded the site to 'the Mayor, Commonalty and citizens of the City of London'.

Against such determined arguments James was advised to let it drop, at least for the time being, and the action of *The Crown v. The City of London* was duly stayed by consent in 1614, a year after it had begun. Proceedings were thus suspended.

It was Mr Justice Hoffman who next weighed the evidence when the case was reopened and he pronounced judgment with a certitude that none of his predecessors had been able to muster: 'Indeed the site was part of the royal demesne until early in the fifteenth century,' he said, 'but Smithfield was indubitably included in land later given to the City under charter granted by Henry VI in 1444 and confirmed by Henry VII in 1505.'

It seemed a resounding defeat for the Crown, yet James I didn't turn a hair. He might well have turned in his grave, though, as by then he'd been dead 367 years. For when Justice Hoffman gave his ruling in the High Court the calendar that day read 6 May 1992.

The time-warp case of all time had resurfaced as a result of the City Corporation's approval in April of plans for a £50 million redevelopment programme to bring the historic meat market in line with EC food-hygiene regulations. A far cry from 1613.

A delay of 368 years to resolve a simple land ownership dispute is some going and, lawyers being mindful of inflation, legal fees were sensibly adjusted in an upward direction to prove what they have known for centuries. It pays not to rush things.

JURY V. BENCH

THE OLD BAILEY, LONDON, 1670

It's certainly unusual for a jury to challenge the authority of the learned legal personages on the bench, but that was exactly what happened in the trial of Penn and Mead in London in 1670. The incident changed the course of legal history in favour of a fair trial for the common man.

On Sunday, 14 August 1670, in Gracechurch Street, London, the English Quaker leader William Penn, then a law scholar, teamed up with a former law student, William Mead, for a spot of gentle street preaching. Nothing manic – it's just not the Quaker way. A crowd soon gathered and presently a couple of London's city officers sidled up, as they do, and promptly arrested Penn and Mead in full flow.

The indictment put before the court when their trial began at the Old Bailey on 1 September 1670 was for 'unlawful assembly'. It spoke dramatically of 'a tumultuous gathering in contempt of the King' causing 'great terror of his people and a gross disturbance of the peace'. In an age of religious intolerance, that was Charles II's way of saying, 'Cut out that Quaker stuff right sharp.'

The nine high-ups on the bench, including the Mayor of London, Sam Starling, may have known they were in for a rough ride when Penn and Mead refused to remove their Quaker hats in court. They were duly given a hefty fine.

The trial commenced and the officers who had made the

arrests gave evidence of 'talking' but certainly not of 'tumult, violence and terror'.

Penn's defence was that he had done nothing more than preach peaceably and he demanded to know by what exact instrument he was being prosecuted: 'Upon common law,' replied the recorder, Thomas Howel. 'Then show it me,' challenged Penn.

When Howel failed utterly to cite particular statutes, Penn suggested that he could surely not be expected to plead 'to an indictment that has no foundation in law'. Howel, now somewhat hot under the collar, promptly called him 'a saucy fellow'. The jury looked on. Eyebrows were raised.

Not at all impressed by Penn's continued argument on a 'point of law', the recorder ordered him to be put into a squalid lock-up adjacent the courtroom. That left Mead, rather irregularly, holding the fort.

He plugged away in like manner, but still the recorder was unable to quote the relevant legislation. In the end Mead did it for him, explaining in an aside to the jury that an unlawful assembly 'is when three or more assemble together to do an unlawful act'. Therefore no unlawful assembly, he insisted, had taken place.

The jury mused. Further eyebrows were raised.

For his insolence, Mead too was put in the lock-up and Penn, buoyed up by events, loudly addressed the jury from there. Doors were quickly slammed shut to put an end to that shenanigan as the recorder summed up. He directed the jury that it was a cast-iron case and they retired to consider on 3 September 1670.

Ninety minutes later, just eight of them trooped back into court. The other four refused to come and they were forcibly dragged in. At that point the rebels' leader, Edward Bushel, took the unprecedented step for a juror of daring to challenge the bench: 'We don't countenance the way this whole matter is conducted, sir.'

After labelling him 'a troublesome and divisive fellow', Recorder Howel insisted they retire anew to give 'a proper verdict'. When they returned later, Foreman Bushel pronounced

Penn 'guilty of *speaking* in Gracechurch Street'. Nothing more.

The recorder made it clear that the jury were fudging the issue and that they must say 'guilty' or 'not guilty' without qualification: 'Go and consider it once more,' he thundered. Again the jury returned. This time they found Mead 'not guilty' but again fudged on Penn. The recorder's response was to lock the jury up for the night, then a standard practice, until they gave a valid verdict. Or, in truth, one he liked. Namely 'guilty' full stop.

They emerged tired and hungry at 7 a.m. the next day but with their resolve intact. Their verdict on Penn was unchanged.

Again they were sent out. Again they came back and again Edward Bushel returned the same verdict.

The bench lost patience: 'I'll fine you, Edward Bushel,' raged Recorder Howel; 'Cut off his nose!' chipped in the mayor, warming to the fray.

Penn seized his chance to say his bit: 'What hope is there of ever having justice done when juries are threatened and their verdicts rejected?'

Howel was unmoved: 'The jury will go out again,' he warned, 'and deliver another verdict, else they will starve and will be dragged around the city as in Edward III's time.'

Out they went for the fourth time and after yet another night locked up without food and water they returned next morning, 5 September 1670, to deliver a historic pronouncement: 'Our verdict is changed, sir,' said Foreman Bushel.

The recorder must have thought they'd cracked, but not a bit of it: 'Both men are not guilty,' said Bushel.

That signalled the end of a bizarre trial, but not of the story, for the jury was fined heavily and put in Newgate Prison. Penn and Mead were fined for contempt of court and sent to join them but they were freed when Penn's father paid the fines.

Edward Bushel, meanwhile, the most defiant juror of all time, appealed to the Chief Justice and ably told the full sorry saga of the bench bullies.

Chief Justice Vaughan found entirely in the jury's favour: 'A jury must be independently and inscrutably responsible for its verdict free from any threat from the court,' he pronounced, before releasing the heroic twelve forthwith.

Bushel and his fellow jurors had stood steadfastly against the worst excesses of kangaroo-court justice and all who have been tried since have something to thank them for. In the hall of London's Central Criminal Court, the world-famous Old Bailey, is a plaque paying tribute to that trusty jury of 1670, ensuring that this strange but seriously pivotal case will never be forgotten.

A TOUCH OF THE BLARNEY

THE TOWER OF LONDON, 1671

It would be difficult to conceive of a more hopeless situation than the one facing Colonel Thomas Blood in 1671. At a time when treason was punishable by a certain and gruesome death he had committed the supremely symbolic and perhaps most overtly treasonable act of all: he'd half-inched the crown jewels.

What's more, he'd been caught red-handed and faced a personal audience with King Charles II, the 'Merry Monarch', who would no doubt cheerfully condemn the wretched Blood to an even more wretched end. To cap it all, poor Thomas had no legal representation. Blood was certainly on the carpet.

No sane betting man would have put money on his walking away unscathed. Yet he was granted a complete pardon, had all his forfeited estates restored and lived a prosperous and influential future life at the heart of the King's court with a personal pension of £500 per annum thrown in. Blood's great escape was an audacious one indeed.

Thomas Blood was born in Ireland around 1618 and, by the time Oliver Cromwell defeated Charles II at Worcester in 1651, sending the monarch into exile in France, he had become fiercely antiroyalist and game for a scrap in support of that cause whenever the opportunity arose. His reward for sundry acts of treachery was a handsome portfolio of Irish landed estates, formerly the property of the King. The rental returns were substantial. When Charles regained the throne by the Restoration in 1660, Blood's ill-gotten gains were promptly taken back from him. He was dispossessed at a stroke, and in turn *became* possessed by the undying desire to wreak vengeance on the monarchy for condemning him to such poverty and loss of face.

He harboured the grudge for fully eleven years and early in 1671 he decided to commit the most scandalous crime of all. He first befriended the rather elderly deputy keeper at the Tower of London, a man named Talbot Edwards, whose job it was to guard the crown jewels. Early in the morning of 9 May, Blood used his acquaintance with the gullible Edwards to gain access to the strongroom. While his accompanying gang made off with the orb, sceptre and other regalia, Blood took the supreme prize, the crown itself.

But the escape wasn't well planned. With the crown stuffed under his cloak, Blood got no further than a few hundred yards before his getaway horse slipped and fell. He was quickly arrested and taken back to the tower, this time as a prisoner rather than a souvenir hunter.

Never had a man's future looked grimmer. But Blood was a cheeky so-and-so, and his cockiness in the face of certain personal disaster amazingly paid handsome dividends.

His capture was the talk of all London. Everybody looked forward to a sensational trial and celebrity execution. But Blood played it cute. As soon as he was arrested he refused to say anything to any of his interrogators, except that he would speak only to the King himself.

Charles was amused and intrigued by such an unconventional request and Blood was duly ushered before the royal presence. He admitted all in a charming and smarmy manner. He then warned His Majesty in the most helpful tone of the consequences of an execution: 'Consider, Your Majesty, that my accomplices are still at large,' he said, 'and may well wreak the ultimate vengeance upon your person.'

Then he played his master stroke, explaining to Charles that he had once been at the very point of assassinating him but had held back at the last moment: 'Although you were at my mercy, bathing unprotected in the Thames at Battersea, the sight of Your Majesty filled me with such awe I was unable to do you any harm.'

More syrupy pronouncements from this consummate licker followed in quick succession and Charles, suitably impressed by such a bold approach and with his ego massively boosted, promptly gave Blood a full pardon. His estates and income were swiftly restored and the only court Thomas Blood appeared in was that of the King, where he swanked for all he was worth and became the talk of all London yet again.

As a demonstration of the art of self-defence, with not a lawyer in sight, Blood's performance was one of the most masterly in history. The Irishman who stole the crown jewels had employed nothing more than a touch of the blarney to escape from the tightest corner in legal history.

WELL, I'LL BE HANGED!

TYBURN GALLOWS, LONDON, 1705

On a small traffic island near the junction of London's Edgware Road and Oxford Street is an unobtrusive plaque bearing the words HERE STOOD TYBURN TREE. REMOVED 1759. What tales that site could tell, for it was there that a permanent gallows, a large triangular structure with three overhead beams known as the Triple Tree, was used to hang as many as 24 men at a time in front of baying holiday crowds.

Yet, of all its tales, one is more remarkable than most. This is the case of John Smith, whose unexceptional name belies the quite exceptional story of survival that was to make him one of the leading criminal celebrities of his age.

A native of Malton, near York, Smith settled in London early in the eighteenth century after spending some years at sea. Once on dry land, he enlisted in the Second Regiment of Foot Guards but soon embarked on a life of habitual crime, by no means unusual for a soldier at that time.

Soon enough, he was in big trouble with the law. On 3 December 1705 he was apprehended on suspicion of breaking and entering and two days later was arraigned at the Old Bailey on four separate indictments. Each involved theft; valuable quantities of shoes, cloth, China silk and gloves were the booty, and each was a capital offence.

Although Smith, then in his forties, managed to talk his way out of blame for two of the alleged offences, he was found guilty of the two others. He had, after all, been caught red-handed on the premises with 148 pairs of gloves ready to go. It was a clumsy burglary attempt and his explanation that he was all fingers and thumbs was a futile one.

He was sentenced to death and incarcerated in the Condemned Hold of Newgate Prison, where he vainly hoped for a reprieve, which didn't come. At least not yet.

On 12 December he was carted to Tyburn, strung up and turned off the wagon to swing. The hangman pulled his legs for good measure, a merciful act intended to prevent undue suffering, for all hangings prior to the nineteenth century were of the 'short-drop' variety involving a fall of just three or four feet and many victims survived for some considerable time before life finally left them.

That proved to be Smith's salvation, for even the final tug didn't finish him off quickly, although witnesses who say he swung for fully fifteen minutes swore that he looked as dead as can be.

As last-minute reprieves go, the one that was then inexplicably and dramatically delivered by a messenger on horseback looked to be a classic case of 'too late was the cry', but Smith was swiftly cut down all the same and conveyed, still apparently lifeless, to a nearby public house.

It was there that John Smith secured his fame. One of the first to be impressed was the diarist Narcissus Luttrell, who wrote: 'He was immediately lett blood and put into a warm bed, which, with other applications, brought him to himself again with much adoe.'

Smith was neither the first nor last man to survive the noose, but what really made his case celebratory was the mileage he subsequently got from his miraculous escape.

When he was taken back to Newgate Prison he quickly became the centre of attention among his fellow prisoners; members of the public queued up and paid to view him as a star exhibit; he related a sensational published account of the hanging itself in which he described 'my spirits in a strange commotion, violently pressing up to my head, then a great blaze of glaring light which seemed to come out of my eyes with a flash before I lost all sense of pain'.

It was all good stuff. Nowadays he'd have employed a PR guru to create the image for him, but John Smith was a natural long before the age of spin, and the hype worked a treat.

His reprieve was followed by an unconditional pardon and he was released from prison on 20 February 1706.

And there his story might end, but, having survived the ultimate penalty, John Smith seemed intent on chancing his arm yet again. Although he kept on the straight and narrow for almost ten years, during which time he kept a pub at Southwark, he was back to his old tricks by January 1715, when he was picked up near Fenchurch Street after breaking into a warehouse. Again it was a capital offence and a date at the Old Bailey beckoned.

But Smith's charmed life continued. He spent eighteen months in Newgate but was at length found not guilty on a technicality. And so it went on: further crimes followed in 1720 and 1721, but on the first occasion he was acquitted and for the second offence he again went back to Newgate.

Only in 1727, when he once more transgressed, did the English legal system finally rid itself of the man they called 'half-hanged Smith'. Twenty-two years after his famous Tyburn appearance he was transported, in his 66th year, to the American colonies.

Had the hangman done his job properly on 12 December 1705, plain old John Smith would be a mere statistic instead of a celebrity criminal akin to a 'soap star' of eighteenth-century society.

Avid strangeologists may be disappointed to know that the late-nineteenth-century executioner William Marwood spoilt all the fun when, in 1874, he introduced the merciful 'long-drop' method of hanging, by which the victim had to fall between six and ten feet based on a calculation involving their state of health, build and weight.

That sure-fire scientific method seemed certain to signal the end of the grand old age of execution cock-ups. But despair not, for where there's technology the gremlins will surely follow. Turn to 'Three-Times-Lucky Lee' (see page 74) for the ropiest hanging of all time.

MORRISON HEARS IT ALL

EDINBURGH, SCOTLAND, 1721

Catherine Shaw had not been on the best of terms with her father William for some time. Like many before her and since, she found to her annoyance that her choice of young man didn't meet with Dad's approval.

William felt strongly that she had 'encouraged the addresses of a man' whom he intensely disliked as 'a profligate and debauchee'. Words passed between father and daughter on many occasions in the tenement flat they shared in Edinburgh, and on one particular night in the winter of 1721 voices were raised to such a pitch that their neighbour, Mr Morrison, could not help but overhear.

Several times he heard the girl cry the chilling words, 'Cruel father, thou art the cause of my death!' followed finally by awful groaning, then the unmistakable sound of William Shaw leaving the house.

Morrison alerted neighbours as the Shaw residence fell ominously silent, but they could not gain entry. A constable was called to break in and poor Catherine Shaw was found, barely alive, weltering in blood and with a knife by her side: 'Has your father killed you?' they asked. She was unable to speak but seemed to those present to have nodded her head before expiring moments later.

When William Shaw returned he trembled violently as he saw his daughter's dead body. He turned pale. The small gathering started to put two and two together, and four began to look a pretty conclusive answer when the constable noticed traces of blood on Shaw's shirt and hands.

He was quickly put before a magistrate and admitted they had had serious quarrels of late over 'the man business'. But on the night in question, he insisted, he had been in another room and had gone out without harming his daughter in any way. He had himself heard the cries, but dismissed them as mere histrionics. The blood was readily explained: 'Some days since, I was bled by a barber and the bandages came untied that night resulting in stains on my shirt and hands.'

The prosecution majored on the evidence of Morrison. He was absolutely sure of the words he had heard: 'Cruel father, thou art the cause of my death!' Catherine's implicit nodding of her head in her last moments was surely an added proof.

Against such evidence William Shaw was convicted, sentenced and executed at Leith Walk in November 1721 with the full approval of public opinion, although Shaw himself maintained his innocence even on the scaffold.

Only in the new year did it emerge that Catherine Shaw was something of a drama queen. The new tenant of Shaw's flat found a sheet of paper, which had slipped down an opening near the chimney.

Evidently placed originally on the mantelpiece, it was written in Catherine's hand and addressed to her father. She reproached him in the letter for his barbarity and said she realised she would never marry the man she loved but was determined not to accept a man of her father's choice. She had decided to end her burdensome existence. The letter finished with a flourish: 'My death I lay to your charge. When you read this, consider yourself as the inhuman wretch that plunged the knife into the bosom of the unhappy Catherine Shaw!'

With that parting shot she had taken her own life with full histrionic sound effects. William Shaw may well have been an inhuman wretch but he was undoubtedly an innocent man.

The authorities made a noble attempt at damage limitation, removing his emaciated body from the gibbet where it still hung and giving the wronged man a decent burial. Contemporary reports say that 'a pair of colours was waved over his grave', but no amount of respect could redress the miscarriage of justice.

Had either the key witness, Mr Morrison, or the court been familiar with the device later used to such good effect by Agatha Christie in a number of her novels, the evidence might have been more closely scrutinised.

A disembodied voice heard from a closed room is not always what it seems. Sometimes even two voices don't prove a conversation with Christie around. One person posing as two, or even the cunning use of a tape recording in an empty room, has been employed to baffling effect by the Queen of Crime.

But Morrison wasn't Hercule Poirot. He hadn't heard the voice of William Shaw but Catherine's words implied he was in the room with her.

If this unusual case proves anything, it is surely that murders, like children, should be seen and not merely heard.

MAGGIE'S REPRIEVE

EDINBURGH, SCOTLAND, 1724

'You are to be taken from this place to a place of execution and there you will be hanged by the neck until you are dead. May the Lord have mercy on your soul.'

Those most chilling words, not heard in Britain since the passing of the Murder (Abolition of Death Penalty) Act 1965, were once commonplace in British courts.

Margaret Dickson heard them in an Edinburgh courtroom on 3 August 1724. So did the jury and all others present at the High Court of Justiciary that day. The finality of that pronouncement could not be denied, yet three centuries later those very words still echo hauntingly, still seem to linger on the long-dead judge's lips, for the case of Margaret Dickson is an odd one indeed.

It was the discovery of a newborn baby's body in the River Tweed at Maxwellheugh, near Kelso, on 9 December 1723, that started it. It was Margaret Dickson's child. Having been deserted by her husband, she had left her two other children behind in Musselburgh, near Edinburgh, and headed south to visit an aunt in Newcastle. She had an extended break in her journey at the small village of Maxwellheugh and there took work with the Bell family. It was one of the Bells' sons who made the gruesome discovery.

Questioning soon revealed that it was Margaret's baby and that she had managed to keep the pregnancy secret from all but the father. Her story was that he was William Bell, another son, who had forced himself on her one night in a drunken stupor. The baby, she said, had been stillborn. She had kept it in her bed for eight days, frantic with worry, before throwing it in the river out of sheer distraction.

It was plausible, but Dickson's secretive manner told against her. Despite her decent and God-fearing Protestant background, she was charged with murder, found guilty, heard the death sentence read, and was hanged in Edinburgh on 2 September 1724.

A baying crowd of thousands witnessed the drop at the Gallows Stone in the Grassmarket. The hangman tugged at her legs for good measure as she swung, and after half an hour she was cut down and placed in a coffin to be taken back to Musselburgh by her friends on a cart.

Scarcely had they left the Edinburgh outskirts before they were attacked by a gang of body snatchers – surgeons' apprentices seeking booty for dissection. They fought the gang off, but not before the coffin had been disturbed and the lid loosened.

They pressed on as far as the village of Peppermill and, still somewhat shaken, stopped there for refreshment. Only then did two passing joiners hear a noise from the coffin, which was duly opened with haste. First, Margaret Dickson's limbs twitched. Then Peter Purdie, one of her friends, opened a vein and a strangled cry of 'Oh dear!' came from Margaret's deathly pale lips. Oh dear indeed.

On 6 September 1724, the Sunday after being hanged, and looking remarkably well, considering, she attended church in Musselburgh amid much sensation. She became a great local celebrity and some months later remarried her former husband. Many a man has dreamed of putting new life into his marriage but Margaret's man surely hit the jackpot.

No attempt was made to arrest her again, as Scottish law deemed the sentence to have been fully carried through. Some said it was an act of God, atoning for a crime she didn't commit. In truth it was a slovenly hangman, a loose coffin lid, a couple of nosey joiners and the remarkable resilience of the human body that gave her the incredible second chance.

No one except Margaret Dickson ever knew the real truth about the body in the river, but everyone said she was the luckiest woman alive. Or dead, as the case may be.

AND THE WINNER IS . . .

CARLISLE, 1746

When Prince Charles Edward Stuart (1720–88), 'Bonnie Prince Charlie', landed from France on the island of Eriskay in the Outer Hebrides on 23 June 1745, he set in motion a chain of events that has become one of the most famous in British history.

His rebellious march south with intent to claim the English throne was to end in defeat for himself, but also in escape. But for many of his rebel forces fate was less kind, being decided by one of the strangest judicial practices in legal history. Anyone fancy their chances at trial by lottery?

Thomas Coppock was one of those who met their gruesome end in that bizarre fashion. He joined the band of rebel forces at Manchester as the 'Young Pretender' marched south towards London, but the closer to the capital they got the more their numbers dwindled. Ever more depleted and in low spirits, they got no further than the Midlands, being repelled at Derby on 6 December 1745. Some say they were merely repelled 'by' Derby and decided the south just wasn't for them. That's one for debate, but at any rate they retreated north, hotly pursued by the Duke of Cumberland, and ultimate defeat was delivered on 16 April 1746 at Culloden.

Now for the trials. But with almost four hundred rebels imprisoned at Carlisle Castle on charges of treason, each requiring a separate hearing, it was more than the courts could cope with. There was nothing for it but trial by lottery!

The procedure was simple but nerve-jangling, and the prize horrific. Prisoners willing to admit their guilt were split into groups of twenty and asked to draw numbers from a hat. The dubious bounty for the one 'winning' ticket was a trial, with its inevitable result. The other nineteen men were 'rewarded' by transportation for life, not always in itself a hugely attractive prospect, it is true, but better than sure-fire death.

With a nineteen-to-one chance of saving their skin, submitting themselves to the lottery was a chance many men took. The Reverend Thomas Coppock, the Oxford-educated chaplain of the rebel forces, was one such, but as he dipped his hand into the hat in September 1746 he was to find that he truly was God's chosen one.

Charged with high treason after conducting a service for the 'Bonnie Prince' in Derby, and already having admitted his guilt, he bore slim hopes of coming out of the trial intact. They were even slimmer when his counsel, a Mr Clayton, failed to turn up to face the five members of the Bar leading the prosecution on behalf of the English Crown. A Scots advocate, David Graham, stepped into the breach to defend him, but neither he nor his client did much to help their cause, as a contemporary account of the trial relates:

> Coppock's counsel said very little in regard to his defence, for the prisoner's behaviour before the court was rude and insolent and impudent beyond imagination.

The jury took less than a minute to find Coppock guilty of high treason, which ensured he would meet his end in a fashion even more dreadful than hanging. The judge pronounced sentence: 'You are to be hanged by the neck, but not till you are dead, for you are to be cut down alive, your privy parts cut off and your bowels taken out and burned before your face, your head severed and your body divided into four parts; and those to be at the King's disposal. And the Lord have mercy on your soul.'

Coppock was duly collected on 18 October 1746. He was dragged on a black hurdle from Carlisle Castle to the gallows on Harrowby Hill overlooking the town. Although he kept his composure and delivered a highly treasonable seven-minute sermon as his parting shot, it was there, so to speak, that he finally went to pieces.

Being hung, drawn and quartered fell into blessed disuse after 1746, as did the drawing of lots, but that was scant consolation for the unfortunate Thomas Coppock, winner of the worst lottery prize of all time.

A FISH OUT OF WATER

CARLISLE ASSIZES, 1776

Many critics of the legal system have bemoaned the tendency of judges and barristers to bamboozle the layman by use of language. Erudite, jargonistic, Latinised, fanciful or plain euphemistic, it's an endless conundrum. Just consider the divorce case:

'And when did you and your wife last have relations?'

'That would have been last Christmas when her mother came to stay, Your Honour.'

It's an old one but it makes the point. How can the ordinary person even begin to understand the language of the law?

That's why it comes as such a comfort to know that even those within the profession are occasionally hoisted by their own petard. Or, in the interests of plain speaking, should I say caught out at their own game?

One such unusual case was related in his memoirs by Lord Eldon, Lord Chancellor for 26 years at the start of the nineteenth century, and it shows how the use of language, even at the most basic level, can paralyse the opposition into submission against their will.

It was at the Carlisle Assizes in 1776 when Eldon, then just a young practitioner on the Northern Circuit working as plain John Scott, was called upon to defend a man accused of salmon poaching. Scott had a yen for such cases, for although he was to rise to become one of the most celebrated English lawyers of his era, he had been born of humble parentage in

Newcastle and had a down-to-earth approach that served him well.

Prosecuting the poacher was a barrister named Bearcroft, rather a star in London, who agreed to make his first ever visit to Cumberland only on agreeing the then enormous fee of 300 guineas. Despite his misgivings about the ways of the far north, Bearcroft confidently expected to bring the case home against the country bumpkins. As it was, he got a rude awakening.

John Scott displayed a canny grasp of the power of language by playing on Bearcroft's lack of a common touch – while conducting his defence he spoke in the broad Cumberland dialect of the Carlisle region and liberally scattered his speeches with vernacular phrases, which the jury fully understood but which the increasingly bewildered Bearcroft could make neither head nor tail of.

The crucial moment came when Scott began to question a witness about salmon caught out of season. Scott knew, as did the witness, that such salmon have white flesh instead of red. He also knew that poachers were in the habit of disguising such illegally caught fish, reddening the flesh by smoking it up a chimney to make what were known locally as 'old soldiers', named after the colour of a soldier's red coat.

Being unaware of country matters, Bearcroft strained to follow the dialogue and when Scott asked the witness, 'Did the salmon make good "ould soldiers"?' the surreal image of an army of fish engaging in battle in their twilight years was more than Bearcroft could stand.

He promptly made the mistake of asking Scott to translate, and Scott's clever but surely entirely just retort won the day in this North-versus-South battle of wits: 'Surely a London counsel marked three hundred guineas on his brief can understand a simple thing like that. Furthermore, it is not for me, with a fee of only five guineas to my name, to help a London counsel whose value is evidently sixty times as great as my own.'

Thus put in his place, Bearcroft floundered like a fish out of water as the jury warmed to Scott's plain-talking submissions.

The salmon poacher was quickly acquitted and Bearcroft left Carlisle sorely stung by the experience of his northern excursion, swearing, 'No fee shall ever tempt me to come among such a set of barbarians again.'

A famous triumph for Scott. A salutary lesson for Bearcroft. But above all a victory for the plain-speaking society.

I would add only one footnote. One must always be careful of assuming from a response that someone has misunderstood the question. For misconstrual on the grounds of ambiguity can, as a rereading of my opening quotation might suggest, sometimes be a two-way affair.

Who's to say, after all, that it *wasn't* 'last Christmas', poor chap?

A UNIQUE ASSASSINATION

THE HOUSE OF COMMONS, LONDON, 1812

Every murder is unique. Each victim, after all, is different. But the classification of murders into distinctive types lends a certain commonplace air even to some of the foulest acts. A classic example of the old adage, 'familiarity breeds contempt'.

But it was not John Bellingham's aim in life to be a commonplace murderer and those present at his trial at the Old Bailey in May 1812 saw the 42-year-old from St Neot's, Huntingdonshire, convicted of a crime that was, and remains to this day, unique in British history. John Bellingham assassinated the Prime Minister.

The esteemed victim, Spencer Perceval, was a Londoner who chose the law as a profession and was called to the bar in 1786. After acting for the government in a number of high-profile cases he was earmarked by Prime Minister William Pitt for higher things and he rose via the office of Attorney General and Chancellor of the Exchequer to become Prime Minister in 1809. Perceval was a Tory but no hint of scandal or sleaze ever tainted his name and he was a family man of high honour – 10 Downing Street echoed to the sound of eleven children during his stay in office. 'Little P', as he became known, was seemingly a thoroughly nice chap; sure, he had vitriolic opponents, but in truth not a serious enemy in the world.

Except John Bellingham. Tall and bony with a long, thin face, Bellingham was a clerk who had worked for years in a

London counting house before branching out to take jobs in Russia and then Hull, where he hoped to make money importing timber. Alas, his Russian contacts let him down and Bellingham suffered huge financial losses, which led him to a spell in prison. It was from his cell that he first began the campaign of blame that was to lead to his immortality as an assassin, and his criticism of the Russian authorities after his release was such that he was soon put behind bars in that country, too.

From there he sent letter after letter of complaint to the British ambassador demanding intervention for his release, but all to no avail. Bellingham's rage rose to fever pitch and he determined that, on his release, someone would pay.

On his return to England his campaign to clear his name and seek what he genuinely believed to be his right to compensation continued relentlessly. Again, he got nowhere and when a Whitehall civil servant one day told him to 'go to the Devil, and take whatever action you like!' that was enough to tip Bellingham over the edge.

Straightaway he stalked to a gunsmith's shop in the Strand, spent four guineas on two pistols and ammunition and passed the rest of the day in target practice on Primrose Hill.

For several days afterwards he lurked around the entrance and lobby to the House of Commons staking out the lie of the land, and on Monday, 11 May 1812, he struck the blow that none before or since has dared to emulate.

It was a fine day and Spencer Perceval, in times far less security-conscious than our own, walked to the Commons from 10 Downing Street rather than take a carriage. It was 5.15 in the afternoon when he entered the lobby and from behind a pillar John Bellingham emerged.

In full view of a crowd of constituents and sightseers, the crazed assassin raised a pistol and fired at close range into Perceval's chest. As the Prime Minister lurched forward gasping, 'I am murdered,' Bellingham was seized without a struggle and as Perceval was pronounced dead at the scene Bellingham addressed police: 'I am the unfortunate man who has shot Mr Perceval. My name is John Bellingham. I know what I have done. It was a private injury, a denial of justice on the part of the government.'

Amid a climate of sensation and outrage, Bellingham was taken to Newgate Prison and stood trial at the Old Bailey later that week, at seven o'clock on Friday, 15 May. He pleaded guilty and he also begged for clemency but, not for the first time, Bellingham's protestations were ignored by authority.

Despite his defence playing the 'insanity' card it took the jury just fifteen minutes to find him guilty and the only man ever to assassinate a British prime minister was hanged on the gallows outside Newgate Prison on Monday, 18 May, within a week of his infamous deed.

It was a strange affair indeed but some would say it is even stranger that Spencer Perceval remains a unique victim, bearing in mind the vitriolic state of political affairs in recent years. Oddly, there was a moment in January 1983 when British visitors to Canada might have been forgiven for choking on their breakfast cereal as newspaper headlines there read, MINISTERIAL HORROR: MURDER OF MRS THATCHER.

This undeniably eye-catching line turned out to refer to Jo Ann Thatcher, the former wife of Saskatchewan's Minister for Energy and Mines, Colin Thatcher. In another sensational affair it was the minister himself who opted to blow his former wife's brains out in an act of revenge after she had divorced him and won the largest settlement ever awarded by a Canadian court.

What a blessed relief it wasn't *the* Mrs Thatcher dispatched to keep her fellow Tory, Spencer Perceval, company.

Or do I hear a dissenting voice? Shame on you!

ELEVEN JUST MEN AND WILSON

CLERKENWELL GREEN, LONDON, 1838

'Juries are like Almighty God . . . totally unpredictable,' wrote the barrister and author John Mortimer in his fictional *The Trials of Rumpole* (1979). Had he been writing in 1838, he might well have called the book *The Trials of Adams*.

When Serjeant Adams, chairman of the bench for the Middlesex Sessions, addressed his fellow magistrates at Clerkenwell Green on Tuesday, 2 January 1838, he assured those suffering New Year blues that 'the calendar is unusually light today'.

But his hopes of an easy session were quickly dashed by the presence on the jury of one Mr H Wilson, whose own eccentric brand of New Year 'resolution' was about to test Adams's patience to hitherto unknown limits.

No sooner had the jury been sworn to try the defendant, Benjamin Dickinson, than Wilson took centre stage: 'I should like to know, Mr Chairman, how I am to be indemnified for my loss of time and the trouble and inconvenience I am put to by coming here.' Adams disdainfully brushed this untimely intervention aside, ordering the deputy clerk, 'Go on with the case.'

'Ay, ay, it's all very well to say "go on" but I won't go on until I know who is to pay me,' whined Wilson in response. Adams replied in patient but firm tone, assuring Wilson that jury service was 'an exceedingly important and essential public duty and one of the most beautiful parts of our

45

admirable constitution for which no remuneration is due', before again ordering the case to proceed.

But yet again the mischievous juryman made the same point and only after several more Wilsonian interruptions of the 'ay, ay' variety did the case proceed.

The evidence against Dickinson for assaulting an officer of the County Court was overwhelming, and Chairman Adams, having finally put Wilson in his proper place, summed up quickly. The jury convened for what should have been an equally rapid decision, but Wilson was game for more.

To the utter exasperation of the jury and all present (except perhaps the accused), he refused to give a verdict without pay. It was time for Chairman Adams to get tough by reminding Wilson that he had sworn under oath to give a verdict: 'And I will place the jury in a locked room without fire or candle until that verdict is delivered.'

At this Wilson remained smilingly uncowed: 'Ay, ay, I have sworn to give a verdict but I did not say *when* or at *what* time. I will do so when I am well and truly ready. Show me the statute that says there is a limit of time or place.'

After more verbal tennis, in which Wilson's argument became ever more semantic, Serjeant Adams ordered an officer to 'remove the jury and lock them in a room until they come to a determination'.

Now it was the rest of the jury who loudly made clear to Adams their disapproval of his orders before turning their attention to Wilson. They reasoned, they pleaded, they cajoled, but all to no avail: 'Oh, let us subscribe and pay him what he wants,' they finally cried in unison, but Chairman Adams would have none of it and again ordered the jury's retention under lock and key.

'I shall not leave this box,' piped Wilson, delivering yet more of the same and a good deal of 'ay, aying' along the way.

'His stubbornness,' wrote *The Times*, 'caused the greatest confusion and utmost anxiety as he sat tight in a manner which induced a supposition that he would not quit the jury-box.'

Then, just as more court heavies moved in to remove him bodily, Wilson calmly rose amid much nodding and winking to his fellow jurors and jauntily acquiesced to the lock-in. It lasted only fifteen minutes and the jury duly delivered a verdict of guilty.

What happened behind the locked door doesn't take much guessing, for Wilson, 'an honest tradesman', emerged much relaxed and smiling contentedly. Evidently, he had got his way.

So what *was* the price of justice? For Adams a restless night after his brush with the most irritating juror of all time.

And doubtless for Wilson a few tankards of decent ale, a goblet or so of wine and a rather splendid dinner.

A NEW LINE OF ENQUIRY

AYLESBURY ASSIZES, 1845

When John Tawell decided to start the New Year with rather more resolution than was good for him it led to a chain of events that created legal history, as an overflowing courtroom at Aylesbury Assizes in March 1845 later listened earnestly to the unprecedented and at that time amazing story of Tawell's capture.

It was 1 January 1845 when the sixty-year-old Englishman murdered his secret mistress, Sarah Hart, at her cottage in Salt Hill, near Slough, Buckinghamshire. A bottle of porter liberally laced with prussic acid was the last drink Sarah ever shared with her somewhat mature lover.

Tawell's entirely selfish motive was partly that he was afraid that his wife, with whom he lived an apparently respectable life in Berkhamsted, Hertfordshire, would discover his double life. But perhaps even more than that was the need to keep the knowledge of his sordid set-up from fellow Friends of the rather purist Quaker movement, of which he passed himself off as a member.

Tawell was a devious man and had a good escape and alibi planned. He had earlier deposited an overcoat in the cloakroom of the Jerusalem Coffee House in London. After the poisoning he planned to catch the train from Slough to Paddington, from where his movements would be entirely unobserved by the law. From there he would go to the coffee house, collect his coat and claim, if questions were ever asked, that he had been in London for the hours conveniently spanning the murder. No one would ever know. The burgeoning railways were certainly the criminal's friend.

Yet circumstances entirely beyond his control led him to stand trial three months later. That an elderly gentleman in Quaker garb had been spotted leaving the murdered woman's house by a neighbour ought not to have mattered bearing in mind his London alibi, nor that a Quaker had purchased a first-class ticket at Slough station and been seen boarding an early-evening train there, for as word got around that the Quaker might be worth watching Tawell was well on the way to Paddington. Of course it must be another Quaker, for *he* had been in London all the time.

But, scrupulous planner that he was, John Tawell was not up to press with the newest technology. Fully 37 years before Alexander Graham Bell invented the telephone in 1876, many a criminal's downfall, William Fothergill Cooke and Professor Charles Wheatstone had managed to interest the Great Western Railway in their latest hi-tech electric-telegraph communication system. GWR gave it a try on the Paddington–West Drayton line in 1839 and extended it to Slough in 1843. Tawell, rather a dinosaur in such matters, hadn't figured on its possible uses, yet it proved to be the unlikely source of his downfall.

Even as he settled into his seat on his journey to safety, the telegraph clerk at Slough was wiring Paddington. The system worked perfectly, although the inability of the equipment to transmit the letters Q and U meant the clerk had to alert police to look out for 'a gentleman in the garb of a KWAKER'. Three times he sent the message before the police twigged it – maybe they were looking for someone dressed as a duck. But even primitive telegraph messages travelled faster than the trains and, as Tawell stepped confidently on to Paddington station, a plain-clothes police officer had no difficulty spotting his man.

He was trailed to the Jerusalem Coffee House, observed for the rest of the day and finally arrested next morning. His story and indignant denials got him nowhere, for thanks to the wires it was incontrovertible that the Slough Quaker and the London Quaker were one and the same.

After he was found guilty and condemned to be hanged he admitted all and before the fatal day many more details of Tawell's double life emerged. Banknote forgery, transportation to Australia and other suspicious deaths all came to light. Tawell was well and truly discredited and a contemporary record tartly reported that 'a respectable garb, sedate demeanour and outward benevolence have seldom concealed a more wicked and unprincipled heart'.

As the first man to be convicted with the aid of the electric telegraph, Tawell, by his unlikely demise, served to deliver a timely warning to all future criminals. If you want to get away with it don't be a technophobe and don't dress as a Quaker.

NO, NO, NO, NO, NO . . . YES

GLAMORGAN QUARTER SESSIONS, 1853

Only the harshest critic would deny that the task of a jury in deciding a verdict can be a very difficult one indeed. But, once the foreman of the jury rises to deliver that verdict, then that part of the procedure is surely simplicity itself. Nay, even foolproof. He must pronounce 'guilty' or 'not guilty'. Nothing could possibly go wrong.

Strange, then, that the leading case of *The Crown v. William Vodden*, heard at Glamorgan Quarter Sessions in 1853, should ever have entered the legal textbooks, let alone be cited on a number of occasions since, even as recently as 1999.

But cited it is, for jury foremen, it seems, sometimes get a little befuddled. The (possibly apocryphal!) case of the Irish foreman who confidently announced, 'My Lord, we find the man who stole the mare not guilty' is not as ludicrous as it may seem, nor is the celebrated procrastination of Tony Hancock in a classic episode of television's *Hancock's Half Hour*.

In the Glamorgan case, Vodden was on trial for larceny, that quaint old term for theft that makes that act sound almost artistic. At the end of proceedings the jury foreman, Owen Hughes, rose to deliver the clear verdict of not guilty. The chairman duly discharged the prisoner but as he did so there was an audible murmur from the remainder of the jury. They had, they quickly made clear, all agreed on a verdict of guilty. As a result of this confusion the defendant was brought back into the dock and the chairman of the bench subjected the jury to a round

51

of 'Is that your final answer?' The first eleven said the intended verdict was definitely guilty and when it came to Owen Hughes he too, perhaps too embarrassed to admit his inexplicable slip of the tongue, said he had definitely said 'Guilty'.

As a consequence, the erstwhile and much relieved defendant was cast into a rather darker humour as the verdict was reversed and he was sentenced to two months' hard labour.

That being a somewhat unpleasant prospect, he decided to appeal for a counter-reversal and the case went to the Court for Crown Cases Reserved. There Chief Baron Pollock established an important precedent: 'What happened was a daily occurrence in the ordinary transactions of life,' he said, 'namely that a mistake was made but then corrected within a reasonable time, and on the very spot on which it was made.' He ruled that the hard labour must stand.

The message to jurors was clear. If you botch it up, admit it pronto. Strange as it is that the wrong wording from a choice of only two verdicts should ever emerge from the mouth of a jury foreman at the crucial moment, the precedent established by the Vodden case has been put to the test throughout legal history. In 1985, in *The Crown v. Andrews*, the jury foreman clearly announced a verdict of not guilty on the charge that the defendant had subjected a child to cruelty. But ten minutes later, during the sentencing of a co-defendant, he sheepishly passed a note to the judge stating: 'We thought we found Andrews guilty; what happens now?' It may sound like an entertaining alternative to *A Question of Sport*, but it was all in deadly earnest and again, much to Andrews's disgust, an about-turn was ordered and a verdict of guilty was recorded. The Court of Appeal later once more upheld the *Vodden* principle and the guilty verdict held.

Only where there has been too lengthy a time lapse in such cases or a change of mind has been deemed to be purely on a whim has the Court of Appeal ordered 'erroneous' first verdicts to stand.

If only juries were perfect such debates would be nonexistent, and *The Law's Strangest Cases* would be a very slim volume, which would never do. So, thank goodness that folly among jurors is an established part of legal history.

Take the farcical goings-on at Snaresbrook Crown Court in 1993. After listening for three days to the case against a man accused of robbery, the jury deliberated their verdict for three hours before losing the plot completely and sending a note to the judge, which asked, 'Is it a question of whether we have to decide if he is guilty or not guilty?'

Nor is the mayhem confined to home shores. In 1960 an Appeal Court in New Jersey, USA, ordered a retrial in an accident case because of 'basic confusion' in the original courtroom. The final straw came, so it seems, when the judge asked the jury foreman, 'Have you agreed on your verdict, Mr Foreman?' The reply – 'My name isn't Foreman: my name is Admerman' – was more than the judge could bear.

And the great thing about these oddities is that, just when you think they can't get any worse, they do.

Back in the realms of the guilty-or-not-guilty conundrum, we again find ourselves in Wales. At Cardiff Crown Court in April 1999 Judge Michael Gibbon sentenced Alan Rashid, charged with making a threat to kill, to two years' imprisonment, after he thought he heard the jury foreman say 'Guilty'. Only when a confused juror asked an usher to explain the sentence did it emerge that 'Not guilty' was the intended verdict. Tapes of the proceedings were played and Rashid was duly freed. Surprise, surprise: no appeal from the accused this time!

The story that appeared in all the newspapers was that an untimely cough had drowned out the vital 'not' when the verdict had been delivered, although Judge Gibbon, perhaps keen not to make a monkey of himself, said that had not been the case. The foreman had, quite simply, he asserted, made a mistake in his delivery. Was there a cough? There was certainly a hiccup.

Lord Devlin (1905–92) once learnedly commented, 'What makes juries worthwhile is that they see things differently from judges. Trial by jury is the lamp that shows that freedom lives.'

He might well have added, 'Once in a while there is a loose connection in that lamp or the bulb goes out. Then, regrettably, we are all left in the dark.'

THE ELEVENTH WITNESS

MILWAUKEE, UNITED STATES, 1855

Some of the law's oddest cases relate to mistaken identity and there is no shadow of a doubt that innocent men have been sentenced, sometimes even to death, on the misguided assertion of a witness that 'this is definitely the one'.

Studies of the phenomenon have been made and controlled experiments have shown that the brain's capacity to absorb, store and later retrieve an image to match to a perceived likeness is by no means infallible. Sometimes, too, the rare existence of a genuine double, the near-perfect doppelgänger, has led to unavoidable errors of identification and it is for such reasons that the police are apt to seek safety in numbers if enough witnesses can be found for a procedure that remains a controversially subjective area of the law.

All of which makes the facts surrounding a case in Milwaukee in 1855 all the more remarkable, for in this instance not one but ten thoroughly 'reliable' witnesses were prepared to say 'yes' when asked the vital question.

This curious story began on the riverbank below one of Milwaukee's bridges on 14 April 1855, when, amid a raft of flotsam at the water's edge, a boy spied what he first thought to be a bag or bundle of rags. Yet a closer inspection saw the boy yell and take to his heels, for inside the loosely wrapped bundle was the trunk of a human body, the head all but severed and the brains dashed out by a blow on the back of the skull. There was a great gash in the throat, the left eye

54

protruded and both legs had been chopped off, never to be found. Importantly, though, the facial features were largely unscathed.

The Milwaukee police wasted no time in seeking identification of the body and a concentration on persons known to be missing for some time was a very sound starting point. It paid dividends, for one name bandied about was that of John Dwire, a well-known face among Milwaukee's residents whom no one could recall having seen for some weeks.

Witnesses were brought forward and the police got the result they wanted as a mass of testimony confirmed the body to be that of John Dwire. All who spoke did so with the utmost assurance. They recognised his face, his features, the colour of his hair and his eyes. There, too, was the 'five-pointed starry scar' on his left cheek, the two missing front teeth, the familiar mutton-chop whiskers, the scars on the finger of the left hand and the thumb of the right. Feature after feature was identified as Dwire's as people who had known him for years nodded sagely as they examined the gruesome remains. First his landlady, then his workmates and finally the owner of the boarding house where he habitually took his meals. Ten sound witnesses provided as positive an identification as it was possible to get.

Yet, even while the inquest before which these statements were made was proceeding, rumours began to circulate that other acquaintances of Dwire's had come forward to say he was alive and well and living upriver, just sixteen miles away: 'He's been up at Kemper's Pier for several months, since Christmas in fact,' they said.

The police were sceptical and those who had identified Dwire knew these latest reports must be bogus. The sightings, obviously, were cases of mistaken identity. Nevertheless, the police sent a delegation to Kemper's Pier to look for the 'dead' man but their journey drew a blank.

Yet back at the inquest events took a conclusive turn, for while they were on their way upriver a new witness appeared at the courthouse to weigh in with his own positive identification.

We've all seen those Agatha Christie stage plays where the audience gasps in the third act. Well, the 'Case of the Unexpected Witness' was a gasper and a half and all present were dumbfounded as the eleventh man delivered his sworn statement: 'Lest anyone here should still think I'm dead I have come in person to assure him that I am not the corpse found in the river last Saturday morning.'

The body was never positively identified, nor was the murderer caught. And the ten most unreliable witnesses in legal history must have been sorely embarrassed as John Dwire achieved instant celebrity status as the only man ever to give evidence at his own inquest.

BAR TALK

DUBLIN, IRELAND, 1860

'Words are a lawyer's tools of trade.' It was Lord Denning (1899–1999), one of just a handful of judges to have become truly household names, who made that succinct observation. The legal luminary was, of course, spot on.

But many a barrister keen to demonstrate such advocacy skills to the bench and jury by masterly wordsmithing has over-egged the pudding to his cost. For every brilliant winning speech from the bar there have been countless losing ones where the question of length, in particular, has done as much damage to a defendant's cause as any amount of damning evidence.

Judge Barrington Black once mischievously marked the card of such bar bores in a tellingly brief missive to *The Times* on 9 March 1999:

> Sir, the new television series of *Kavanagh QC* is so true to life that I fell asleep during the last ten minutes of counsel's speech to the jury.

In defence of the windbags it must be said that legal history is full of stirring long speeches. Indeed, entire books have been written in celebration of such gems. But brevity, just as it is said to be the soul of wit, also lies at the heart of many examples of classic advocacy, which is, in its purest form, merely the art of saying the right thing in the right way at the right time.

It's for that very reason that a short speech made in 1860 by an Irish lawyer during a very workaday case is even today quoted in full as an example of its art. Odd that it should have survived into its third century, but if a nail was ever to be hit on its head then a counsel by the name of Dr Webb was surely the man to wield the hammer to best effect.

He was appearing before the Recorder of Dublin for Peter Mulligan, a respectable young man of 25, who was applying for a licence for a public house in the fair city. The police objected on the grounds of the applicant's youth and the learned recorder echoed that view, stating gravely to Webb, 'He is very young for such a responsible position.'

It was then that Dr Webb earned his fee in a memorable manner: 'My Lord,' he said, 'Alexander the Great at twenty-two years of age had crushed the Illyrians and razed the city of Thebes to the ground, had crossed the Hellespont at the head of his army, had conquered Darius with a force of one million in the defiles of Issus and brought the great Persian empire under his sway. At twenty-three, René Descartes evolved a new system of philosophy. At twenty-four, Pitt was Prime Minister of the British Empire, on which the sun never sets. At twenty-four, Napoleon overthrew his enemies with a whiff of grapeshot in the streets of Paris. Is it now to be judicially decided that Peter Mulligan, at the age of twenty-five, is too young to manage a public house in Capel Street?'

One eminent barrister once took seventeen days to deliver his final speech and still lost his case. Dr Webb took no more than 45 seconds to deliver his. Little surprise that he was later raised to the bench and became County Court Judge for Donegal. Little surprise, too, that pints were raised in his honour at the grand opening of 'Mulligan's Bar'.

SWEET FANNY ADAMS

ALTON, HAMPSHIRE, 1867

Only a very singular case could bestow on the English language a phrase still in everyday use well over a century after the event that gave birth to it. This is a singular case indeed.

'Sweet Fanny Adams', 'Sweet FA' or 'Sweet . . .' you know what. Whichever strength of the well-known phrase one elects to use, the meaning amounts to the same: 'not much at all' or 'nothing of any consequence'. What a dreadful tale those words allude to.

Fanny Adams was a pretty village girl with long blonde hair and bright blue eyes, just seven years old, living in the village of Alton, near Winchester, Hampshire. 'The village stood on the Pilgrim's Way,' a tourist guidebook tells us, 'and in summer the fields hereabouts are green with trailing hops to supply Alton's breweries.' It is a description that conjures up the quintessential English scene of idyllic long hot summers, and it was just such a scene in Alton in the summer of 1867. But the guidebook does not tell us what happened on the afternoon of Saturday, 24 August.

A solicitor's clerk, Frederick Baker, saw no point in being cooped up in the office all Saturday, so he used his tea break to good advantage, strolling out into the meadows near the hop fields by the River Wey.

Fanny Adams and her two friends were playing happily when Baker passed them. He gave them halfpennies to run races for him and then sent two of the girls home while he took

Fanny into the hop field, later stopping off for a beer at the Swan Inn before returning to his office.

After Fanny was reported missing the horrified villagers found the body. Baker was arrested and at the inquest in the Duke's Head Inn three days later the jury viewed the body and heard the gruesome details of the discovery of the dismembered corpse.

The severed head was stuck on the top of a hop pole with the eyes gouged out and one ear torn off; the upper torso, cut off at the diaphragm, had the heart scooped out, left on the ground nearby; each arm was deposited separately, with two halfpennies still being clutched in one hand; one foot was discovered in a field of clover; both eyes were found in the River Wey; the legs were assumed to have been taken by the river's current; there was no evidence of a sexual assault because the lower abdomen was never found.

All the evidence suggested Baker had battered the poor child with a large stone and then butchered her with his penknife. He was unable to explain bloodstains on his cuffs and his main defence, that his knife was too small to have done the damage, was weak.

That any man should have behaved in such a way was an abomination and that Baker was a man who worked in the business of law seemed only to make it worse. Under magisterial examination at Winchester Town Hall on Thursday, 29 August, he strongly protested his innocence and asked for more time to prepare for calling a fellow clerk, Mr French, as a witness. The extra time was granted, but to no avail. Baker was found guilty of wilful murder and was hanged at Winchester at 8 a.m. on Christmas Eve 1867 before a high-spirited crowd of five thousand.

His case had not been helped by the discovery of his diary in the drawer of his desk. The final entry for Saturday, 24 August, read: 'Killed a young girl. It was fine and hot.'

That so little was left of sweet Fanny Adams's body lends graphic meaning to the phrase we now use. It explains, too, why 'Fanny Adams' became navy slang for the canned mutton first introduced into sailors' rations in 1869 and why the term was used as a generic name for meat stew as late as the 1940s.

Those who say the world today is cruel are right. But there are also those who say, after the latest child abduction makes the tabloid headlines, 'It never used to happen in the old days; children had freedom and fun back then; now they've got sweet FA.'

If only they knew what they were saying. Make no mistake – child murder is as old as the hills. Even in the hop fields of Alton in that golden summer of 1867, there was evil under the sun.

THE VOICE OF CONSCIENCE

NORWICH, 1869

Like the little boy who runs to his mother to say, 'It wasn't me who broke the vase' – even before his dastardly crime has been discovered – criminals of a rather more serious breed have long suffered the seemingly unbearable torture of the guilt complex, which makes remaining undetected almost as much of an ordeal as getting caught.

Police know from experience that the urge to place the blame elsewhere, to revisit the crime scene or to make a confession is a strong one indeed and many criminals would have remained undetected but for succumbing to one of these strangely seductive and often overwhelming desires.

One of the oddest cases of this type is that of the 'Norwich Murderer', William Sheward, who had so completely got away with killing his wife that he had nothing to fear whatsoever. Yet so badly did the incident play on his mind that he eventually issued a full confession to a startled police officer. Odd, in the circumstances, that he should do so at all – but even odder that he should wait fully eighteen years to spill the beans.

It was in June 1851 that the Norwich tailor William Sheward, living with his older wife Martha in a somewhat strained relationship, committed the crime that was to haunt him. After what he was later to describe as 'a violent altercation about money matters', he attacked his wife with a razor and slit her throat. Having then gone out drinking, he

62

spent the night in the house with his wife's corpse before embarking next morning on the painstaking and gruesome disposal of evidence.

It took him five days to complete a full dismemberment and the resulting body parts were either thrown down sewers or buried at various locations in the suburbs.

When Martha Sheward was missed he told friends and relations she had left him for another man in London and he had no idea where they were. Some of Martha's relations felt this to be out of character and suggested to police that they investigate, but when they interviewed Sheward they were more than satisfied with his story, regarding him as nothing more than a mild, inoffensive, if somewhat weak, creature.

Nasty moment number one was over for Sheward but far worse looked set to come when an inquisitive dog out for walkies in Lakenham, a suburb of Norwich, discovered a hand and then a foot loosely buried in undergrowth. Over the next few days Norwich police discovered many more body parts in the vicinity and were able to reconstruct an approximation of an entire corpse, which William Sheward knew only too well to be that of his 55-year-old wife.

The outcome of the investigation depended on forensic evidence, not nearly as scientific in the Victorian era as it is now, and a police surgeon got it spectacularly wrong: 'The well-filled understructures of the skin,' he wrote, 'its delicacy and the neatness of the foot, the clean well-trimmed nails of both hands and feet, suggest a person not accustomed to toil and aged between 16 and 26.'

That truly stunning own goal led police to accept that the body parts were those of 'a missing young person unknown' and with that erroneous verdict Martha Sheward was assumed to be just one of many women drawn to the metropolis in search of a better life. William Sheward was off the hook for the second time.

Left with his own guilt and conscience he must have had a scare two years later when police again knocked at his door asking after Martha Sheward, but all it was on this occasion was that she had been left a £300 inheritance and needed to claim it in person. Again William Sheward said she was 'somewhere in London'. With this third and final let-off the case was as good as closed.

The Norwich tailor continued his trade, remarried and had two sons. Yet friends said he seemed unsettled. He suffered bouts of depression, took to heavy drinking and talked of leaving Norwich for good. And that he did, moving to London, where he was led seemingly by irresistible forces to Walworth, the very spot where he had first made acquaintance with his murdered wife.

It was 1869 when his conscience could stand no more and he resolved to commit suicide – 'but the Almighty would not let me do it,' he later told police.

That left only one way of escape from his tortured world. Confession. He duly made a full statement to police, who at first discarded it as the ramblings of a crank, but, when the case was reopened and the same police surgeon was interviewed again about the certainty of his deductions, they accepted that the mystery remains must indeed have been those of Martha Sheward.

Fully eighteen years after his crime, William Sheward was tried for murder, found guilty and hanged at Norwich in 1869. He had been betrayed by nothing but his own conscience.

This cautionary case should be a lesson to us all. Unless we are prepared to spend a lifetime racked by guilt, assailed by doubt and in danger of breaking the Olympic high-jump record each time the doorbell rings, it pays to leave wife-murdering to those with a touch more bottle than poor William Sheward.

WAY OUT WEST

LANGTRY, UNITED STATES, 1882

'Extreme justice is extreme injustice.' When the Roman statesman Cicero (106–43 BC) made that shrewd observation, America's Wild West was unexplored territory. Yet almost two thousand years later the phrase seemed tailor-made to describe the remarkable courtroom capers of Judge Roy Bean, lawmaker extraordinary of the wild frontier.

My choice of date is entirely random: 1882 just happened to be the date Roy Bean began his judicial career by discharging a man accused of murder because 'it served the deceased right for getting in front of the gun'. Any one of the twenty years in which Judge Bean dispensed his peculiar brand of justice in Texas would have done just as well because all the proceedings in Bean's courthouse were of the strange persuasion.

All for the very simple reason that Judge Roy Bean was arguably the most colourful and strangest judge in all legal history, leastways in the good old US of A.

Born around 1825 in Mason County, Kentucky, he followed the railroad gangs as a young man, working in construction or as a trader and bartender. He later settled in San Antonio, Texas, and finally 'retired' early in 1882, replete with a lifetime of experience among the hardest of men and roughest of women, to run a crude saloon in the tented camp of Vinegaroon in the desolate Lower Pecos valley right on the Mexican border.

Was a man ever better qualified to dispense justice in a town where lawlessness was a way of life? The locals thought not and on 2 August 1882 Roy Bean was duly appointed Justice of the Peace by the very road-gang workers who drank regularly at his bar, the Jersey Lilly.

The bar was named (and given an extra 'l' for luck) after the beautiful English society actress, Lily Langtry, who took to the stage in 1881 and secured herself a big fan in Vinegaroon. In fact, so smitten was Roy Bean that he renamed the burgeoning town Langtry in honour of the actress with whose picture he was said to have fallen in love.

No one complained of this dictatorial move, perhaps because Vinegaroon, the Spanish for a large and rather ugly type of scorpion, wasn't the sort of name too many would campaign to keep. Nonetheless, Judge Roy Bean decided he liked the power that his position gave him, and, from thereon in, there was just no stopping him.

Doubling up the use of his ramshackle wooden saloon as a courtroom, he erected signs reading JUDGE ROY BEAN, NOTARY PUBLIC and LAW WEST OF THE PECOS next to the one saying ICE BEER.

This curious hybrid of bar room and courtroom made for interesting proceedings as the bearded Bean regularly interrupted his trials to serve bottled beer or a slug or two of something stronger. He started all his important cases by requesting that everyone should buy a bottle to oil the wheels of justice and he introduced a special house rule that no one was allowed to mention the name of Lily Langtry without buying a drink and toasting her picture, which hung behind the bar.

As the money rolled in, the strangest judge in the West branched out into weddings and inquests at two and five dollars apiece and, despite having no judicial power to grant divorces, he decided that was a nice little earner, too: 'If I can marry 'em,' he said, 'I guess I got a right to unmarry 'em if it don't take.' He generally alerted couples to the possibility of future business by finishing his marriage ceremony with, 'May God have mercy on your soul.'

Bean was equally noted for his unusual touches when wearing his coroner's hat. When a railroad worker fell 500 feet from a viaduct Bean pronounced him dead but felt the $5 fee wasn't big enough. Quickly changing into his Justice of the Peace character, he searched the body and found a pistol and $40. A ready-made solution – 'I find this corpse guilty of carrying a concealed weapon, and I fine it $40,' he boomed, while promptly pocketing the proceeds.

Bean became noted for his wild sense of humour, famously informal style and leniency in his treatment of his favoured locals. Dropping the case against one of the Jersey Lilly's tough Irish regulars for murder, he gave the reason that the victim was Chinese. Examining his famous handwritten 'statoot' book, which contained such gems as 'Cheating and horse theft is hanging offenses if ketched', he enlightened the court thus: 'Gents, this here court finds the law is explicit on the killin' of a fellow man, but there ain't nothin' about knockin' off a heathen Chinee – case dismissed and the drinks is on Paddy there!'

Despite (or perhaps because of) such scandalous judgments, the locals rather liked Judge Roy Bean. Most of them were, after all, habitual lawbreakers and Bean was later officially elected by majority to the Justice of the Peace post he had originally been arbitrarily appointed to.

Late in his career he became a celebrity in his own right and many visitors travelled out of their way to Langtry to see the legendary judge sitting on the front porch of his famous courthouse.

With the next nearest court some two hundred miles away, Bean's own brand of justice was given full rein. Yes, but was it effective? I hear you ask. Of course – as Bean once told a visitor: 'Everything is perfectly peaceful here: there hasn't been a man killed in four hours.'

Bean died just short of his eightieth year following a major bender in San Antonio in March 1903 in which he drank himself into a coma. He was carried back to Langtry and died in the back room of his courthouse the next day.

So there is way-out justice way out West. Thank goodness our British judges have all been upright fellows of the first order. God forbid there could ever be such eccentricity this side of the Atlantic.

And, if you like to believe that, might I suggest you read the rest of this book with a sharp pair of scissors to hand.

MAN'S BEST FRIEND?

COUNTY CORK, IRELAND, 1883

'Is there any other point to which you would wish to draw my attention?'
'To the curious incident of the dog in the night-time.'
'The dog did nothing in the night-time.'
'That was the curious incident,' remarked Sherlock Holmes.

The dialogue above, between Inspector Gregory and the world's greatest consulting detective, is from the short story *The Adventure of Silver Blaze*, first published in 1892. Holmes's lateral thinking led him to believe that the dog of the household must have known the intruder on his master's premises.

One wonders if Holmes's creator, Arthur Conan Doyle, had half a mind on turning on its head a real case from just a few years earlier, for in 1883 a dog named Sam gave evidence of a most singular kind, which left a couple of violent house-breakers feeling more than a little betrayed. The game is afoot.

Mrs Fitzgerald, an elderly widow, lived with her daughters in a house at the foot of Mushera Mountain in County Cork. One of the less welcome legacies of her late husband was an agrarian dispute with members of the Twohey family, who, even in the face of Mr Fitzgerald's death, were not prepared to let the matter lie.

Two brothers of the family, Jeremiah and James Twohey,

broke into the Fitzgerald home, threatened and assaulted the old lady and beat up her daughters. It was a violent and cowardly act but one they looked like getting away with.

They were charged on the evidence of an informer, at that time termed an 'approver', named Connell, but to make the charge stick the law in Ireland in those days required corroborative evidence from an independent source. Connell gave full details of the Twohey brothers' preparation for and participation in the raid, but no further evidence was forthcoming.

Mother and daughters were too shaken to identify their assailants with confidence and in any case suspected they may have been in disguise. There was a servant who seemed prepared to identify the Twohey brothers, but that evidence, too, was thought by the police to be too shaky to lead to a conviction.

Leading the prosecution at the court case in Cork in 1883 was to be Peter O'Brien, then a Senior Crown Prosecutor but later to be Lord Chief Justice of Ireland. Even his burgeoning advocacy skills looked set to struggle to bring the case home against the Twohey boys. Nor was he yet practised enough to bring to bear the shrewd but rather naughty jury-packing tactics that he was later so notorious for trying in an effort to secure cast-iron convictions – tactics that earned him the famous nickname 'Peter the Packer'.

Peter O'Brien looked like needing help, and he got it from an unusual source. When police had attended the scene of the crime they found a dog wandering close to the premises, seemingly lost. It didn't belong to the Fitzgeralds and when it was taken to the police station no one claimed it. Before the trial, on the hunch that the mystery pooch may have been left behind by the assailants as they fled the scene of the crime, Sub-Inspector Starkie and his sidekick Captain Plunkett bundled it into a sack and released it within sniffing distance of the Twohey brothers' home.

The results would have been most gratifying even to the great Sherlock Holmes. Sam, the unwitting canine informant left behind by his owners as they scarpered, did what came naturally and made straight for the Twohey household.

There the entire family made great efforts to shoo him away, but Sam was pleased to be home and greeted his owners in the time-honoured fashion of a faithful friend, wagging his tail furiously and reserving particular affection for his master, James Twohey. Sam's reaction might not have been admissible evidence in its own right but, when a search of the Twohey household revealed disguises and hidden ammunition, the vital independent supporting evidence was in place.

At the subsequent trial both prisoners were found guilty and Peter O'Brien made sure Sam was present in court to help press home his prosecution, where again the dog recognised the prisoners without needing a second glance.

Many is the time in history when dogs have protected their masters, sniffed out bodies or led police, Lassie-style, to hidden booty or badly injured victims. That's why they're called 'man's best friend' and why an old Irish proverb says, 'The dog that's always on the go is better than the one that's always asleep.'

Try selling either of those old chestnuts to the Twohey brothers, instinctively betrayed by the heroic Sam. They each got seven years' penal servitude.

THERE'S ALWAYS PARKER

THE HIGH COURT, LONDON, 1884

The Queen v. Dudley and Stephens was one of the strangest cases in Victoria's reign, which is saying something for an age in which bizarre occurrences were seemingly two a penny.

It is one of those rare cases that beg the question, 'What would *you* have done?' It's certainly a tough one to call.

The tale begins with the shipwreck on 5 July 1884 of the yacht *Mignonette* in the South Atlantic nearly two thousand miles from land on a journey from England to Australia.

Blessedly there were survivors. Three men, Captain Thomas Dudley, Edwin Stephens and Ned Brooks, were able to take to a small open boat. With them was seventeen-year-old Parker, the cabin boy, whose parents had taken the sensible precaution to name him Richard rather than Roger.

Without food or fresh water the foursome drifted for eighteen days, managing to catch and consume just one small turtle in that time. As hunger raged and minds became distorted, the survival instinct kicked in.

Dudley and Stephens suggested to Brooks that one of their number should be sacrificed for food, for all four would surely perish otherwise. Their intentions were all too clear. A kill, then cannibalism. Parker, undeniably a boy of tender years, was ominously left out of the debate.

Brooks made it clear he was repulsed by the idea and would have nothing to do with it, but, by day twenty, Dudley and

71

Stephens could hold out no longer. They resolved to eat and their menu plan had Parker on every course.

Dudley did the deadly deed, ably assisted by Stephens. The weak and defenceless cabin boy was slaughtered in cold blood and duly ripped apart. Over the next four days they ate his flesh and drank his blood. And that included Brooks, who, once the murder was done, seemed to acquire a sudden taste for the P-plan diet.

Their survival instincts paid off, as they were rescued on the 24th day by a passing German barque, the *Montezuma*, which brought them to Falmouth. When their grisly story unfolded the three survivors were surprisingly embraced by the public as heroes, and when it became clear there must be a trial there was a widespread popular clamour for their acquittal, which those on the other side of the law, undoubtedly thinking of Parker, found extremely hard to swallow.

The case was first heard before Judge Baron Huddleston at Exeter Assizes on 6 November 1884. The judge was so anxious to secure convictions that he took the unusual step of directing the jury to deliver a 'special verdict', which permitted them merely to state what they perceived as the true facts of the case, relieving them of the onerous responsibility of delivering an ultimate verdict. 'Upon the matter of the prisoners being guilty,' Judge Huddleston announced in his summing up, 'the jury are entirely ignorant. I therefore refer it to a higher court.'

When the case was heard before the five judges of the Queen's Bench Division of the High Court of Justice in London, the central question was whether Dudley and Stephens were guilty of murder or whether, on a legal technicality, the doctrine of necessity overrode that verdict. Brooks, by the way, although himself morally culpable of a rather shameful duplicity, was not charged with murder.

Lord Coleridge presided amid huge media interest. The defence argued that four human lives would have been lost but for the act. Being the weakest, Parker would surely have gone first and the taking of his life merely pre-empted what appeared to be inevitable by natural causes, they asserted.

In a long summing up Lord Coleridge was sympathetic and conceded that 'these men were subject to a terrible temptation and to sufferings which might break down the bodily power of the strongest man and try the conscience of the best'.

Yet he was unable to reconcile the facts completely and finished without ambiguity: 'It is therefore our duty to declare that the prisoners' act was wilful murder and that the facts stated are no legal justification for what they did.'

Lord Coleridge duly passed the death sentence on Dudley and Stephens but reserved more sympathy for them than he would ever have accorded to common murderers by suggesting that 'the Crown may wish to consider the possibility of a pardon in such extraordinary circumstances'.

It was indeed a supreme irony that, having fought so desperately to preserve their lives, the men should then face losing them at a stroke. After due consideration the Crown did show mercy and the death sentences were commuted to just six months' imprisonment without hard labour.

It was a truly extraordinary case, which divided the opinions of those who took an interest in it. But who can say with any certainty how *they* would have reacted adrift on the high seas? Starvation or Parker? An indigestible question indeed.

THREE-TIMES-LUCKY LEE

EXETER, 1885

During the early hours of 15 November 1884 Miss Emma Keyse was brutally murdered at her pretty thatched cottage in Babbacombe, near Torquay. The local community was outraged, for Miss Keyse, a former lady-in-waiting to Queen Victoria, was a wealthy and much-respected elderly spinster who lived a blameless life.

The police investigation quickly identified a twenty-year-old footman, John Lee, as the prime suspect. He had argued with Miss Keyse over household discipline, his duties and wages and had apparently cut her throat and battered her head at the dead of night in a cold-blooded act of revenge.

Lee was arrested and committed to trial at Exeter. Proceedings began on 2 February 1885 but in three days it was all up. The prosecution case was overwhelming and the jury took only forty minutes to find the prisoner guilty of murder.

As Mr Justice Manisty passed the inevitable sentence of death, he remarked on Lee's curiously calm and collected demeanour during the trial and suggested he spend his few remaining days alive in preparation for the next world. The condemned man's reply has entered legal history as the most prophetic of all time: 'The reason, my lord, why I am so calm and collected is because I trust in my Lord, and he knows I am innocent.'

Such bravado in the face of certain death was by no means unusual and Lee was removed from the courtroom and taken

74

back to Exeter Prison, where he remained in the condemned cell until 23 February, when the sentence was to be carried out. His execution was to be by the infallible long-drop method of hanging – once the trapdoors opened and the body plummeted down, a broken neck and instant death was a medical certainty. A few lucky men and women had survived the old-fashioned nonscientific hangings that had preceded the new method but the long-drop had been 100 per cent effective. Survival was impossible.

In the face of that, Lee's faith in God seemed naïvely misplaced, and his claim to have had a dream on the eve of his execution in which he survived three attempts to hang him was dismissed as nothing but desperate wishful thinking.

The executioner, James Berry, wasn't interested in Lee's dreams. He was too preoccupied checking and testing the trapdoor mechanism above the eleven-foot-deep pit in the prison coach house. He found everything to be in perfect working order.

Just before eight o'clock on the morning of 23 February, John Lee was led to the place of execution, his legs were strapped together, the rope was placed around his neck and a white cap pulled down over his face. Ten newspaper reporters watched as Lee remained impassive while a chaplain concluded the burial service. As the chaplain finished, James Berry pulled the lever to open the double trapdoor through which John Lee would hurtle to his death.

But an astonishing thing happened. *Nothing* happened. Despite Berry's continued movement of the lever to and fro the trapdoors remained firmly closed.

The noose and the cap were removed from Lee's head and he was moved forward while emergency repairs were effected with an axe, a saw and a plane. The apparatus was then tested and found to be working perfectly. Once again Lee was put in position and Berry pulled the lever. Yet once again, to the astonishment of all present, the trapdoors stayed firmly closed.

This was new territory for Hangman Berry and the prison officials, but after frantic discussions they determined to go for another attempt. Again they tested the apparatus. Again it worked. Again Lee was led forward. Again he survived despite Berry's stamping furiously on the trapdoors as he pulled the lever on this third attempt to hang John Lee.

As all present looked on dumbfounded it was the prison chaplain, the Reverend John Pitkin, whose presence of mind then called the shots. He wrote in his memoirs that 'we were all mentally paralysed by the hopelessness of the task we were by law expected to perform. Three times I had concluded the service and I announced that I would remain at the place of execution no longer.'

In that way Lee *was* saved from death by the act of a man of God, for further attempts to dispatch him could not legally be made without the chaplain's participation.

Lee was taken back to his cell and large crowds gathered outside Exeter Prison when the news of his three-times survival was broken. Although the prison authorities were determined to try again, and indeed Lee himself encouraged them to do so, public opinion clamoured for the prisoner's death sentence to be lifted.

That very same afternoon the Home Secretary, William Harcourt, put Lee's sentence on hold and it was later commuted to life imprisonment. While he was waiting for the news, Lee wrote to his sister and expressed his view that his survival was 'a miracle worked by the Lord'.

After a detailed investigation of this strange affair the prison authorities suggested that damp conditions had caused the trapdoors to swell and wedge together when Lee's weight was applied to them.

Whatever the reason, the failure of the mechanism permitted John Lee to spend 22 years in Portland Prison, Dorset, which he had never expected. He was released on 17 December 1907 and went back to live with his widowed mother in the village of Abbotskerswell, Devon. Many members of the public, in particular the victim's relations, were outraged that he had been allowed to survive at all. Equally large numbers thought he deserved his luck and great interest was aroused when *Lloyd's Weekly News* serialised his life story.

Lee further capitalised on this interest by having the story published in book form as *The Man They Could Not Hang*, and he made enough money from this to live very comfortably for some months. A year after his release from Portland Prison he married, moved to London and subsequently fathered two children. Although he worked as a humble barman his celebrity status was perpetuated when a silent film based on his life was shown around the country to enthusiastic audiences.

His later life is shrouded in some mystery but he is generally believed to have split from his wife and then travelled, ending up in Milwaukee, USA, where he died in 1933 aged 68. What is certain is that John Lee lived nearly fifty years of extra life because of nothing more than gremlins in the works. His astonishing survival of the hangman's noose remains the most remarkable case of its type of all time.

A SHOCKING AFFAIR

NEW YORK, UNITED STATES 1890

When William Kemmler, of Buffalo, New York, took a hatchet to his mistress, Tillie Zeigler, on 29 March 1889, he might well have known that the brutal murder would lead him to the courtroom.

But that he would be immortalised as a result of the verdict was not what he had in mind. The reason for his fame is clear, though, for William Kemmler was the first ever person to be condemned to death by the electric chair. And it didn't go well.

When the jury found him guilty of murder they marked a historic moment in legal history, the moment the barbaric, unreliable and primeval practice of hanging was swept aside in America for something quicker, cleaner and far more humane, something more befitting of a civilised nation that embraced new technology and recognised human dignity. That's the theory, but it proved a tougher cookie than the Americans had bargained for.

Even before the conviction strange forces were at work, for Kemmler's defence was sponsored . . . by an electricity company. There was method in this apparently distasteful madness, for the electrocution, if it happened, was set to take place using the Westinghouse Electric Company's new-fangled Alternating Current. This was being promoted by them as a cheaper and *safer* form of electricity supply than the direct-current system pioneered by Thomas Edison, and the idea that it could kill in an instant wasn't at all good for the ad campaign. The Westinghouse Company wanted to get Kemmler off, guilty or not.

They didn't, and Kemmler's execution was set for 6 August 1890 at New York's Auburn Prison. The death chamber was a large room with viewing seats provided for officials and reporters. Kemmler was led in and introduced by the warden in the manner of a master of ceremonies. This was theatre.

After a short speech Kemmler removed his coat and was strapped into the wooden chair before electrodes were secured in place by Deputy Sheriff Joseph Veiling, one on his head and another on his back. Kemmler's last words were to the point: 'Don't get excited, Joe, I want you to make a good job of this.'

On a signal from the warden, the executioner, hidden from view in an adjoining room, threw the switch and for fully seventeen seconds 1,000 volts pulsed through Kemmler's body, which contorted and strained, eyes bulging, as the current did its deadly job. When it was all over doctors gathered round the chair to confirm the deed was done as reporters looked on. The next day's *New York World* described what followed:

Suddenly the breast heaved. There was a straining on the straps. The man was alive! Everybody lost their wits and someone gave a startled cry for the current to be switched on again. The handle could be heard as it was pulled back and forth time and again to break the deadly current into jets.

They let it run this time for four minutes before the prisoner was finally pronounced dead. Although Kemmler had been unconscious throughout the ordeal it was accepted that it was a bungled operation and most of the press described it as 'horrific'. Only the *New York Times* stuck their neck out by saying, 'It would be absurd to talk of abandoning the law and going back to the barbarism of hanging.'

They were proved right, for voltages were subsequently increased and the electric chair flourished, although even as late as 1983 it still took nearly ten minutes to finish off John Evans in Alabama's Holman Prison. Meanwhile, the worst fears of the Westinghouse Electricity Company over negative publicity were unfounded, for they and their new system also went from strength to strength.

There is a humorous postscript to the unsavoury case of William Kemmler. Later in 1890, as news of the ongoing use of the electric chair spread worldwide, Emperor Menlek II of Abyssinia (now Ethiopia) was so impressed by stories of its efficiency that he ordered three from New York. He had overlooked one vital factor though. Abyssinia had no electricity!

Two of the chairs were promptly thrown out and he used the third as a throne, so Emperor Menlek is one of just a handful of men to have sat in the electric chair and lived to tell the tale.

A UNIQUE DISCOVERY

NECHOCHEA, ARGENTINA, 1892

The quality of strangeness, particularly in relation to the scientific techniques of criminology, is one that shifts with time, for by today's standards the capture and conviction of a murderess in the province of Buenos Aires, Argentina, in July 1892, was a tediously routine case.

Yet, at the time, the methods used to incriminate the culprit were as 'cutting-edge' as any of the myriad computer-aided techniques now increasingly being applied. It is odd that the small town of Nechochea should have secured a permanent place in legal history, but then the first ever use of fingerprints in a successful detection is certainly something worth shouting about, bearing in mind the subsequent use of that method in bringing millions of criminals to justice.

The build-up to this celebrated case is interesting because the concept of fingerprints had been talked about long before their use in a real situation. A Scots-born doctor and teacher, Henry Faulds, submitted a short monograph on the uniqueness of this human 'calling card' and its potential use in catching criminals to the magazine *Nature* and it was published on 28 October 1880. Alas, the British authorities took little notice of his 'cranky' views, and, just eight years later in London, a certain Jack the Ripper was able to leave his prints all over the place without ever being caught.

Even writers of fiction were more ahead of the game than police. The American author Mark Twain mentioned thumbprinting criminals in his 1883 *Life On the Mississippi*, and two years before that, in the December 1881 edition of *Chambers' Journal*, a ripping yarn entitled 'The Story of a Thumb-Mark' described how a murderer was caught by use of Henry Faulds's recently publicised technique.

It was only a matter of time before science fiction became science fact and the unlucky first victim of this advance was Francesca Rojas. When her two young children were found with their throats cut Francesca was also found to have a superficial throat wound and she laid the blame for the murders and 'attempted murder' firmly at the door of her neighbour, Velasquez.

He was arrested and questioned but police were unsure of his guilt and wrote to the police Bureau of Anthropometric Identification in La Plata for help. In charge of the bureau was Juan Vucetich, an enthusiast of the Faulds methods, and he instructed his colleague Inspector Edward Alvarez to make a detailed examination of the crime scene.

When Alvarez found bloody fingerprints on a door jamb he sawed out the relevant section and sent it back to Vucetich with sample prints taken from the mother and suspect. The prints were quickly shown to belong to the mother and, since she had denied ever touching the children after she had supposedly 'found' them dead, it was certain she was lying. When confronted with the scientific 'proof' she broke down, offered a full confession and was duly tried, found guilty and given a lengthy prison term.

Vucetich had undeniably triumphed in making a major breakthrough and as a consequence he started the world's first fingerprinting bureau to put Argentina at the forefront of new detection techniques.

Yet the strangest postscript to the pioneering Francesca Rojas case is how slow other forces were to cotton on and how it was the nations we would now call 'Third World' who were first to react.

Outside Argentina the first use of fingerprints in a murder case was in Bengal, India, in May 1898, when a thief called Kangali Charan was charged with murdering his former employee. Again, prints linked him inextricably with the theft and murder, but the Indian court, evidently wary of the power of this new technology, perversely saw fit to find him guilty only of the theft.

It wasn't until the conviction of Henri Scheffer on 14 March 1903 for murdering a dentist's manservant in Paris that prints were used in a capital case in Europe, and it was fully 25 years after Henry Faulds's 'cranky' monograph that a British murderer was finally convicted on fingerprint evidence.

Maybe Scotland Yard were making up for lost time, for at the Old Bailey on 23 May 1905 the Stratton brothers were found guilty of the double murder of an elderly man and his wife at their chandler's shop in Deptford High Street, south London.

Now we have DNA profiling and sophisticated computer-aided analysis of voice, facial characteristics, handwriting and personality. There will undoubtedly be more discoveries to come and the thanks for setting the ball rolling must go to the Scottish scientist and Argentinian police chief so willing to stick their necks out over a century ago.

IN THE FOOTSTEPS OF
SWEENEY TODD

CHICAGO, UNITED STATES, 1897

The People's Periodical and Family Library, published in
Fleet Street, London, began to sell particularly well from
November 1846. For it was in that issue of the 'penny
dreadful' that a serial entitled *The String of Pearls* first
introduced readers to the fascinatingly macabre character of
Sweeney Todd, the 'Demon Barber of Fleet Street'.

The barber who would regularly dispatch his customers
from the chair through a trapdoor into a subterranean morgue,
after using his cutthroat razor exactly as the name implies,
provided a storyline likely to do the next issue's sales figures
no harm at all; that the hapless victims were then butchered
and ended up in the famously 'tasty pies' sold by Mrs Lovett
in her shop at Bell Yard was enough to create record sales of
The People's Periodical for the eighteen issues in which
Sweeney appeared. Pie sales, however, dipped alarmingly for
the same period.

So legendary did the tale become that by the end of the
century Sweeney Todd joined Sherlock Holmes in the psyche
of many members of the general public as one of those
characters who really did exist beyond the pages of fiction.

Yet, far-fetched as his extracurricular tonsorial activity may
have been, legal history has thrown up some strange cases of
its own that come closer to Todd's dreadful deeds than might
be imagined. May I introduce the master sausage maker

84

Adolph Luetgert (1848–1911)?

When he emigrated from Germany to the United States in the 1870s he settled in Chicago, showing great entrepreneurial spirit and opening a sausage factory in the neighbourhood of Lakeview.

His appetite for making money was matched by his appetite for women, and when his first wife died he married Louisa Bicknese. He cemented the relationship by giving her a gold ring embossed with her new initials, 'LL', but despite this loving gesture he still took mistresses whenever it pleased him and soon became bored with Louisa.

On 11 March 1897 he decided on positive action, buying 325 pounds of potash and 50 pounds of arsenic. Neither was required in the sausage-making process. After 1 May, his wife Louisa was noticeable only by her absence and Luetgert explained to all enquirers, including her brother Diedrich, that she had gone visiting relatives in Kankakee, Illinois.

Diedrich Bicknese, unable to track his sister down, subsequently informed the police and Captain Hermann Schluetter was put on the case. It was on 15 May, acting on information from two factory employees, that he decided to examine the contents of a five-foot-deep vat, which contained a pungent and greasy slime. It was Officer Walter Dean who made the gruesome discovery of human bone fragments and a small section of gold ring. The initials 'LL' were still clear.

Police soon concluded, despite strenuous denials from Luetgert, that he had ground up the body and then boiled it in the vat usually used for sausage meat. Witnesses spoke of suspicious behaviour and having caught sight of Louisa with Luetgert in the factory on the night she disappeared.

When he was charged with the crime the residents of Chicago were revolted by the details and, since they themselves were familiar with tales of Sweeney Todd, rumour soon had it that Louisa Luetgert had been made into sausage. In truth she never was, because the factory was being refurbished and wasn't manufacturing at that time, but suffice to say the butchers of Chicago saw banger sales slump for some weeks after Luetgert's unsavoury deeds were revealed.

No further body parts were ever discovered and, as such, the evidence remained circumstantial. It was that which saved Luetgert's skin, for at the first trial, on 21 October 1897, opinion was split as to whether he should suffer the death penalty or life imprisonment.

At the second trial, on 9 February 1898, he got the benefit of the doubt, being convicted of murder but sentenced to life imprisonment as a result of the rather fragmentary evidence.

Luetgert died in the Joliet State Penitentiary in 1911, a shadow of his former robust self, claiming his wife was haunting him. His attorney, Lawrence Harmon, too, suffered extreme mental strain as a result of losing the case. So convinced was he that Louisa would one day turn up to save the day that he spent $2,000 of his own savings searching for her. She never did appear and Harmon died insane in a mental institution.

Although the sausage factory burnt down in 1902 and was never rebuilt, Chicago folklore has it that the ghost of Louisa Luetgert still walks the site. That would be strange, but, in a world where the line between fact and fiction is an indistinct one to a public ever susceptible to the sensational and macabre, it may also be true.

This case remains one of the oddest murders on record, and still without an entirely conclusive solution. Could the haunting spectre of the 'sausage lady' be the missing link?

A THEATRICAL PERFORMANCE

THE OLD BAILEY, LONDON, 1898

The similarities between a courtroom scene and the stage are legion. Elaborate costume, stirring speeches, witty asides and the serried ranks of the 'audience' make for everything from high drama to cruel tragedy and hilarious farce.

But once in a while, when genuine thespians really do appear in court, the worlds of the stage and the law become one, and invariably to theatrical effect. Enter, stage left, Richard 'Mad Archie' Prince.

Dundee-born Prince, christened Richard Millar Archer, the son of a humble ploughman, was everything the archetypal 'wannabe' invariably is – full of ambition, full of himself, but entirely devoid of all but basic talent. The eccentric Scotsman was, it has to be said, a 'cannabe' of cringeworthy averageness – at best.

He'd reached the age of 39 scratching nothing more than a meagre living from occasional small parts, and as Christmas 1897 loomed he was 'resting' for the umpteenth time. His Actors' Benevolent Fund maintenance payment had just been stopped and he was pondering where his next decent meal would come from. He was also looking for someone to blame.

Enter, stage right, William Terriss, a handsome and hugely popular actor-manager of the flamboyant world of Victorian theatre who was everything 'Mad Archie' aspired to.

Terriss, affectionately known as 'Breezy Bill', had tried his best to help Prince by giving him small parts but had once had him thrown out of a play for offensive remarks. Even so, when Prince's 'resting' became a permanent state of affairs, Terriss was kind enough to give him free stage passes and the odd handout.

But none of that washed with Prince, who blamed his misfortune entirely on Terriss and planned to wreak vengeance.

On the evening of 16 December 1897 Richard Prince lurked under the awning of the famous Rules Restaurant in London's Maiden Lane, not the best place for a hungry out-of-work actor to soothe his troubled brow. The woodcock with chestnut purée looked particularly inviting.

As fifty-year-old William Terriss approached the rear entrance of the Adelphi Theatre opposite, prior to his performance in the play *Secret Service*, the years of frustration finally caused Richard Prince to act as he'd never acted before.

Who knows what really caused him to flip? But flip he did. He dashed across the road and plunged a kitchen knife deep into William Terriss's back. As the hero of melodrama turned and fell, a second blow slashed his side and a third inflicted a chest wound for good measure.

Terriss got the final curtain prematurely that night, dying in the Adelphi greenroom shortly after the stabbing. The evening's performance was cancelled and elsewhere in theatre land all the stages of the West End observed a minute's silence as news of the tragedy quickly spread. Richard Prince was a leading player at last.

He made no attempt to escape, but strode up and down Maiden Lane delivering a dramatic soliloquy justifying his deed. When the police arrived he meekly gave himself up and when they later offered him food at Bow Street Police Station, he burst into tears, sobbing, 'I'm so hungry.'

Act Two of Prince's gripping performance saw the scene shift to the Old Bailey on 13 January 1898. He first answered the charge of murder with a plea of 'guilty with provocation' but changed this on the advice of his counsel to 'not guilty by reason of insanity'. This was backed up by medical evidence demonstrating his 'insane delusions' and, rather less scientifically, by his loving mother. She took to the witness box to declare loudly, 'My son is soft in the head.'

Throughout the one-day trial Richard Prince wore an Inverness cape and conducted himself in a thoroughly theatrical manner, seemingly much pleased to be centre stage at last. The jury needed only half an hour to find him 'guilty but not responsible for his actions'. He was duly committed to the criminal lunatic asylum at Broadmoor and speedily removed from the courtroom as he attempted to make a dramatic closing speech of thanks.

Thus spared from the hangman's noose, Prince was, according to reports of his later life, much happier in the surreal world of the asylum than he had been in the real world outside. There were frequent opportunities to take meals with Napoleon Bonaparte or indulge in a game of draughts with Alexander the Great, and Prince took a keen interest in all the entertainments put on by the inmates.

Mad Archie's new company might well have performed to audiences a few short of a full house but rave reviews were guaranteed.

ROUGH JUSTICE

FLEMINGSBURG, KENTUCKY, UNITED STATES, 1903

It is unusual for a man to be convicted of the same crime three times but that is exactly what happened to William J Thacker after he murdered John Gordon in July 1900. But what singles out this case as more remarkable still was that Thacker's third conviction was not in a court of law, for the callous murderer was subjected to the roughest justice of all: the lynch mob.

In 1900 Thacker, a burly hard-drinking man in his early forties, lived in the small hamlet of Noah in northeast Kentucky, where he owned a general store and doubled as the local postmaster. His true passion, though, was an interest in the baser manifestations of politics and he was a firm devotee of the Republican Party, which had been dominated by the Democrats for almost fifty years since the Civil War.

It was on 30 July 1900 that Thacker, accompanied by his sixteen-year-old son Robert, left his home to go hunting for what he considered to be the most dangerous quarry in the entire United States. Thacker was after Democrats.

Buoyed by a few slugs of liquor, he accosted John Gordon, a local sawmill worker in his early twenties, and asked him if he knew any local Democrats. When Gordon unwisely admitted being one himself, Thacker goaded him into a fight and as Gordon advanced with a knife Thacker drew a gun and shot him in the head. He covered the body with brush and left Gordon to die.

In the cold and sober aftermath of his treacherous act, Thacker confessed to the murder, was taken to Flemingsburg jail and convicted in January 1901. His sentence was life imprisonment but he appealed against this, unsuccessfully as it turned out. Exactly a year later he was again convicted and once more sentenced to life.

Yet once again Thacker found grounds on which to appeal and it seemed likely that even more time and money would be wasted on an abjectly guilty and vicious killer. Public feeling in the area ran high and Democrats, understandably, spared little sympathy for Thacker.

It was just after midnight on 15 July 1903 that an angry mob, which had gathered outside Flemingsburg jail, decided that the machinery of the unwieldy American legal system needed a little oiling. They stormed the building, dragged the screaming Thacker from his cell, stoned him and ripped his clothes to shreds. Then they hanged him from a honey locust tree.

It was natural that there should be an inquest but the coroner returned a verdict of death by persons unknown and no action was ever taken against any of the lynch mob, despite the fact that the identities of some would have been easy to ascertain.

It was an unusual way for justice to be dispensed but a surprisingly common one in the Southern and Western states of the USA, where law enforcement could be notoriously ineffective and fear of Negro domination or extreme religious indoctrination was a very real problem to many Americans. Between 1882 and 1927 nearly five thousand persons were lynched in the USA.

Although the last lynching there was reported to be in 1954, the lynch-mob mentality still prevails, even in England, where angry crowds habitually gather outside courtrooms or prisons when particularly reviled characters are set to make an appearance.

Without the stringent security measures now in place, who knows what might happen in the heat of the moment?

Certainly there is an ingrained and primitive desire for justice of the most direct kind in sections of most societies. It may be more than two hundred years since the Quaker Charles Lynch set up his own court to dispense summary justice in the town now known as Lynchburg, Virginia, back in the eighteenth century, but the spirit of the uniquely practical brand of the law to which he is generally acknowledged to have given his name is still alive today.

ELEMENTARY, MY DEAR HOLMES!

GREAT WYRLEY, STAFFORDSHIRE, 1903

At the risk of disillusioning admirers of Sherlock Holmes, the world's most brilliant detective of all time, it is my sorry duty to report that the great man never solved a single case in his life. He was, regrettably, a fictional character – a shock, I know, to the countless fans who have written to him at 221B Baker Street over the years, but there it is. Sooner or later someone will be telling us that Santa Claus doesn't exist – it's a cruel world we live in.

Yet strangely enough the razor-sharp intellect and unique powers of observation we associate with Holmes did help to shape the course of British justice, because his creator, Sir Arthur Conan Doyle, used his own considerable knowledge of the art of detection to help solve a singular crime and usher in a law that has benefited the wrongly accused for almost a century since. 'The Case of the Mutilated Beasts' might sound like one of Doyle's more far-fetched short stories but this one was played for real.

In the latter years of the nineteenth century the vicar of Great Wyrley in Staffordshire was Shapurji Edalji, a Parsee Indian married to an Englishwoman, who had a son named George. The family met with considerable uncharitable xenophobia from parishioners and in 1888 a series of threatening anonymous messages were scrawled on walls around Great Wyrley parish. When a disaffected servant girl admitted writing them Edalji let the matter rest, not wishing to create a fuss.

Then, between 1892 and 1895, anonymous letters, in a

93

different hand, were sent to the Edaljis and many cruel practical jokes were played on the family. Deliveries of goods were made to their home as a result of bogus orders, advertisements under the vicar's name were placed in the newspapers, rubbish was strewn on their lawn and, mysteriously, a key from Walsall Grammar School was left on their doorstep. The local Chief Constable, the Honourable G R Anson, investigated the incidents and told Edalji that it was his own son George, a pupil at Malvern School, who was responsible – a 'difficult teenage phase', nothing more.

Despite George's protestations of innocence, believed by his father completely, the matter was again put to rest.

But from February to August 1903, by which time George had entered into practice as a Birmingham solicitor, Great Wyrley was again back in the news when a bizarre series of animal mutilations occurred in the parish – sixteen sheep, cattle and horses had their stomachs ripped open and letters were sent to the police accusing George Edalji of being 'The Great Wyrley Beast Killer'.

He was duly arrested and put in jail to await trial. Police had found 'horse-hairs and blood' on his jacket cuffs and other circumstantial evidence, which they said linked Edalji firmly to the outrage.

George was a quiet, studious and very sensitive young man and he wrote to the press from his prison cell offering his life savings of £25 to anyone who could give a clue that would lead to the real culprit. No one came forward until a hysterical farmer's son, Harry Green, sensationally confessed to the mutilations himself.

The police rejected his statement and promptly ushered him from the scene by assisting his passage for an extended visit to South Africa. Edalji, meanwhile, was tried, found guilty and sent to prison for seven years late in 1903, despite the fact that the animal mutilations had continued even while he was in custody.

It was an outrageous stitch-up fuelled entirely by racial hatred – one Birmingham newspaper said the killings were 'sacrifices which were part of Edalji's elaborate Black Magic rituals'.

The police and public were happy with the conviction but a number of solicitors and barristers sent a petition to the Home Office expressing their outrage. It was ignored, although it may have contributed to Edalji's early release for good behaviour in 1906.

Once free of his prison nightmare Edalji, barred from legal practice, promptly gave his own account of the affair in a sporting magazine called *The Umpire*. Sir Arthur Conan Doyle read that account.

Doyle instinctively believed Edalji and arranged to meet him to discuss the evidence in detail, and he subsequently wrote the serialised 'Story of Mr George Edalji' in the *Daily Telegraph* in January 1907.

Using all the techniques with which he had imbued Sherlock Holmes, Doyle was able to expose the police 'evidence' as an utter sham – armed with a special dispensation from Scotland Yard he was allowed to examine the exhibits.

Edalji's clothes were indeed covered in horsehair, but only because they had been taken to the police station bundled up in a box with a horse's mane. The bloodstains on his cuffs were indeed cattle blood – splashes from a joint of rare beef Edalji had enjoyed for Sunday lunch. Blood on Edalji's razor was rust, and the hairs on it were human, not equine. The anonymous letters were written by two people jealous of Edalji's respectability. Doyle was unsuccessful in getting Edalji the compensation and retrial he pushed for because the Gladstone Commission charged with re-examining the case shamefully fudged the issue.

But Edalji's name was cleared in the eyes of the public and the Law Society readmitted him to the roll of solicitors. Such was the public support, too, for Doyle's campaign, that the widespread national criticism played a major part in leading to the creation of the Court of Criminal Appeal in 1907, which has helped to furnish justice to countless men and women ever since.

In as much as Sir Arthur Conan Doyle *was* Sherlock Holmes, the greatest detective of all time has, after all, shaped the course of British justice and 'The Case of the Mutilated Beasts' was one of his most singular triumphs.

A MAN AHEAD OF HIS TIME

HARLESDEN, LONDON, 1905

Countless murderers throughout history have been caught and convicted because they didn't plan ahead. But Arthur Devereux knew precisely that and he aimed to get away with murder by foolproof planning of the most meticulous kind. Alas for poor Arthur, though, his forward-thinking approach proved to be the very thing that finally convinced the trial jury of his guilt and condemned him to the gallows.

Devereux was working for a chemist in Hastings when he met his future wife Beatrice there in 1896. They married two years later in Paddington, but after the birth of their first son, Stanley, they began to struggle financially. Beatrice was an accomplished musician and might well have contributed significantly to the family income but for the untimely arrival of twins, Evelyn and Lawrence, in 1903. Devereux doted on young Stanley but he resented the twins from the moment they were born.

Feeling all the pressures of being the sole breadwinner, Arthur Devereux struggled to hold down his job and began to suffer emotionally. In an effort to dig himself out of the hole, he resorted to illegal and bizarre behaviour, first forging false references to get himself a position and then posing as an American millionaire.

But these excursions into fantasy land paid no dividends and by December 1904 the Devereux family were in dire straits. It was in that month that they moved into a top-floor flat in Harlesden, northwest London, under the assumed name of Egerton, by which time Arthur Devereux had already decided to rid himself of the main drain on his resources, his wife and the twins. The catalyst for the dreadful deed surely occurred on 2 January 1905, when Arthur was released from his post as a chemist's assistant in Kilburn. Mrs Devereux and the twins were last seen alive on 28 January.

Although Arthur told neighbours and the milkman that they had gone to Plymouth for a rest cure, Beatrice Devereux's mother proved tougher to convince and her tip-off to the police ultimately led them to a trunk deposited in a warehouse by Devereux. It was opened on 13 April and was found not to contain the bottles of chemicals that Devereux had insisted it did. Instead, tightly crammed inside the trunk, were the bodies of Beatrice Devereux and her twenty-month-old twins, both still wearing their nightgowns.

Devereux was picked up by police at his new place of work in Coventry and charged with murder, to which the 34-year-old pleaded not guilty at his trial in June. On the face of it, the jury seemed to have a simple task, but Devereux concocted an elaborate story that might have sown the seeds of doubt in the minds of the more susceptible members of the panel.

His version was that on the morning of 28 January he had argued with his wife, taken young Stanley out for the day and returned to find his wife and twins dead in bed smelling of chloroform. It was a clear case of suicide, he said, and only the fear that suspicion would fall on him had led him first to pack the trunk with its gruesome cargo, then to pack Stanley off to boarding school in Kenilworth and finally to pack himself off to a new life in Coventry just a few miles away.

It might just have washed with the jury but for Devereux's peculiar brand of forward planning, for he had 'imagined' the deed done before it actually occurred.

Members of the jury began seriously to wonder when they heard the landlord of the Harlesden flat testify that Devereux said he would 'only need it for six weeks' but the real clincher was Devereux's reply to a job advertisement, which he sent off on 13 January, a full fifteen days before his wife's death.

It proved to be unlucky 13 for Devereux, for in his letter he described himself as 'a widower'. It is a fatal trait in many walks of life to glimpse the winning post too early and Devereux's wishful thinking proved his final undoing. Having unwittingly announced himself as a murderer ahead of his time, he was pronounced guilty by the jury after just ten minutes' consultation.

As an object lesson in forward planning the case of Arthur Devereux is best treated with caution by all those intent on murder. One word out of place had cost him his life and he was hanged at Pentonville Prison on 15 August 1905.

MURDER BY REQUEST

GUILDFORD ASSIZES, 1919

It is unusual for a man to stand up in court, openly admit to stabbing someone to death, yet still expect to be found not guilty. Yet this was exactly the scenario at Guildford Assizes on Thursday, 3 July 1919, as seventeen-year-old William Nelson Adams described how he stabbed sixty-year-old George Jones but asked the court to consider the special circumstances surrounding his apparently cold-blooded act.

George Jones had befriended young Adams, a market porter from Blackfriars, London, and given him lodgings in his home. He treated the lad to meals and drinks and after one such excursion to a pub in Tooting on the evening of 10 June 1919 their unlikely friendship took a curious turn.

They left the pub late at night in the company of another man, Charlie Smith, and caught a tramcar to Sutton. Shortly before midnight they alighted and walked into a local park, where Adams stabbed his elderly friend six times with a shoemaker's awl, three times in the throat and three times in the chest.

Jones was later found half alive, wearing only his trousers and vest, with his shirt wrapped awkwardly about his chest and neck as if someone had tried to stem the flow of blood. He lived for three more days and was able to tell police that he had no idea why Adams had attacked him: 'I had done nothing to him,' he said.

When Adams was arrested he told police a different story

altogether, one that he repeated in court, and one that gave the jury a dilemma that no jury had ever encountered before. Adams made no effort to deny the killing, but explained that Jones had made a request that he should perform a special service in gratitude for his kindness: 'During the tramcar journey he gave me the weapon,' Adams explained. 'He said to me, "I've done you a good turn, now you do one for me. Will you kill me?"'

This curious affair became known as the 'Murder by Request' case and Adams related to the court in detail how Jones had told him he was worried out of his life because of an income tax bill he couldn't pay.

'When we got to the park,' said Adams, 'George said to me, "The best way is to stab me in the left side of the neck." I hesitated for a quarter of an hour but at last had the temptation to do it.'

The court was told that Charlie Smith, a man never found by police, watched the whole scene but did not participate. Although Adams told the court that he had tried to stem the flow of blood, his cause wasn't helped by the fact that he had stolen Jones's money after the crime and fled the scene.

The jury retired after hearing Adams's final cry for mercy that he had 'only been trying to oblige the old gentleman'.

No one but Adams, the missing Charlie Smith and the dead man ever knew the real truth but there was a strong feeling in the contemporary press reports that Adams's bizarre tale might well have approximated to the truth. The jury, though, undoubtedly conscious of the possibility of setting a hugely unwise precedent, found Adams guilty of murder and the seventeen-year-old was sentenced to death.

Adams, though, did not hang. Home Secretary Edward Shortt commuted the 'Murder by Request' prisoner's sentence to life imprisonment.

In the wake of Adams's case, a number of subsequent murderers have used the 'request' defence, most entirely without justification, but one or two have been cited as possibly genuine.

Most famous of these, and proven to be true, was the South

African case of a 23-year-old bodyguard, Marthinus Rossouw, who shot his boss in the head near Cape Town in March 1961. The boss, a playboy-landowner named Baron Dieter von Schauroth, had an unhappy marriage and was suspected of being involved in illegal diamond trading. He gave Rossouw a revolver and a cheque for 2,300 rand to do the deadly deed.

At the trial in 1962 Rossouw's defence again proved a spurious one but, as the baron had recently insured his life heavily, the aftermath of the crime was a bitter wrangle between his widow and the insurance company, who said that von Schauroth's death was not 'murder' but 'assisted suicide'.

There are variations on this unusual theme. Murderers have claimed to have been hypnotised, taken over by evil spirits, guided by God or instructed by aliens. Although such cases have required a closer examination of the legal implications than most, the defendants are seldom successful, although 'killing while sleepwalking' and being in a state of 'automatism' have been allowed as valid defences on rare occasions, as has murder during the course of an epileptic fit.

On balance, though, I would suggest that anyone with murder in mind should prepare to take full responsibility for their act. Even if you are begged to do it, there is only one person who will be truly 'asking for it' – and it won't be the victim.

MONKEY BUSINESS

DAYTON, USA, 1925

Think of the USA in 1925. The jazz age. Gangsters. Illicit drinking dens. The movies. All the latest inventions. A worldly-wise nation at least ten years ahead of Britain and centuries ahead of the world's less developed cultures.

Then think again, for the curiously anachronistic case of *The State of Tennessee v. John T Scopes* might have been straight from the Middle Ages. And it put the tiny town of Dayton, Tennessee, under the world spotlight as unprecedented press coverage reported on the opposing religious principles that lay at the core of this extraordinary affair.

The catalyst was the passing of the Butler Act in 1925, an act intended to reflect the deeply fundamentalist religious beliefs of much of America's population. It was made law in the State of Tennessee on 21 March and the legislators claimed it would 'uphold the foundation of the Bible on which Christian belief depends and preserve the truth for our children of the Biblical story of the creation'.The terms of the bill itself provide a more telling translation of that fundamentalist view, for in short the Butler Act was an anti-evolution measure which forbade the teaching of Darwin's Theory of Evolution in school biology classes. Forget the scientific evidence. Ignore the fossils. The only truth was Genesis, Chapter 1, verses 25–7. And that in 1925.

The God-fearing parents of Tennessee's children had, as a body, no objection to this hugely blinkered Act, but the

American Civil Liberties Union determined to challenge it and advertised for a teacher willing to volunteer to be prosecuted in a test case. A Dayton businessman, George Rappelyea, saw the advertisement and, seeing it as an ideal opportunity to put his sleepy town on the map, persuaded a 24-year-old biology teacher, John T Scopes, to act as guinea pig.

His plan worked perfectly. Four days after he had reported Scopes for flouting the law and corrupting the pupils at Rhea County High School, the young teacher was indicted by a Rhea County grand jury for violating the Butler Act. And several months later, when the trial commenced on 10 July 1925, the whole of America and much of the world beyond had heard of Dayton, population just 2,000.

An old Southern plantation house served as a courtroom and a thousand people filled the hall to capacity on day one as committed fundamentalists in the gallery sang hymns and prayed for a guilty verdict.

Leading the prosecution was William Jennings Bryan, himself a committed Christian fundamentalist and a powerful Bible Belt personality. Against him was Clarence Darrow, confirmed religious sceptic, who agreed to defend Scopes without a fee. Holding court was Judge John T Raulston, staunch upholder of the literal truth of the Bible.

If ever a stage was set for a national debate, this was it, and the fireworks soon began. Judge Raulston refused to allow Darrow to use any scientific evidence. Eleven of the jury were self-declared fundamentalists and the twelfth could not read. Darrow's chances of pulling off a victory looked slim indeed.

By 15 July, with the nation listening for the first time ever to live radio broadcasts of court proceedings, the outcome of 'The Scopes Monkey Trial', as the press quickly dubbed it, looked a foregone conclusion as Judge Raulston formally announced to the jury that the theory of evolution was entirely inadmissible: 'All you need to decide,' he instructed them, was 'whether or not Scopes has taught the theory'.

Darrow complained bitterly and was promptly cited by Judge Raulston for contempt of court and denied all recourse to expert witnesses from the scientific community. Thus left in complete isolation, he launched a last desperate bid to discredit Bryan's fundamentalist theories by questioning him on the literal interpretation of the Bible.

His barrage was relentless and huge gaps in Bryan's knowledge of his own 'good book' were exposed before the packed court as many of the Bible's literalisms were shown to be ludicrous. Darrow encouraged religious sceptics in the courtroom to laugh loudly each time he scored a point and finally Judge Raulston put the embarrassed Bryan out of his misery by instructing him to stand down from the witness stand.

It was a classic technical knockout but perversely, on the brink of possible victory, Darrow asked the jury to find Scopes guilty. He had in mind an appeal, which would give the case even more publicity and turn the screw even more painfully on the hapless Bryan.

Sure enough, Scopes was found guilty and fined the nominal sum of $100, but those who firmly believed God had acted as an agent for the prosecution case were stunned just five days later as William Bryan died of a brain haemorrhage.

This undeniably dramatic case reached a halfway-house conclusion in 1926, when the Supreme Court of Tennessee in Nashville overturned the verdict on a number of technicalities. John T Scopes, the evil teacher of that monkey business called evolution, was an innocent man.

But the wheels of change still moved slowly in Tennessee. Clarence Darrow quickly declared that the entire anti-evolution Act was 'as brazen and as bold an attempt to destroy learning as was ever made in the Middle Ages' – but it wasn't until 1967 that the Act was repealed and the theories of Charles Darwin could be legally taught in the schools of Tennessee in the 'Land of the Free'.

ONCE PICKLED, FOREVER TOASTED

PAISLEY, SCOTLAND, 1928

When May McAllister was born in Cambuslang, near Glasgow, on 4 July 1898, that she would one day alter the course of legal history would have been a fantastic notion to her plain-living steelworker father James and his wife Mary.

Yet their daughter was destined to become the pivotal figure in a bizarre incident that has become one of the most famous and influential in common-law history.

May married Henry Donoghue in 1915 but life was unkind to her in the years that followed. By 1920 she had given birth to four children, three of whom died within a matter of days, and she endured a life of harsh deprivation. In 1928 she parted from Henry and moved to her brother's flat at 49 Kent Street, Glasgow. By way of a pick-me-up she arranged to meet a friend on the pleasant summer evening of Sunday, 26 August 1928, taking a tram to nearby Paisley and strolling into Mr Minchella's inviting café for a little refreshment.

After scrutinising the menu she made the decision that would write her name indelibly into the legal history books. She ordered a ginger beer to mix with her ice cream to make a soda. As she poured some of the sparkling mineral from its opaque bottle she would have been blissfully unaware that ginger beer already had a legal record of sorts, but thereby lay the rub of the tale that was to unfold.

In 1913 a Mr Bates had bought a bottle of Batey's ginger beer from a retailer. It carried more wallop than he bargained

105

for when it exploded in his face, causing injury. He decided to sue the manufacturer but the verdict from *Bates v. Batey and Company* was that, while the manufacturer had a contract with the retailer and the retailer had a similar relationship with the consumer, there was no bridging contract between manufacturer and consumer. Bates lost his case as the missing link won the day.

That was still the status quo when May Donoghue licked her lips at Minchella's as her friend poured out the last remnants of the bottle. But they weren't the only last remnants she saw that day as the decomposed body of a long-drowned snail slithered uninvited and uninvitingly into the glass.

Perhaps all the frustrations of May Donoghue's life came to a head at that moment. Suitably shocked and feeling physically sick, she suffered an attack of restaurant rage and vowed, like Bates before her, to sue the manufacturer.

The case dubbed the 'Battle of the Bottle' began on 4 April 1929, but the manufacturer, Stevenson, and his representatives played the *Bates v. Batey and Company* card incessantly. It took until June 1930 for the Scottish Courts to rule that the case could proceed at all. Then in November they got cold feet and reversed their decision. By this time May Donoghue was a woman with a mission and she refused to accept that her fight was over. Even two years down the line the slimy image of that sluggardly snail would keep repeating on her.

She went right to the top and appealed to London's Law Lords for the right to take the case forward. Speaking for Donoghue, George Morton, unlike the dregs in question, was clarity itself: 'The ginger beer was bottled and labelled by Stevenson, it bore his name and was sealed with a metal cap by him; it was the duty of Mr Stevenson to provide a system of working which would not allow snails to inhabit this bottle and to provide an efficient system of inspection of the bottles before the ginger beer was poured into them. He failed in those duties and caused harm to my client May Donoghue.'

Five Lords sat in judgment and a majority of three needed convincing for the case to go forward. In the legal equivalent of a penalty shootout, Lord Buckmaster struck first for

Stevenson: 'It is ludicrous for him to be responsible to the public for every bottle which issues from the works. This appeal should be dismissed.'

Atkin stuck his neck out and got one back for Donoghue. Tomlin put Stevenson ahead by stating that to find otherwise could have 'alarming results'. Thankerton levelled for Donoghue and Lord Macmillan stepped up calm as you like to make the casting vote in Donoghue's favour.

It had taken three years to decide that the case itself could be heard but what a historic decision it was. Yet ironically the action for damages never did reach court. Perhaps it was the strain, for the beleaguered Mr Stevenson promptly died and in December 1934 an out-of-court settlement for £200 brought the case to a close. It had dragged on for six long years, but then most snail-related cases are inclined to be slow.

To May Donoghue, then a Glasgow shop assistant, the money was nice but her life thereafter was scarcely a bed of roses. She finally divorced Henry in 1945 but began to suffer mental illness and on 19 March 1958 she died in Gartloch Mental Hospital, Glasgow, aged 59. Her entire estate was just £364 18s. 8d. (£364.94).

So May Donoghue was made neither rich nor happy by her unprecedented crusade but the case of *Donoghue v. Stevenson* established the legal link between manufacturer and end-user which allowed the litigation floodgates to open. Those who have sued successfully since have May Donoghue to thank for their good fortune. But the manufacturers forced to cough up might well rue the real cost of the day a wayward mollusc took to the bottle and got pickled.

May I offer a toast in ginger beer to that trailblazing snail? But do check the glass first.

THE WORST CRIMINAL OF ALL TIME

FORT LEAVENWORTH, UNITED STATES, 1930

When Carl Panzram was executed in Fort Leavenworth jail on 5 September 1930, the world rid itself once and for all of the man who has been labelled by some as 'the worst criminal of all time'.

It would be something of an understatement to say that Panzram was 'no stranger to the law'. Successions of juries had to listen to accounts of his vile and violent deeds but time and again Panzram lived to offend once more.

Deciding on the 'worst ever' of anything is a subjective business – all I can do is present the evidence of Panzram's notorious career. It is for you to pass judgment.

Carl Panzram was born in 1891 on a farm near Warren, Minnesota, son of immigrant Prussian farmers. His father deserted the family when Carl was only a boy and the youngster quickly fell into bad ways. In 1899 he was brought before the juvenile court on a drunk-and-disorderly charge – at just eight years old, his lifelong career of crime had begun.

After graduating to acts of petty thieving the courts decided a spell at the Minnesota State Training School might set him on the right track but, the rigid routine not being entirely to his liking, he responded on the night of 7 July 1905 by setting fire to the school workshop, causing $100,000 worth of damage. The fourteen-year-old did not own up and in January 1906 he was released back into an unsuspecting society.

On 29 March of that year he hitched a ride on a westbound

108

freight train and committed a series of assaults and robberies, which landed him in the Montana State Reformatory.

That wasn't to his taste either – he escaped and by way of celebration robbed and burnt down several churches.

Undetected for these crimes, he joined the army but found that military life wasn't his cup of tea. He was court-martialled on 20 April 1907 for gross insubordination and pilfering and was sentenced to three years in Fort Leavenworth jail, where this time he served his full term and spent much of his time in the archetypal convict's pastime of rock-breaking. He was released in 1910, still only nineteen.

After a spell in Mexico he roved California enhancing his ever-growing tally of misdemeanours, adding brutal sexual attacks to his varied repertoire. He was later to boast in his memoirs, written in prison, 'I have murdered twenty-one human beings, committed thousands of burglaries, robberies, larcenies, arson, and last but not least I have committed sodomy on more than 1,000 male human beings.'

Bearing in mind that record, most of which was yet to come, the sterner advocates of crime prevention among you might by now be arguing that he shouldn't have been released from prison at all. Nor, when he inevitably served his next term in Montana State Prison, should he have been allowed to escape after just eight months.

But escape he did, to commit further crimes under the alias Jeff Rhoades. Yet again he was caught and after this time serving two years in Montana State Prison he was released in 1914, a criminal veteran at only 23.

Yet again he wasn't out long, being arrested in Oregon for burglary and sentenced to seven years in Salem State Prison. Another seven years was added to that after he attempted to lead a prison riot. Panzram didn't take to the bread-and-water diet he was put on for his latest misdemeanour but he did take to spending many voluntary hours toiling assiduously in the prison workshop. A breakthrough perhaps? In fact a 'breakout', as the prisoner from hell, using tools he'd made inside, escaped in May 1918 after serving just a fraction of his sentence.

Next stop Frederick, Maryland, to rob a hotel. Then New

York to sign up as a merchant seaman, jumping ship in Peru and travelling to Chile, where he got a job as a foreman with an oil company. Their Human Resources Department soon regretted their cursory screening procedures as Panzram set fire to an oil rig and went on the run.

Eluding capture just long enough to slip back into the United States, he bagged $7,000 from a jewellery store and then had the audacity to break into the New Haven home of the former US President William Howard Taft, who was about to become Chief Justice of the United States. As well as taking the Michael, Panzram netted booty worth $40,000.

He escaped undetected and used the money under the alias John O'Leary to buy a luxury yacht. Ten sailors were hired to refit the boat and when they'd completed the task Panzram invited them to stay on board for a night of celebration. He made sure there were no hangovers next morning: 'When they were asleep,' he wrote, 'I got my Army Automatic and blew their brains out.' The bodies were weighted down and dropped into the harbour.

Again Panzram escaped suspicion but was arrested in Bridgeport for burglary and spent six months in jail.

Next stop Europe, then on to West Africa, where it seemed only natural that he should unwind by trying his hand at a spot of hunting. He hired six black porters to guide him on a crocodile shoot, and how deadly his shooting proved. In the deserted backwaters he shot all six men in the back and tossed them to the waiting crocs.

Is there no end to this man's depravity? I hear you ask. Regrettably not, because back in the USA, in 1922, Panzram made a twelve-year-old Salem boy, Henry McMahon, his next tragic victim: 'I killed him with a rock to the head,' wrote Panzram. 'I tried a little sodomy on him first and then left him laying there with his brains coming out of his ears.'

Although I hate to say it, there's more. Back with the boating set, Panzram became a night watchman for the New Haven Yacht Club. Not the ideal man for a security role, he promptly stole a boat and dispatched another man overboard to a watery grave.

Caught again for robbery, Panzram was given five years in Sing Sing jail but, after guards there said they couldn't cope with him, he was transferred to Clinton Prison in Dannemora, New York, generally regarded as the end of the line for the hardest cases. Yet astonishingly, with the blame for his worst atrocities still not laid at his door, Panzram was released in 1928.

It was a glorious reprieve for a man committed to crime and violence. In the space of a few months, Panzram added eleven burglaries and one murder to his list before he was arrested on 16 August 1928.

Finally the trial judge, Walter McCoy, got tough. As he sentenced Panzram to 25 years in Leavenworth, the 'worst criminal of all time' glared at the unfortunate jury: 'If I live I'll execute some more of you,' he shouted. 'Visit me!'

At last Panzram was safe inside for a long stretch, but safety for his fellow inmates was a different matter: 'I'll kill the first man who bothers me,' he warned Fred Zerbst, the deputy warden, who gave Panzram duties in the prison laundry. That wasn't a healthy decision for the laundry's civilian supervisor, Robert Warnke, who on 20 June 1929 met his end at the wrong end of an iron bar after he had reported Panzram for breaking the laundry rules.

That *was* the last straw and after a hasty trial Panzram was sentenced to hang. Even when the do-gooders from the Society for the Abolition of Capital Punishment tried to get him off, Panzram didn't have a nice word for them: 'Forget it. Hanging will be a pleasure and a relief. The only thanks your kind will ever get from me is that I wish you all had one neck and I had my hands on it. I believe the only way to reform people is to kill 'em. My motto is "Rob 'em all, rape 'em all and kill 'em all." I don't believe in man, God nor Devil. I hate the whole damned human race, including myself.'

And with that final tirade, on 5 September 1930, 39-year-old Carl Panzram was hanged.

The worst criminal of all time? This has been the longest summing up in *The Law's Strangest Cases* – you may now retire to deliver your verdict.

A CLERICAL ERROR

CHURCH HOUSE, WESTMINSTER, LONDON, 1932

Doctors who murder their patients, bent coppers, corrupt solicitors or judges who break the law all provoke a strong sense of public disquiet, outrage even. But when it comes to men of the cloth it seems wry smiles and great hilarity of the nudge-nudge, wink-wink variety are more the order of the day. A dodgy vicar, it seems, is fair game for entertainment.

Naturally *The Law's Strangest Cases* must include one of these clerical tales and, just as naturally, the star of the show must be the Reverend Harold 'Jumbo' Davidson, the rector of Stiffkey in Norfolk. In 1932 he put the ecclesiastical courts in a right tizzy but the public were royally entertained by the newspaper reports of this singular affair in which the man dubbed 'the Prostitutes' Padre' was both disgraced and defrocked.

Harold Davidson descended from a long line of Protestant churchmen and after being ordained in 1902 held a position as an assistant curate in Westminster. In 1906 he left London, opting for a quiet existence as rector of the parish of Stiffkey with Morston, a sleepy fishing community in northwest Norfolk.

But he evidently missed the bright lights of London. Finding that he could tend the needs of his Norfolk flock by putting in scarcely more than a couple of days a week in Stiffkey, he took to staying in London for much of the time and became a tireless campaigner for just about every cause

112

going, writing to MPs and influential families begging for donations for 'the less fortunate'.

Newsboys and waitresses were two of his favourite causes, but they were eclipsed by his 'concern' for actresses and prostitutes. Davidson became, with the full backing of the Bishop of Norwich, the accredited chaplain to the Actors' Church Union; he took to appearing backstage at West End theatres, where he was later variously remembered as 'a well-meaning innocent' and 'a voyeuristic pest' – 'Sorry, ladies, I didn't know this was your changing room', spoken in a suitably bumbling-vicar sort of way, was the sort of 'mistake' he was apt to make with startling regularity.

It was when he started taking London prostitutes back to stay at his home in Stiffkey with his wife and five children that some of the Norfolk locals got a bit twitchy. As yet there was no real evidence that Davidson himself was 'playing around' but some of the antics between the girls and local lads were thought to be shocking.

A serious complaint was bound to arise, and did, but not until 1931, when Davidson was late for an Armistice Day service. A Norfolk landowner promptly wrote to the Bishop of Norwich and incorporated charges of 'impropriety' in his complaint. On 2 February 1933 the *Eastern Daily Press* briefly reported that 'complaints concerning the moral conduct of the rector of Stiffkey have been lodged'.

From there it quickly became an affair of national interest – Davidson was proving an embarrassment to the church and the bishop had to act. He was duly hauled before the Church Consistory Court at the Great Hall of Church House, Westminster, and his trial was to last for fully 25 days.

There were five charges, including 'embracing a young woman in a Chinese restaurant', 'making improper suggestions to waitresses' and 'maintaining an immoral liaison with a "named woman" for 10 years'.

In truth the evidence was wishy-washy but there was a lot of it. He had never been caught *in flagrante* and indeed Davidson and many of his supporters claimed that none of his liaisons had ever been consummated. He was simply, like

Prime Minister William Gladstone before him, 'very much committed to the idea of salvation'.

Yet many of the witnesses called were prepared to testify before the Worshipful F Keppel North that Davidson's behaviour was not what might reasonably be expected from a churchman. There was much talk of 'fondling', 'whispering' and 'brushing against', all of which lent an air of high farce to proceedings – Davidson himself added to this at one point by doing an impromptu tap dance in the witness stand.

It was probably the photograph of Davidson, complete with dog collar, standing alongside a half-naked teenage girl, that sealed his fate. Davidson insisted that this was a set-up taken on the eve of the trial, when the girl walked up to him and whipped off her shawl with a photographer conveniently on hand. This was very likely true, and indeed some say the church authorities themselves set it up to nail their man, but nail him it did.

Amid intense media interest Harold Davidson was found guilty on all charges on 8 July 1932. His attempted appeal was dismissed and he was duly defrocked.

And there this odd affair should end but doesn't, for the famous rector of Stiffkey, described by his own son as 'mad, quite mad' and his own lawyer as 'a troublesome busybody', seemed determined to achieve even greater immortality.

Still needing to earn a living, he set himself up as a circus-style sideshow on the promenade at Blackpool; punters paid to listen to the famously defrocked cleric protesting his innocence while sitting in a barrel, from where he wrote his memoirs. Betweentimes he made a general nuisance of himself, interrupting church services and instigating law suits, or preaching from the mouth of a stuffed whale and undertaking a 35-day hunger strike 'until the church reinstates me'.

It didn't, and Davidson was arrested for 'attempted suicide', although appearing remarkably robust for a half-starved man – not surprising, as a hidden stash of food was discovered, which had sustained him during his so-called toilet breaks.

Shameless publicity stunter he may have been but the financial rewards were significant and it has been written of

Davidson that he 'raked in up to £20,000 in the mid-thirties', a huge sum for the time.

Can this story get stranger? Well, yes, actually, for Davidson's final stunt was to appear in Skegness in 1937, again protesting his innocence but this time from a cage he shared with a couple of mangy old lions. He billed himself 'Modern Daniel in the Lion's Den'.

Geriatric the lions may have been but they obviously had a macabre sense of humour because one of the beasts, Freddy, mauled the crazy cleric in an unsympathetic manner; Davidson was rescued, appropriately by a sixteen-year-old girl, but died of his wounds two days later on 30 July 1937.

The most famous cleric in legal history has been the subject of an opera, a number of folk songs, several biographical studies and an underground film directed by Ken Russell. The case still provokes controversy and many say he was an innocent victim of the gossipmongers. His grave in the churchyard at Stiffkey is neatly tended by loyal villagers to this day.

At worst his behaviour might have been shockingly immoral. At best that of a harmless buffoon. But it was, surely, unwise. I have no intention of including any further clerics in *The Law's Strangest Cases* because the rector of Stiffkey always was an impossible act to follow. Reverend, you have given lots of people lots of fun – and how many clerics can we say that about?

A SELF-INFLICTED WOUND

THE HIGH COURT, LONDON, 1933

A London stockbroker, William Lewis Rowland Paul Sebastian Blennerhassett, was proud of his name. His ancestor Alan de Blenerhayset had been Mayor of Carlisle in 1382 and members of the family had been MPs for that city right from the reign of Richard II to that of James I.

He was proud, too, of the Distinguished Service Order awarded for his wartime conduct. Proud of serving as a delegate to the League of Nations. Proud of his thirty years as a stockbroker in Throgmorton Street. Safe to conclude, then, that Mr Blennerhassett was a proud man. Pity he didn't remember that 'pride comes before a fall'.

He had enjoyed a pleasant lunch on 26 May 1932 but was much perturbed on his return to work to be greeted by jeers, ribald laughter and much nodding and winking. Only when he was shown that day's *Evening Standard* did he get the joke, for there was a full-page advert for the latest novelty-toy craze, the yo-yo, telling the story of a man who bought a 'Cheerio 99' for each of his two children but became obsessed by it and ended up in a mental institution. It was an amusing yarn nicely illustrated, but Mr B stared aghast at some of the copy:

> Take warning by the fate of Mr Blennerhassett, as worthy a citizen as any that ever ate lobster at Pimm's or holed a putt at Walton Heath. 'Sound man, Blennerhassett', they said on Throgmorton Street. But Yo-Yo got him and today he is

116

happy in a quiet place in the country under sympathetic surveillance as he practises Yo-Yo tricks. So beware of Yo-Yos, which start as a hobby and end as a habit.

An amazing coincidence and nothing but. In fact the copywriter had taken the name from an amusing episode in a book by the American author Mark Twain. But Blennerhassett convinced himself the advert *was* based on him. Throgmorton Street. Pimm's. It all added up.

Completely unable to work that afternoon, he repaired to the sanctuary of his club but was horrified that there too he was met with much mirth. Restrained mirth, yes, but mirth all the same. There and then he resolved to sue for libel.

Blennerhassett v. Novelty Sales Services Ltd and Another was heard at the Royal Courts of Justice in the Strand on Thursday, 19 May 1933. But his day at the High Court descended into high farce as Blennerhassett succeeded unintentionally in doing what Groucho Marx, as the attorney Waldorf T Flywheel of Flywheel, Shyster and Flywheel in a classic radio show, did so brilliantly. The law became a vehicle for humour and Blennerhassett brought the house down.

His counsel stated that 'the advertisement was understood by various persons to refer to him and that it depicted him in a ridiculous and ignominious manner.' He was, stated J F Eales KC, 'the only man of that name associated with the Stock Exchange, and in Throgmorton Street, and had for some years eaten at Pimm's Restaurant'.

But as soon as Blennerhassett was cross-examined by the defence lawyer Sir Patrick Hastings the fun started. Witness the transcript highlights.

HASTINGS: The name Blennerhassett is a very well-known Irish name, is it not?
BLENNERHASSETT: Certainly not, it's English. (laughter)
HASTINGS: Oh, I didn't mean to cast aspersions on it. (laughter) [First point to Hastings.]
HASTINGS: Were you in the habit of eating lobster at Pimm's?

BLENNERHASSETT: Much to my cost, I'm afraid I was. (laughter)

HASTINGS: And are you a regular there for luncheon?

BLENNERHASSETT: Yes.

HASTINGS: When was the last time you ate there?

BLENNERHASSETT: 1928. (laughter)

HASTINGS: Have you ever played golf at Walton Heath?

BLENNERHASSETT: No.

HASTINGS: Have you ever holed a putt anywhere?

BLENNERHASSETT: No, I don't play golf. (laughter)

HASTINGS: What age do you think the two children are in the picture?

BLENNERHASSETT: About five or six.

HASTINGS: Do you have two children?

BLENNERHASSETT: No, one, a son.

HASTINGS: And how old is he?

BLENNERHASSETT: 21. (laughter)

HASTINGS: Tell me, have you any sense of humour?

BLENNERHASSETT: You must ask other people about that. (laughter)

After several more questions and answers in which Blennerhassett unfailingly emerged as the fall guy, a stockbroker colleague, Mr Stubbs, was called as a witness, but succeeded only in scoring an own goal of head-clutching proportions.

STUBBS: I think the advert does refer to him but also people may think he has done it himself to advertise his name to the public as a stockbroker, which is against the Stock Exchange rules. Therefore it is a defamatory innuendo.

HASTINGS: If you wanted to advertise yourself as a member of the Stock Exchange would you select a picture of yourself being escorted into a madhouse with a Yo-Yo? I don't think I should! (gales of laughter)

With each passing exchange Hastings belittled Blennerhassett with consummate skill and not a little poker-faced glee, until the presiding judge, Mr Justice Branson, stepped in to put Blennerhassett out of his misery by stopping the case forthwith: 'No reasonable being would after reading the advertisement have thought it referred to a living person. Even if they did, it is not capable of bearing a defamatory meaning and there is no case to go to the jury.'

Judgment was duly entered for Novelty Sales Services with costs and, next day, *The Times* ran verbatim details of the case across two columns. The entire floor of the Stock Exchange enjoyed their morning read immensely that day, and at Mr Blennerhassett's club the newspapers appeared unusually well thumbed.

William Blennerhassett had succeeded where the advert had failed. His sense-of-humour bypass cost him dear. He had shot himself in the foot. Now he really *did* look ridiculous.

If only he had heeded the wise words of Samuel Johnson (1709–84) on the real truth behind damage ensuing from libel: 'Very few attacks either of ridicule or invective make much noise but with the help of those they provoke.'

MOST UNSAVOURY EVIDENCE

SYDNEY, AUSTRALIA, 1935

Many are the times that members of a packed courtroom have been shocked or revolted by physical evidence put before them, but the general public are invariably spared such grim confrontations. Not so in Sydney in April 1935, though, when evidence of a vile underworld crime came up in a remarkable and particularly repulsive way.

The man who murdered a forty-year-old former boxer, James Smith, knew that an untraceable disposal of the body was paramount if he was to avoid detection. Not for him a clumsy shallow burial, an impromptu bonfire or a well-packed tin trunk deposited at the left-luggage office of a railway station. They were the province of mere amateurs. All had been tried time and again but sooner or later the bodies invariably came to light. All it took was an inquisitive dog out for walkies, a fragment of charred bone or a railway porter with a good nose for curious smells and a sharp eye for telltale seepage. All too soon the game was up.

Smith's murderer needed to be sure, so the body was first cut up and packed in a weighted tin trunk. True, it was a mistake not to use a trunk quite big enough to house all the bits, but the arm left over was firmly secured by a rope round its wrist and then tied tightly to the outside of the trunk. When the murderer dumped the gruesome cargo from his boat into Sydney Harbour early in April 1935 he was confident that his foul deed had been consigned to the deep for ever.

But he bargained without two fishermen landing an unexpected catch just a week later. If you're expecting the trunk, just hold on a second. That's far too simple for *The Law's Strangest Cases*. What they did get tangled in their lines was a shark, not at all what they were after but a fine-looking specimen all the same. Being good citizens, they handed it over alive and apparently well to the Coogee Beach Aquarium, where it was put in a tank for the delectation of the public. Kids, in particular, were fascinated by the fearsome new arrival.

Although 25 April 1935 was just another day for the aquarium, it was not so for the shark, which was decidedly sluggish and suffering digestive troubles. As many a child knows from bitter experience, what's gone down must sometimes come up – these things will happen. In front of a band of admiring onlookers the shark was promptly sick.

Not pleasant at the best of times, but this was a particularly stomach-churning sight, for it was the arm that came up in its entirety, complete with a length of rope still attached. The aquarium publicity promised AN EXPERIENCE YOU WILL NEVER FORGET and the punters certainly had one that day.

The police acted quickly. The shark died shortly afterwards but no signs of other body parts were found in its stomach. A search of the shore drew a similar blank but close examination of the regurgitated arm revealed a distinctive tattoo of two boxers. After that the identification of James Smith, missing since telling his wife he was going on a fishing holiday on 8 April, was mere routine.

But this already bizarre case was yet to continue its odd course to the very end. Patrick Brady, a known forger and acquaintance of the dead man, was named by Smith's wife as one of the fishing holiday crowd and was swiftly arrested. He in turn named a billiard hall owner, Reginald Holmes, who employed Smith as a helper. Holmes was closely watched by police but both he and Brady denied all knowledge of the murder despite the fact that evidence found at their holiday cottage linked one or both of them firmly to the crime. A missing trunk, in particular, helped police to piece together what they thought had happened.

Three days after Brady's arrest, Reginald Holmes was spotted by police steering his speedboat in a wayward manner in Sydney Harbour. When they finally pulled him in after a four-hour pursuit he had a bullet wound in his head and claimed somebody was trying to kill him. It was Brady, he said, who had killed Smith and dumped the body in the harbour. And yes, it had been in the trunk.

After further questioning Brady was duly charged with murder on 17 May, but there were still twists to come. On the night before the coroner's inquest Reginald Holmes, now regarded as the key witness, was shot dead under Sydney Harbour Bridge. Forty other witnesses, though, did give evidence at the inquest and the case began to look decidedly grim for Brady.

That was when his lawyers played a master stroke. The severed arm, they said, while undoubtedly Smith's, did not prove he was dead. There was, after all, no complete body.

The Supreme Court promptly issued an order to curtail the inquest and in September, when Brady was tried for the murder of James Smith, he was acquitted for lack of evidence.

Police were convinced that Brady, involved with Smith in drug trafficking, had killed him as a result of a typical gangland dispute, but Brady lived a free man until his death in 1965, always protesting his innocence. Nor was Reginald Holmes's killer ever brought to justice.

This unusual case demonstrates how crucially important the existence of a body can be in proving that a murder has been committed.

Never has the production of evidence been more dramatically effected than by a queasy shark partial to an unexpected savoury snack. Unmissable it was. Admissible it wasn't. A murderer was thus spared a date with the gallows and the case was never solved.

DEATH OF A SWEET OLD LADY

NEW SOUTH WALES, AUSTRALIA, 1944

On 10 April 1944 at a hospital in Strathfield, near Maitland, New South Wales, the death of 100-year-old Ruth Emilie Kaye aroused no suspicion, and rightfully so.

Miss Kaye was just a sweet old lady. Those who had known her since she arrived in Australia from England more than fifty years before remembered her first as a nurse who had helped lepers and underprivileged girls and later as the caring and well-educated matron of her own nursing home. Make no mistake, Ruth Emilie Kaye was a lady of the right sort.

But what none of her fellow hospital patients knew in 1944 was that the lady they knew as 'Miss Kaye' had been christened Constance Kent one hundred years earlier and could have told a tale that would surely have exposed her elderly colleagues to the risk of instant heart failure, a story of one of the most sensational murder trials of Victorian England, which involved an equally sensational mode of confession and is still debated by criminologists to this day. Time travel may not be possible but Ruth Emilie Kaye was proof that if you live long enough, or change your name, the past can indeed become 'another country'.

This is that sweet old lady's story.

Constance Kent was born on 6 February 1844 in Sidmouth, Devon, the ninth child of respectable factory inspector Samuel Kent and his first wife, Mary Anne Windus. When Mary Anne died in 1853, Samuel Kent married the children's governess,

Miss Pratt, and the family moved to Road Hill House at Road (now Rode) on the Somerset–Wiltshire border.

Nine-year-old Constance took the marriage badly. She became moody and unsettled, and when the new Mrs Kent gave birth to a daughter of her own and then a son, Saville, Constance convinced herself that the new members of the family, especially baby Saville, were favoured by their mother.

The night of horror occurred on 29 June 1860, when Constance was sixteen. In the small hours her stepbrother Saville, aged only three years and ten months, went missing from his cot and was found next morning halfway down the cesspit of a remote old privy in the house's beautiful gardens. His throat had been slashed with a razor and there was a four-inch-deep wound in his chest.

The police found many clues and much circumstantial evidence that pointed to Constance as the killer of the innocent child as he slept. Scotland Yard was brought in because of the public outrage at the crime and Inspector Whicher of the Yard became convinced that Constance was guilty, a confused affection-starved adolescent who had killed in a fit of misguided jealousy.

She was arrested and charged on 20 July 1860 but, at the committal hearing at Devizes on 27 July, Constance's denials were convincing, and Saville's nurse, Elizabeth Gough, gave evidence that the girl's attitude towards her stepbrother had been nothing but a loving one. Although others voiced their suspicions forcibly, there just wasn't enough hard evidence to make the accusations stick. Suspicion fell, too, on both Elizabeth Gough and Mr Kent before the case collapsed unsolved, much to Inspector Whicher's chagrin, amid fierce public criticism of 'police incompetence'.

Following Constance's release through lack of evidence, her father sent her away to a convent school in France to help her forget the trauma and she stayed there two years and was noted for her kindness to children. When she returned to England in 1863 she attended a religious retreat, St Mary's Home in Brighton, under the care of the Reverend Arthur Douglas Wagner.

She became convinced there of the value of confession and early in 1865 she made a full admission of her guilt to Wagner and told him at Easter that she would like to go public.

On 25 April 1865 she went up to London, dressed all in black, walked into the famous Bow Street Magistrates' Court and handed in a written statement. Two days later it was printed in full in *The Times* amid much sensation.

Although there were anomalies in the confession, Constance pleaded guilty to murdering the infant Saville and was duly found so at Wiltshire Assizes in Salisbury on 21 July 1865. The twenty-year-old was sentenced to hang and one contemporary reporter wrote that 'her quiet fortitude was such that observers, the jury and even the judge himself could not restrain their tears when he passed sentence, and as he did so, she too pushed back her veil and sobbed uncontrollably'.

With emotions running high, the sentence was commuted to life imprisonment four days later and Constance spent the next twenty years in Millbank, London, and Portland, Dorset, before being released in 1885, aged 41. She maintained throughout that she had committed the crime alone, not from jealousy of Saville, but to avenge her own mother, who she felt had been let down by her father and usurped by his second wife.

Many anomalies remained and many outlandish further theories have been put forward over the years, not least that Constance Kent later became 'Jill', not 'Jack', 'the Ripper'.

That one we *will* discount, but only Constance Kent, Ruth Emilie Kaye to her Australian friends, knew the whole truth of what happened on a summer evening in Rode in 1860 – and she, you will recall, died just a sweet old lady, aged 100, in a New South Wales hospital in 1944.

A DOSE OF ILL FORTUNE

SOUTHPORT, 1947

The air in Southport can be quite bracing but it evidently didn't suit the wealthy heiress Amy Victoria Burnett Clements, who died at the Astley Nursing Home there on 27 May 1947.

The death of his wife must have been a particular blow for Dr Robert George Clements because, despite his eminent position in the medical profession, he'd had the incredible misfortune to lose his three previous wives in similar circumstances. In 1912 he had married Edyth Annie Mercier, who tragically expired in 1920. Only the fact that she was a wealthy woman might have softened the crushing blow for Dr Clements.

Newly enriched, he overcame the heartbreak to marry Mary McLeery just a year later, but she too expired after just four years of married life. Again, only a substantial inheritance made such tragic misfortune bearable to the unfortunate doctor.

Once more, he mustered the courage to remarry, but Katherine Burke, Mrs Clements number three, died in 1939 of cancer. Although the police became suspicious at the completion of such an unlikely hat-trick they didn't conduct an autopsy – such was Dr Clements's grief that he'd had her cremated quickly before it could be carried out.

Remarkably, having suffered more misfortune in 27 years of married life than any man could be expected to endure, he held himself together and met Amy Victoria Burnett. He and

'Vee' got on quite well and when her father died unexpectedly in 1940 the good doctor must have felt she needed the stability that only marriage could offer her. The £22,000 she'd been left was all very well, but what she really needed was a husband. She duly became Mrs Clements number four.

When she had the seizure and went into a coma on 26 May 1947 Dr Clements acted quickly to get her into the nursing home, but she died the next day. He carried out his own diagnosis of myeloid leukaemia and suggested this strongly to his young colleague Dr James Houston, who studied the post-mortem report and duly signed the death certificate despite harbouring personal doubts as to the real cause. Hadn't the staff surgeon, Andrew Brown, noticed the pinpoint pupils of the corpse, sure sign of morphine poisoning? But Dr Houston passed it over.

Grief-stricken once more, Dr Clements quickly arranged the funeral, but this time so many tongues were wagging in Southport that the police stepped in to stop it and ordered a second post-mortem, which concluded that poisoning was indeed the cause of death.

It seemed a certainty that Clements would be charged, found guilty and hanged and that the deaths of all four of his wives would ultimately be laid at his door.

Yet Robert George Clements, 57-year-old member of the Royal College of Surgeons, never did stand trial for murder. When police called at his Southport home to arrest him they found tellingly large amounts of morphine and his own dead body. He had died from a huge overdose of cyanide administered by his own hand.

Evidently, with five deaths now his responsibility, Clements didn't believe that doctors should save lives. And it was soon to be one more as this extraordinary affair came to its end. On 2 June 1947 Dr Houston, unable to live with the knowledge that he had been professionally negligent, was found dead in his lab. He left his colleagues no room for error at his post-mortem – his body contained 300 times the lethal dose of sodium cyanide.

Dr Robert George Clements joined a small but notorious

band of medical men who took life instead of saving it. Indeed for some time he had a reasonable claim to be the doctor with the worst bedside manner of all time, but even as he took his deadly dose in 1947 a sweet little toddler by the name of Harold Frederick Shipman was contemplating his own future as the undisputed holder of that particular title.

CAPSTICK MAKES AN IMPRESSION

BLACKBURN, 1948

Crime detection 21st-century style is certainly different from the 1948 variety. DNA profiling and instantaneous computer matching of fingerprints were still in the realms of science fiction half a century ago.

Nor had the police force then established a corporate image. Undying pledges of service and letters to victims headed 'We Care' were simply unheard of. We know we're in safe hands now, but there was nothing so positive in 1948. All the police had then was a sense of duty, due diligence, old-fashioned determination and sensible shoes. Without a 'mission statement' from the constabulary there was surely little hope.

Consider the task facing Detective Chief Inspector John Capstick in May 1948. During the early hours of 15 May three-year-old June Anne Devaney was found to be missing from the ground-floor children's ward of the Queen's Park Hospital in Blackburn, Lancashire. Two and a half hours later she was found in the grounds just a hundred yards away. She had been raped, then brutally murdered, her head having been bashed forcefully against a boundary wall.

There were no witnesses to the abduction or murder and all the Blackburn police had to go on were some fingerprints left on a bottle in the ward and a few fibres found on the dead girl's body.

Such was the terrible and emotive nature of the crime that the Chief Constable of Blackburn feared serious public

129

disorder in the town. Mindful of that, he immediately called on Scotland Yard for assistance. 'Have you the resources to help?' he asked. 'Of course,' came the prompt reply.

Within just a few hours of the clarion call, John Capstick and his colleague, Detective Sergeant John Stoneman, arrived to take charge, but hopes of an early arrest were dashed when the fingerprints were found not to match those of any known criminal.

The way forward for Capstick was clear as mud. All he had in mind was that the man was likely to be local as he seemed to have knowledge of the hospital layout. But Capstick was made of stern stuff, as his next proposal illustrates.

His suggestion was supremely logical if not a touch outrageous. Every male person in Blackburn between the ages of fourteen and ninety would be fingerprinted. Only the bedridden would be spared.

The Mayor of Blackburn made a public announcement asking for cooperation and promising that all prints would be destroyed after they had been manually compared with those left by June Devaney's murderer. The words 'added to our data bank', 'civil liberties' and 'invasion of privacy' were conspicuous by their absence as the operation began in earnest.

The first 5,000 prints yielded no match. Nor did the second and third. After 20,000 tries the task looked hopeless. At 30,000 the officers engaged on checking must surely have been flagging but no claims for repetitive-strain injury were lodged. The 40,000 mark was duly passed, but on the afternoon of 12 August the cry was 'Eureka!' as set 46,253 yielded an exact match.

That evening 22-year-old Peter Griffiths, a former Guardsman working as a packer in a flour mill, was arrested at his home. No armies of lawyers mobilised in his favour. No social-services personnel rushed to proffer extenuating circumstances on his behalf. Instead, thoroughly ashamed by his actions, Griffiths calmly admitted the offence. His only mitigation was that he had been drunk at the time. He told the officers who arrested him, 'I hope I get what I deserve,' but pleaded not guilty on the grounds that he had not been responsible for his actions.

Fibres from his suit were quickly matched to those on the body and at the trial at Lancashire Assizes the jury took only 23 minutes to find Peter Griffiths guilty. He was hanged at Walton Prison on 19 November 1948.

It had taken Detective Chief Inspector Capstick three months to bring the killer to justice. Compared with today's techniques his unsophisticated methods were as PC Plod's to the Rapid Response Unit's. It might have been Toytown. And the mayor, no doubt, had worn his ermine-trimmed robes and ceremonial chain when making his impassioned appeal to the doughty burghers of Blackburn from the town hall steps.

But then all life was surreal in 1948. As Griffiths was being held in custody, Manchester United lost 2–1 at home to Derby County, beer was sold at elevenpence (4½p) a pint and 'Big Brother' was the snotty-nosed kid who nicked your gobstoppers.

Who would ever wish to return to those strange Dark Ages when the police had nothing better to do with their time than catch criminals?

A SUSPENDED SUSPENDED SENTENCE

THE OLD BAILEY, LONDON, 1948

Prior to the abolition of hanging in 1965 the only 'suspended sentence' really likely to be accorded to a cold-blooded murderer was the sort that involved a noose around the neck.

Sentence was sometimes mercifully commuted to life imprisonment, it is true, but any bookmaker would surely have set the odds for Donald George Thomas getting lucky at several thousand to one, for in 1948 Thomas committed the most socially unacceptable crime of that era, murder of a policeman.

In January 1948 a sudden spate of housebreaking and burglary in the Highgate and Southgate areas of north London led police to deploy plain-clothed officers in the locality to keep watch for suspects.

The operation worked a treat, and on the evening of 13 February 1948 PC Nathaniel Edgar and his colleague spotted a man behaving suspiciously. When the suspect gave the officers the slip they separated to search the Oaklands Estate in Wynchgate, and at 8.15 several people reported hearing three shots. PC Edgar was found seriously injured and died in the North Middlesex Hospital two hours later. The final entry in his notebook was found to be the name and address of Donald George Thomas, who, police records showed, had deserted from the army towards the end of the war.

Thomas was on the run from military police for two years

before being captured, but again went missing on his release from 160 days' probation. Police quickly formed the opinion that 23-year-old Thomas was their likely murderer and he was traced to lodgings in Mayflower Road, Clapham, where he had holed up with his lover, a mother of three, Mrs Winkless.

A party of four policemen opted to pay Thomas a surprise early-morning visit, co-opting his landlady, Mrs Smeed, into the covert ambush operation. Mrs Smeed was to take the couple's breakfast up to their room as usual, leave it outside their door and knock, an uncomplicated role, which she nevertheless performed to perfection. And a futile one in the culinary sense, for her early-morning magic with the frying pan went entirely to waste that day.

When Thomas opened his door wearing just his underpants he was greeted by rather more than freshly cooked bacon and eggs and a nice pot of tea, as he was unceremoniously jumped on by the avenging police presence.

Although Thomas went for the Luger pistol hidden under his pillow, he was overpowered before telling the officers, 'You were lucky. I might just as well be hung for a sheep as a lamb.'

Seventeen rounds of ammunition, a jemmy and a rubber cosh were found in the bedroom and Mrs Winkless, still in bed at the time of the raid, told police that Thomas had confessed to her that he had committed the murder. Thomas, rather unconvincingly, denied this and pleaded not guilty.

He was brought to trial at the Old Bailey in April. A police murderer who had happily admitted to further intent, and an army deserter to boot, his cause was as grim as any could be. To nobody's surprise Thomas was duly found guilty of the murder of PC Edgar and sentenced to death.

Yet to everybody's surprise he lived to tell the tale and was released from prison fourteen years later in April 1962, for Thomas had unwittingly selected the only window of opportunity in which to commit his capital crime and remain alive into the bargain – at the time of his conviction the future of capital punishment was being debated in the House of

Commons and a temporary suspension of hanging had been enacted during the discussions.

Donald George Thomas's claim to be the luckiest murderer of the twentieth century would seem a valid one, and such was the publicity surrounding the case that it inspired the plot of the 1949 film *The Blue Lamp,* in which the legendary PC George Dixon, of Dock Green fame, played by Jack Warner, was shot and killed by a delinquent played by Dirk Bogarde.

Despite his death halfway through his film debut, Dixon of Dock Green went on to serve many years in the force, single-handedly coining the much-lampooned phrase, 'Evening, all', which has dogged the force ever since.

Nor was the memory of PC Edgar allowed to die, for in 1998 a commemorative fiftieth-anniversary plaque was placed in his honour at Muswell Hill Police Station.

No such affectionate tributes were given to Donald George Thomas, the only police murderer for whom suspension meant life instead of death.

NO HALF-MEASURES

THE HIGH COURT, LONDON, 1959

When the seventeenth-century essayist Thomas Hall wrote 'Lie lustily, some will stick', he proffered some advice that many a man intent on belittling another has since followed with gusto.

While the tactic has sometimes led to the greatest degree of satisfaction on the part of the critic, it has also led to some widely publicised libel claims in the face of the strongest possible invective.

And never, surely, has the 'no half-measures' ploy been put more spectacularly to the test than in the 1959 libel case of *Wladziu Valentini Liberace v. William Connor and Daily Mirror Newspapers Limited.*

When Liberace, musical entertainer extraordinaire, stepped off the *Queen Mary* at Southampton on 25 September 1956 after his voyage from New York, and stepped on to a special six-carriage train that transported him to Waterloo Station, few men or women would have denied that here was a man who was rather an individual. Liberace had style, a style that women in particular found irresistible.

Three thousand screaming and swooning fans met his train at Waterloo, some leaning forward to kiss the carriage as it drew to a halt. But Liberace and his syrupy sweet piano act wasn't everybody's cup of tea. William Neil Connor, writing as the *Daily Mirror* columnist 'Cassandra', wasn't altogether keen and he made little effort to disguise this in his report of Liberace's arrival:

> I have to report that Mr Liberace is about the most that a man can take. I spoke to men at this newspaper who have met every celebrity arriving from the United States for the past thirty years and they all say that this deadly, winking, sniggering, chromium-plated, scent-impregnated, luminous, quivering, giggling, fruit-flavoured, mincing, ice-covered heap of Mother Love has had the biggest reception since Charlie Chaplin arrived at Waterloo in 1921.

How much more critical could a critic be? Quite a lot more in fact:

> He reeks with emetic language that can only make grown men long for a quiet corner, an aspidistra, a handkerchief and the old heave-ho. Without doubt he is the biggest sentimental vomit of all time, slobbering over his mother, winking at his brother and counting the cash at every second. This superb piece of calculating candyfloss has an answer for every situation.

Maybe the choice of the word 'superb' heralded a change of tune. Might Cassandra enjoy Liberace's music, perchance?

> Nobody anywhere ever made so much money out of high-speed piano playing with the ghost of Chopin gibbering at every note. There must be something wrong with us that our teenagers longing for sex, and our middle-aged matrons fed up with sex, alike should fall for such a sugary mountain of jingling claptrap wrapped up in such a preposterous clown.

OK, so let's assume Cassandra wouldn't be buying tickets to the show. But the more serious question that arose from this attack was how far a critic, paid, after all, to give his opinion, could justifiably go in giving it.

Liberace and his entourage were understandably not best

pleased by Cassandra's little outburst and the feud led eventually to a High Court libel case, which opened in London on 8 June 1959.

Astonishing though William Connor's attack was, even more remarkable was that Liberace complained seriously about only one small phrase. He objected strongly to being labelled 'fruit-flavoured' on the grounds that it suggested he was homosexual, something he was at pains to deny vigorously in that more innocent time when being 'out' meant nothing more than having popped to the grocer's to do the weekly shop.

Liberace was represented by 74-year-old Gilbert Beyfus QC, a man who, according to Liberace's camp when they first saw him, 'lacked charisma'. 'We might as well fly back,' they said, especially when they saw that Gerald Gardiner QC, altogether more suave and youthful, was acting for the defence.

But Liberace's famous charm started to work in court as he told the rather bemused jury how lovable he was in the eyes of his fans, which was after all what really mattered: 'I get a mail bag of six thousand to ten thousand letters a week and twenty-seven thousand Valentine cards each year,' he purred. 'I have sixty suits, eighty pairs of shoes and a diamond-studded tailcoat worth ten thousand dollars.'

That may be what Elton John puts in a charity bag nowadays but in 1959 it was sensational stuff. The jury were falling under Liberace's spell and so was his counsel, Beyfus, who was later inspired to give Cassandra a real roasting during cross-examination.

The trial proved to be a serious but entertaining seven-day case in which everything in essence revolved around the meaning attached to the words 'fruit-flavoured'. Did it or did it not imply homosexuality?

Sections of the public certainly had their views, for when Liberace travelled to a concert in Sheffield he was greeted with shouts of 'Fairy' and 'Go home, queer'. The press were less direct. Not a single newspaper picked up on the fact that the trial was being held in the Queen's Bench Division of the High Court.

Seeking to win the jury over, Liberace addressed the court in the manner of a wounded soul: 'I have never indulged in homosexual practices in my life,' he said. 'In fact I am against the practice because it offends convention and offends society. The words "fruit-flavoured" are commonly used of homosexuals and I am in court because the article has attacked me below the belt on a moral issue.'

When Connor gave his evidence he rather unconvincingly denied that he knew the word 'fruit' had connotations in the United States: 'I used it purely to refer to his sugary manner, purely in a confectionary sense.'

A string of witnesses were called to Court Four. The comedian Bob Monkhouse, himself quite adept in the syrup-tongued department, spoke very sincerely of Liberace's qualities. But the turning point was Beyfus's ferocious cross-examination of Cassandra by which he showed the jury how vitriolic a pen the critic wielded: 'Did you attack the medical profession by referring to "their smooth, lying inefficiency and their blunt assumption that the disease-laden clients have the mentality of sick cattle"?'

Cassandra could not deny it.

'And did you refer to the broadcaster Richard Dimbleby as "quietly sizzling and gently bubbling like an over-rich Welsh rarebit"?'

Cassandra could not deny it.

After Beyfus had also shown that the columnist had written in a disparaging manner about poodles, 'what many people think to be a very brave and rather sporting race of dog', he added, the game was all but up.

The judge, Mr Justice Salmon, duly summed up and the jury retired for three and a half hours. They came back to announce that the words in the article did allege that Liberace was homosexual and that they were neither true nor fair comment. They awarded him £8,000 damages, of which £2,000 was attributed to the false allegation regarding his sexuality.

The money meant nothing to Liberace. What was important was that his name was cleared. Yet time was to show that there were more twists to this bizarre affair. Liberace was subjected to unsavoury court proceedings on a number of further occasions and books and television documentaries have examined his life in the greatest depth.

By the time of his death in February 1987 of an AIDS-related illness only a blindfolded troglodyte would have been unaware which flavour of fruit Liberace favoured.

It seems with the benefit of hindsight that William Connor, arguably the most vindictive libellist in legal history, was vindicated. His novel pen name proved in that sense to be an apt one, for Cassandra was a Trojan prophetess whose curse it was always to be right but never to be believed.

LET'S HEAR IT FOR PARLIAMENT

THE HOUSE OF LORDS, LONDON, 1960

It is all too easy to forget that the law has to be 'made' by Parliament; tempting, too, to regard the laborious process of British government that steers laws through the upper and lower Houses as being dry, boring and utterly remote from the person in the street.

As a four-year-old child in 1960, I viewed the law as simply the local bobby telling me to be careful as I crossed the road behind the ice-crean van, clutching my cornet for dear life. But little did I know that, as I licked off the last drop of raspberry sauce on a glorious summer's day in 1960, the highest authorities in the land were at that precise same moment ensconced within the stifling confines of the House of Lords protecting my welfare on that very issue, for Monday, 18 July 1960 was the day of the great ice-cream debate.

I am obliged to the verbatim account from *The Times* for revealing how our great nation's lawmakers go about their business.

PEERS' RESISTANCE MELTS, said the headline to the 'Parliament' column:

> The Lord Chancellor took his seat on the woolsack at half past two o'clock to consider the Noise Abatement Bill at Report stage with particular reference to clause 2 regarding the restriction of operation of loudspeakers on highways.

Boring stuff? Not a bit of it, for the fun started as soon as Lord Taylor moved an amendment to permit the use of a speaker between noon and 7 p.m. if it was on a vehicle used for the conveyance of a perishable commodity for human consumption (to wit ice-cream) and if it was operated solely for the purposes of informing the public (to wit four-year-old me) that the commodity was for sale and gave no cause for annoyance.

It seems that the drafters of the Bill had entirely ignored the nation's ice-cream men and their peculiarly British chimes and charms, and Lord Taylor, perhaps because he was partial to a choc ice, sought to protect their interests.

Why should the nation's Mr Whippys, Mister Softees and Tonibels be left out in the cold? That was the question for Parliament to debate – and what a lively affair it proved to be.

Lord Taylor met with immediate objections:

LORD REA: I oppose the amendment, not because I don't like ice-cream vendors or their product but because we must remember this is a Noise Abatement Bill, not an Ice-Cream Bill. The picture of the Pied Piper of ice-cream men with all the little children following may be appealing but it is false. There has been much lobbying by those interested in the money to be made from ice-cream. That is the truth of it.

LORD TAYLOR: Do you have any evidence?

LORD REA: No, but there is hearsay. It is a rich industry and it would be in their interests for this amendment to pass through.

LORD TAYLOR: That is a monstrous statement. Accusations against an industry should never be hearsay.

As the volume of debate over the Noise Abatement Bill rose ever higher, other Lords of the Realm pitched in:

LORD ATLEE: I concur with Lord Rea. Many people seem to think these chimes an extraordinarily bad nuisance. I have received a pitiful letter from a night watchman whose only time for rest coincides with the very times the bells would be allowed to ring.

LORD AMWELL: I fear we are making ourselves a little

ridiculous over the idea of special legislation to deal with a little industry peddling ice-cream up and down the streets. Why not let it be? There are far more infernal noises. Why, every night beneath my window I have motorcycles starting up after midnight. It is abominable. Noise should be dealt with in a fundamental way.'

He didn't actually add 'especially when it's underneath my window' but his sorry tale elicited the sympathy of the Minister of Agriculture, who stuck his own two penn'orth in forthwith and provoked gales of laughter from the benches.

LORD WALDEGRAVE: I agree. I hope the House sees fit to allow the amendment. After all, the amendment mentions perishable goods and I read in *The Times* only this morning that vintage port may be considered such a commodity. If we send the Bill back to the Commons unchanged we may lose it altogether and then there would be no control. Surely half a loaf is better than none.

All this talk of food must have aroused another eminent Lord who further unbalanced the menu by introducing a fish course:

LORD MILVERTON: Lord Taylor's speech is a wonderful example of how ice-cream can turn into a red herring. I have a shoal of correspondence commending the house for their help on this issue. I'm not saying the ice-cream lobby are getting at me but privately there has been pressure brought to bear.

I would like to report that someone then shouted, 'Stick a flake in it!' Regrettably not, but the response was indignant all the same.

LORD SHACKLETON: I resent the suggestion that the amendment is the result of the ice-cream lobby. No one has approached me!

That sounded suspiciously like a complaint.

LORD BURDEN: Nor me. I know nothing of any ice-cream lobby.

He then rather spoilt the impression of his affected innocence by showing a remarkable insight into the business of Cornish-wafer shifting by adding: 'Without audible means of advertising, the van's sales fall off by 50 to 70 per cent I believe. They perform a useful community service. Are we to prevent small traders earning an honest living?'

LORD SILKIN: The amendment has nothing to do with small traders. It's the big merchants who are behind it.

The continued debate proved all too much for Lord Taylor, who rather felt his fellow peers had lost sight of the issue: 'May I remind this house that the amendment is *not* put down in the interests of *any* ice-cream people, traders *or* merchants – this Bill is solely in the interests of *noise abatement*,' he shouted vociferously.

It did the trick and with that the amendment was duly agreed. REPRIEVE FOR ICE-CREAM CHIMES, screamed *The Times*'s sub-headline. It was entirely thanks to their Lordships that the children of the sixties were able to contemplate the delights of a 99 and suck on their Zooms and Rockets safe from the fear of the nasty men from the Noise Abatement Office.

So now you know how laws are made and what serious debate goes on in the House of Lords on a typically rigorous day.

TRIAL OF A LADY

THE OLD BAILEY, LONDON, 1960

Nineteen sixty was a year in which a number of curious literary cases were heard but the one heard loud and clear above the rest was the somewhat dull-sounding *The Crown v. Penguin Books.*

But dull it certainly wasn't, for the case popularly known as the trial of *Lady Chatterley's Lover* seemingly caused an entire nation collectively to hold its breath before releasing a gasp of unrepressed relief as the verdict effectively cast aside the final remnants of Victorian prudery in favour of a new era of sexual liberalism, an era that made it OK for decent people not only to read about 'it', but to talk about 'it' and, glory be praised, to actually do 'it' without having to pretend to the outside world that 'it' didn't really exist.

An apparently routine announcement by Penguin Books on 25 August 1960 set the legal machinery in motion – they intended to publish a 'popular' unexpurgated 3s. 6d. (17½p) paperback edition of D H Lawrence's 1928 classic, *Lady Chatterley's Lover*, a book previously available in Britain since 1932 only in an expensive, abridged and much-censored version.

But only a matter of weeks before the proposed publication date, with 200,000 copies already printed awaiting release, the office of the Director of Public Prosecutions informed Penguin that, having read the book, they intended to prosecute under the Obscene Publications Act 1959. The book was put on hold.

144

Not even the best publicity guru could have hyped it better.

The case opened in Court No. 1 at the Old Bailey in London on 20 October 1960; Mr Justice Byrne was the judge, Mervyn Griffith-Jones led the Crown's prosecution, Gerald Gardiner QC fronted the defence, the jury contemplated the huge moral responsibility that their decision would carry and the person in the street contemplated the prospect of reading all the juicy bits if Penguin won – especially pages 176–85.

The prosecution's case was that the book's content would tend to 'deprave and corrupt' those exposed to it. The sex act, they were at pains to point out, was openly described on a number of occasions and the coarseness and vulgarity of both the thought and language that the book contained was 'obscene'. Mervyn Griffith-Jones told the court in the gravest tones possible that he had counted 76 'four-letter words' and he even forced himself to read a selection of them out. The case to him was crystal clear – Lady Constance Chatterley was a shameless adultress and Mellors, the gamekeeper whose rugged attentions she enjoyed, was nothing but a rough, depraved, sex-crazed degenerate.

The case for the defence encouraged the jury to take a more balanced and modern view. Gerald Gardiner QC said Lawrence's use of four-letter words in the work was merely 'an attempt to talk about sex without shame' and he suggested that all the jury must read the book themselves before passing judgment. As a result of this request, Justice Byrne ordered that a suitable reading room with comfortable armchairs be set up at the Old Bailey and he declared a three-day break for the novel to be read from cover to cover.

Such an unusual interlude created massive public awareness and the newspapers of the day whipped up a frenzy of interest in the affair of 'Lady C'. Certainly, public opinion seemed to be moving in favour of the publishers by the time the defence started calling their 35 witnesses on 27 October. A stream of distinguished academics, critics, literary editors, authors and journalists all spoke strongly in favour of the book, and even the Bishop of Woolwich, referring to the 'purple passages' in the prose, suggested that Lawrence was merely 'trying to portray this relationship as an act of holy communion'.

In ending the case for the defence, Gerald Gardiner ridiculed the reactionary views of the prosecution and Mervyn Griffith-Jones did little to dispel the view that he was well out of touch with developments in society when he implored the jury of ordinary men and women to consider 'if the book is one you would even wish your servants to read'.

With that one ludicrous question the case for the prosecution almost certainly foundered. Judge Byrne, though, completed his summing up on day six of the trial in a style that suggested he assumed the jury were repelled by what they had read. He vehemently disparaged the views of the expert witnesses, roundly condemned Lady Chatterley again as a shameless adultress and implied to the jury that he expected them to 'pass moral judgment on the behaviour the novel describes'.

It took the jury three hours on 2 November 1960 to decide to ignore the judge completely. They had enjoyed the book. 'It' was not a problem. The verdict on 'Lady C' was not guilty.

There was loud clapping and applause from the back of the court and that day's *London Evening Standard* ran a banner headline on its front page, THE INNOCENCE OF LADY CHATTERLEY . . . SHE'S CLEARED AFTER 6-DAY TRIAL.

The days that followed witnessed what is surely the most intense physical reaction to any trial decision as queues, mostly of men, formed at the bookshops and street stalls, which announced 'LADY C' NOW ON SALE.

A television reporter famously interviewed some of those making the purchase and astonishingly some men covered their faces with their newspapers or issued a terse 'no comment' when asked why they were buying the book. One rather prim-looking woman, meanwhile, asserted very firmly, 'I'm buying it for someone else.'

Needless to say, despite this rather furtive reaction from some quarters, the book became a bestseller. Judge Byrne, meanwhile, severely piqued at the jury's decision, never presided at another trial as the shameless 'Lady C' led a newly liberated Britain into the 'Swinging Sixties'.

A VERY QUIET TENANT

RHYL, NORTH WALES, 1960

A cursory glance at the results of court proceedings from the Quarterly Assizes at Ruthin, Denbighshire, for 1960 wouldn't suggest that the trial of a 65-year-old widow, Mrs Sarah Harvey, was particularly unusual.

Falsely obtaining £2 a week under a court order that had in truth become invalid some time ago was naughty but hardly sensational. That she had claimed it on behalf of a dead woman was macabre, it is true. That the woman had been dead fully twenty years did rather seem to worsen the crime and that the claims had persisted throughout that time certainly smacked of deliberate deception rather than absent-mindedness. Maybe it was fair, then, after all, that the seemingly harmless pensioner was sent to prison for fifteen months.

Yet the bare facts hide a much stranger story, one straight from the realms of horror fiction, which, had it come from the pen of a scriptwriter for Hammer films, might well have been considered too far-fetched to be believable.

This is the story of Sarah Harvey and her lodger, Mrs Frances Knight, the quietest tenant of all time.

It was early in 1939 that Frances Knight, a semi-invalid, moved into the home of Sarah Harvey. She was around for only a matter of months, apparently just passing through.

It was 21 years later, when Mrs Harvey was away for a few days in hospital, that her taxi-driver son Leslie decided to

147

surprise his mother by redecorating the house for her. But it was Les who got the surprise of *his* life when curiosity got the better of him and he forced open the door of the landing cupboard with a screwdriver – he remembered from his childhood it had always been locked. Now was his chance, on 5 May 1960, to reveal its secret.

There, still dressed in nightdress and dressing gown, although they were little more than rags, was a cobweb-covered, mummified body. Not the sort of discovery you want to make at any time, let alone in the very year that Alfred Hitchcock's *Psycho* was showing at the cinema: the body had a definite air of Norman Bates's mother about it. Maybe it was the dry hair and the hollow gaze. Who knows?

Les duly called the police and when their surgeon arrived he found the corpse entirely rigid and stuck to the linoleum floor – he had to use a garden spade to prise it loose.

Scientists concluded that the mummification, rather than a more natural rotting process, had occurred due to the circulation of air via a gap in the door frame. The dead female might well have had an illness but at least she'd been cured in a manner of speaking.

Forensic examination suggested the body was that of a female between fifty and sixty with a pronounced limp, and when Mrs Harvey was interviewed about the unexpected find she confirmed that it was her lodger, Mrs Knight. Her story was that she had found Frances Knight dead after a bout of illness just months after she moved in and, not being sure what to do with the body, she had hidden it in the cupboard.

The police accepted implicitly that the body was Frances Knight but they were suspicious of marks on the neck that suggested possible strangulation with a stocking. Sarah Harvey was duly charged with murder.

All the macabre facts emerged at the five-day trial, at which the evidence presented was largely scientific. Death, so the experts suggested, was probably due to disseminated sclerosis, from which Mrs Knight was known to have suffered. Mrs Harvey, meanwhile, strenuously denied murder and the jury concluded she was not guilty on that count but did find her guilty of claiming Mrs Knight's £2 a week.

Did she kill her lodger? Only Mrs Harvey really knew, but what is certain is that Frances Knight was the only tenant in history to pay £2 a week to live in a cupboard for 21 years without once complaining to her landlady.

Frances Knight, though, is not entirely alone in living an extended 'life' of sorts after death.

Robert Farrell of Boise, Idaho, kept the mummified body of his deceased mother in his house for six years. Georgia Farrell was found lying on her sofa in March 1993 and it was estimated that she had died in 1987 at the age of 88. Robert, who lived with his mother, never reported the death and whenever the self-styled mummy's boy was asked by neighbours where she was his stock reply was a casual 'Oh, she's in.'

Robert evidently got used to mother's being part of the furniture but first prize for ingenuity on that front must go to a man in Derby who, faced with the disposal of the body of a man he'd murdered, opted for the most novel solution of all time. After his efforts to cut it up proved unsuccessful he had the brainwave of tossing a throw over it, and when police discovered the hunched corpse early in 2001, it was being used by the murderer as a coffee table. If he'd been six foot five instead of five foot six he might have been a tall boy. Such is death.

MISTAKEN IDENTITY

PHOENIX, ARIZONA, UNITED STATES, 1963

Legal history is riddled with cases of mistaken identity but it's seldom the woolly witnesses who suffer for their errors. It's invariably some poor innocent who cops it instead.

But there has been at least one instance where a litigant with a cast-iron case failed to win the day, not because someone else erred on the recognition front but because the litigant himself had an identity crisis that apparently led him to believe that *he* was an entirely different person.

This is the rather poignant case of the actor Raymond Burr, who for one fleeting moment in 1963 seemed truly to fancy himself as the television super-lawyer Perry Mason, whose character he had played so convincingly for the previous six years.

When the American lawyer-turned-author Erle Stanley Gardner had his first Perry Mason novel published in 1933 he could have had little idea that it would be just one of 83 worldwide bestsellers featuring the celebrated defence counsel and his secretary Della Street. But how could he possibly fail with titles like *The Case of the Grinning Gorilla*, *The Case of the Stuttering Bishop*, *The Case of the Musical Cow* and *The Case of the Singing Skirt*? Film and radio success followed but it was the television series that began in 1957 that really made Perry Mason a household name.

Only three times in 245 episodes did Mason lose a case. He was undeniably the greatest lawyer in the world and Raymond Burr played him to such perfection that the finely drawn line between character and actor became ever less distinguishable, especially to the viewing public.

On one occasion when Mason lost a case because his client refused to reveal a piece of vital information that would have saved her, Burr received three hundred letters saying 'Never do that again'. Between 1957 and 1966, Raymond Burr surely *was* Perry Mason.

And thereby lay the source of an embarrassing episode for Burr. Unfortunately *The Case of the Addled Actor* didn't come from Gardner's pen – the hapless Burr was entirely responsible for this one, and the ribald publicity that accompanied it.

When Ward George Sheehan claimed that Burr owed him $1,085 from a debt created in 1949 the chances of Burr's having to legally pay up after fully fourteen years were remote indeed. All Arizona law required was for Burr to answer the summons through a lawyer and *The Case of the Spurious Debt* looked likely to be quickly closed. But something told Burr he had no need of lawyers, not with the spirit of Perry Mason straining from every pore of his body ready to see some real live action for once. Burr decided to act for himself.

Things began to go awry when he was requested to appear for a court-ordered deposition in June 1963. Burr failed to deliver a clear statement to the court, largely because he forgot the date and failed to turn up at all.

Further embarrassment soon followed three months later, when, in September 1963, a court in Phoenix, Arizona, ordered Burr to discharge the historic debt in full. Judge Charles C Stidham later explained that he would certainly have dismissed the case because the debt was so old if only Burr had pursued the matter through the correct legal channels. 'Pleading his own case was most improper,' he chided. 'It is not good law.'

Although Burr received much gentle ribbing for his abject failure he was reported not to have seen the funny side of his fruitless courtroom caper. He subsequently played Perry Mason many more times on television, maintaining the great man's startling success rate with elegant ease, but he never played Perry Mason in real life again and *The Case of the Second Identity Crisis* remained blessedly unpublished.

THE FULL MONTY

COURT OF APPEAL, LONDON, 1964

'The first lesson of libel is, if you don't like losing, don't play the game.' That eminently sensible piece of advice was given in January 1994 by Thomas Crone, legal manager of the *Sun*, to the *EastEnders* actress Gillian Taylforth after she had been given a particularly sound licking by the newspaper in one of the most notorious (and therefore most entertaining) libel cases of the 1990s.

If only someone had given the same advice to the unusually named Moses Fairchild Gohoho in 1964, the Court of Appeal might have been spared one of the most bizarre episodes in its history; thank goodness Gohoho's advisers were slow on the uptake.

Mr Gohoho was a Ghanaian politician, author and publisher who wasn't at all happy about some of the things said about him in an article in the *Ghana Evening News* in March 1959. He decided to sue two companies involved in the placement of the piece, Lintas Export Advertising Services and West Africa Publicity Ltd. Like many a litigant before him and since, he decided that London, libel capital of the world, would be the scene of his triumph.

It was a long hard slog and it wasn't until 24 October 1963 that his case was heard. Having been declared bankrupt in May 1962, he could not have denied that the substantial damages he anticipated would come in useful. All he needed was a sympathetic jury.

When Mr Justice Thesiger announced the first verdict, with costs, in favour of Lintas Advertising, Gohoho's spirits must have sagged. But, when the verdict went in Gohoho's favour against the second defendant, the triumphant litigant stood on the brink of untold riches.

He was then to experience, though, the sort of devastation more recently suffered by the least successful contestants on television's *Who Wants To Be a Millionaire?* as Justice Thesiger sent him home with an award from West Africa Publicity of one solitary halfpenny.

Being awarded derisory damages can feel even worse than losing. After all, if a man's reputation isn't even worth the price of a penny chew, what's the point in having a reputation at all? Why not just blow it?

That was precisely what Moses Fairchild Gohoho did. Not for him a spot in a quiet corner licking his wounds. He decided to appeal.

The big day was Monday, 20 January 1964. Lord Justices Sellers, Pearson and Russell sat in judgment as Gohoho prepared to conduct his own defence. But he was tripped up at the first hurdle as the defendants' representatives made an unexpected but entirely reasonable request.

'Gohoho still owes our clients £273 costs from the first hearing,' they said. 'We therefore make application that he should lodge security for the costs of this present appeal lest he should again be unsuccessful.'

Gohoho was riled, asserting to the panel that such an application was 'frivolous and vexatious'. But their Lordships were unmoved by his passionate plea and gave him a period of 21 days to lodge £50. Unless he did so, the case would be dismissed. To add insult to injury the court granted the defendants the costs of preparing their security application.

Gohoho's bill, it seemed, was already mounting. So was his blood pressure. Becoming increasingly hot under the collar, he removed his jacket and adopted a lying-down position on the bench, from where he had addressed the court. Their Lordships turned a blind eye and called the next case while Gohoho exclaimed that he would 'come to court every day until this is resolved'.

It isn't often that the rather dry Law Report columns of *The Times* have recourse to an eye-catching headline, but CLOTHES REMOVED was one of their better moments. As the next case proceeded, Gohoho stripped off his trousers and underpants and reclined naked, except for his shirt, on the bench.

As a female litigant sitting next to him fled to the sanctuary of junior counsel's seats, their Lordships adjourned proceedings and called for the court tipstaff and police to remove the reclining figure. The court was emptied and Moses Fairchild Gohoho was carried out in the strong arms of the law, protesting loudly.

Lord Justice Sellers committed Mr Gohoho to prison for one week for his intransigence and the Ghanaian politician's case still raises a 'ho-ho' nearly forty years on.

MIND YOUR LANGUAGE

THE HIGH COURT, LONDON, 1970

It was the end of the swinging sixties, a time when 'rights' and 'free expression' were as much on the mind of the nation's student fraternity as free love and the price of a pint in the union bar.

It was a time when Welsh students, in particular, had a very personal axe to grind – campaigning for the Welsh language to be more widely recognised as an official form of communication. The touchpaper being thus prominent, all that was required was a spark of ignition and it was unfortunate for Mr Justice Lawton that it was his court that proved in 1970 to be the scene of the resulting fireworks in a case that occupied more column inches in the newspapers than almost any other of that year.

The spark was provided by a 25-year-old folk singer, Dafydd Iwan, chairman of the Welsh Language Society. In 1969 he was caught daubing Welsh translations on English road signs and fined £56 for his perceived vandalism. He refused to pay and as a result, early in 1970, was sentenced to three months in Cardiff prison. Aberystwyth University students first demonstrated their support of Iwan's cause in January 1970, when a fifty-strong group barricaded themselves in the courtroom at Carmarthen, and these scenes were mirrored in Aberystwyth when 27 students settled in for an all-night sleepover in the courtroom there.

Although these acts of defiance made the news, they were

on Welsh soil and didn't have the intensity of impact the students had hoped for. There was only one thing for it, and that was to strike at the heart of the English legal system, which meant London and the Royal Courts of Justice in the Strand.

It was 4 February 1970 when Mr Justice Lawton was hearing a libel action in the High Court in which a respected naval commander was suing an author of a book that called into question certain aspects of his wartime conduct. The case had nothing whatsoever to do with Wales and a high-ranking admiral was in the middle of giving evidence when the 'Celtic Hairies', as *The Times* described them, made their mark.

On an otherwise entirely routine Wednesday, a protest squadron of 22 students invaded the courtroom at 11.50 a.m. singing songs in Welsh, distributing leaflets and causing general mayhem as the group's leader addressed the court, in English at this stage, to say, 'This is a demonstration against the imprisonment of Dafydd Iwan. The English legal system is acting against the interests of the Welsh language.'

As a rousing chorus of 'We Shall Overcome' echoed around the hallowed halls of English justice and a stupefied admiral looked on open-mouthed, Justice Lawton acted swiftly by adjourning the hearing and leaving the courtroom.

Now the students might well have regarded this as mere high jinks but as an act of disrespect it was rather akin to holding a rave in St Paul's Cathedral. It just wasn't done.

It was twenty minutes before police rounded up the students and put them in a jury room, and Justice Lawton had already determined to make swift reprisals unless unconditional apologies were received forthwith.

Although eight did decide to grovel, the other fourteen were in no mood to compromise and Justice Lawton might have known he was in for a bad time of it when he questioned the first youth, only to receive an answer in Welsh: 'That is impertinent, young man,' he said. 'Is there anything you wish to say as to why you should not be committed to prison for gross contempt of court?'

Again the reply contained rather more double-L's and

rather fewer vowels than Justice Lawton could cope with and, undoubtedly feeling somewhat affronted by this provocative behaviour, he summarily sentenced fourteen students, including five females, to three months in prison.

If there had been a fan in the court that was the moment when the proverbial would undoubtedly have hit it with a vengeance as Justice Lawton's strong stance divided the opinion of the nation and roused supporters of the students, including some influential MPs, to speak out strongly in their favour.

The result was that eleven of the demonstrators, encouraged by their leader, Griffith W Morris, went to appeal and the case of *Morris and Others v. the Crown Office* was heard under the full glare of the public spotlight on Monday, 9 February.

The Master of the Rolls Lord Denning, Lord Justice Davies and Lord Justice Salmon were in a tricky position, for the students, all but one under the age of 21, were perceived by many as nothing more than 'young kids who didn't realise the gravity of their actions' as described by Mr Gwynfor Evans, nationalist MP for Carmarthen, whose daughter was one of those arrested.

In the event, Lord Denning described their strike at the very heart of the system as 'unprecedented' but opted to show 'exceptional mercy' by releasing the eleven appellants from prison and binding them over to keep the peace for twelve months.

The students were duly photographed linking arms in a display of jubilation outside the scene of their invasion to cap an affair in which a headmasterly ticking off from the Law Lords sufficed to calm the turbulent waters and dig Justice Lawton out of a hole of his own making.

Although this is the most celebrated language-related case in the record books, it is by no means the only time that members of a court have been linguistically challenged.

Let's finish on a light note with a visit first to Wood Green Crown Court, north London. In February 1990, as a witness with an exceptionally broad Scottish accent gave evidence, the eyes of everyone in court began to glaze over, for no one could understand a word he was saying. The problem was resolved only when James Graham, a Scottish usher, was sworn in to provide a running translation service.

That further brings to mind the tale of the Scottish trial in which the sheriff told the prisoner, 'Although I find you a fecund liar I will not send you to prison.' The prisoner's reply was: 'Thank you, Your Honour, and you're a fecund good judge.'

Not that the English, either, are entirely masters of their own tongue. At London's Horseferry Road Magistrates' Court in a 1996 neighbour-dispute case the noise-abatement officer amused the court by reading out a verbatim statement taken from a neighbour at the scene: 'It's the decimals! It's the decimals! It's her next door, isn't it? I'll sue her for definition of character.'

So that's the Welsh, Scottish and English taken care of. Who does that leave?

Just one from a veritable embarrassment of Irish linguistic riches must suffice. In Dublin in 1880 on the twentieth day of the trial of a home-rule campaigner, Charles Stewart Parnell, for seditious conspiracy the jury returned the uniquely Irish verdict: 'We are unanimously of the opinion that we cannot agree.'

A MOVING EXPERIENCE

THE HIGH COURT, LONDON, 1970

There is an apparently trifling geographical distinction between London's two most famous court buildings. The Royal Courts of Justice, sometimes referred to as the High Court or more commonly simply the Law Courts, are in the Strand. The Central Criminal Court, meanwhile, generally known as the Old Bailey, is merely a stroll down Fleet Street away, less than a mile distant.

But that puts only the Old Bailey in the City of London itself, and it was this fact that proved significant enough one day in 1970 for general mayhem to ensue.

There are some who say there is no such thing as a truly effective short cut, but when the case load at the Old Bailey began to outstrip the court's capacity it seemed a pretty good idea to transfer some of the backlog to the Royal Courts of Justice.

One such case concerned a matter of fraudulent dealing by directors of the crashed 'Rolls Razor' Washing Machine Company and the expected marathon trial began on Wednesday, 8 April. But, only seconds after Mr Justice MacKenna took to his seat in New Court No. 4 to commence proceedings, there was an unexpected turn of events.

A juror asked to be excused duty because his wife was ill, and he was immediately granted that privilege. This was by no means unusual – a new juror would be quickly commandeered and sworn in without delay. Or so the judge thought.

159

Not so, My Lord. A barrister was quick to point out that under the Supreme Court of Judicature Act of 1873 jurors in cases originally allocated to courts within the City could be sworn in only in the City itself. He might have been a jobsworth but he was darn well right and months of tortuous proceedings could have been made invalid at a stroke on such a technicality.

There was only one thing for it. In order to conduct the swearing-in procedure properly and kick off the case in a valid manner the entire court needed to decamp temporarily to the Old Bailey.

It was at this point that the vagaries of legal hierarchy emerged to graphic effect, for the judge travelled in his official chauffeur-driven car, the barristers hailed taxis and the jurors were allotted Shanks's Pony.

After the valiant eleven's unscheduled walk they met the somewhat bemused twelfth man at the Old Bailey and he was duly sworn in within the City confines 57 minutes after the adjournment.

Then it was back to the High Court, the judge by chauffeur-driven private car, the barristers by taxi and the full complement of jurors again on foot. That the smooth operation of the machinery of British justice should have been disturbed by such a spanner in the works was certainly embarrassing at the start of such a high-profile trial but there was more to come.

Back in Court No. 4 the number of jurors still didn't add up and there was a near panic when an usher was heard to say, dispensing with any pretence to legal jargon, 'Blimey, only nine of 'em have come back.' Much to the judge's relief the missing three were quickly rounded up – they had got lost after a visit to the court toilets – and the case commenced at 12.10 p.m., nearly two hours after it should have started.

Embarrassing, yes, but just one of those excusable one-offs that will happen. Well, two-offs, actually, for as Court No. 4 settled down to normality there was a stir in the adjacent Court No. 5 as Judge Grant was about to begin a long and complicated income tax case.

A woman juror, it appeared, feared her delicate health

would not stand the strain of a lengthy trial. Again a twelfth person was needed. Again the procession began – first the limo, then the taxis and finally the footsloggers. As they scurried along to the Old Bailey as if their lives depended on it, passing tourists must have thought they were witnessing a quaint Olde English custom, the ancient art of court racing, perhaps. In any case, they made it back to Court 5 in record time, bang on schedule for the lunch adjournment.

Wednesday, 8 April 1970, wasn't the proudest day in English legal history but it was the only day two judges, a score of barristers and 24 jurors went court-hopping at the behest of a barrister whose anorak knowledge of an 1873 Act led to this strangely moving experience.

A VERY VEXING SEXING

THE HIGH COURT, LONDON, 1970

'A judge is not supposed to know anything about the facts of life until they have been presented in evidence and explained to him at least three times.'

If those words of Lord Chief Justice Parker (1900–72) even approximate to the truth then Mr Justice Ormrod must have had a pretty educational time of it in the High Court in February 1970, when he became the first judge in an English court ever called upon to decide an individual's sex. He was to find that the question of sexing can indeed be very vexing and that the case of *Corbett v. Corbett (otherwise Ashley)* was one more suited to the medical books than the law courts when it came to the intimate discussion of the mechanics of the matter.

The genesis of this mind-boggling case lay in seemingly romantic enough circumstances back on 10 September 1963, when the Honourable Arthur Corbett, 43-year-old heir to Lord Rowallan, married the 27-year-old fashion model April Ashley in Gibraltar. The couple were to live in a splendid villa near Marbella, Spain, and all looked set for a long and happy future.

Not that there wasn't a strong whiff of scandal about the affair, for in truth Corbett had grown tired of his life with his first wife and four children and they divorced in June 1962, leaving the way clear for the future Lord Rowallan to marry his glamorous model.

But all was not as it seemed. Vital parts of the story were

missing. April Ashley's parts to be precise.

Or, more accurately still, George Jamieson's parts, for April Ashley was born as George Jamieson in Liverpool in 1935, was brought up as a boy and joined the Merchant Navy in 1951 when he was sixteen.

That was when the doubts began to surface and after a voyage and a half at sea the young sailor sought psychiatric advice and by 1953 was telling the medical men he wanted to be a woman.

By today's multiple-choice gender-bending standards it was a straightforward case, but almost fifty years ago this was weird stuff indeed. George, though, was determined, and after a course of hormone treatment, which encouraged breast development, he went all the way, and on 11 May 1960 had the cuts that most males would consider the unkindest of all when he underwent what was then called a 'sex-change' operation, which also involved the construction of artificial female genitalia.

The name change by deed poll to April Ashley quickly followed. The 'he' became a 'she' on her passport and for National Insurance purposes, but the Registrar General refused to change the birth certificate. April Ashley behaved and lived as a woman though, and was attractive enough for the modelling career to take off during 1961. The wedding followed two years later.

Perhaps not surprisingly, the marriage to Arthur Corbett didn't work out. He later intimated that it had never been consummated and the couple spent only fourteen days together throughout the seven-year relationship. Corbett agreed to a divorce and pursued the grounds that the marriage was null and void because he had 'married a man'. April Ashley did not contest the divorce in principle but insisted that the grounds should be nonconsummation.

It was left to poor Justice Ormrod to decide whether April Ashley was in law a man or a woman and whether any intimacy that may or may not have taken place could be construed as 'normal relations'.

If there was ever a moment he regretted becoming a judge

it was probably as he took his seat in the High Court on 2 February 1970.

Even before the fundamental bits and pieces of the case were debated with medical experts, there were surprises in store, for the court heard that Arthur Corbett had been made fully aware of his wife's background when they met in November 1960 and that Ashley's story had appeared in the newspapers a year before the marriage. Furthermore, Corbett himself had long experienced the desire to dress in women's clothing and he had mixed in the most unusual social circles.

Justice Ormrod didn't allow these facts to cloud the issue and he duly added to the remarkable records of English legal history by pronouncing that 'the biological sexual constitution of an individual is fixed at birth at the latest and cannot be changed by the natural development of organs of the opposite sex or by medical or surgical means'.

A huge oversimplification by today's standards but good enough for 1970 and a landmark decision in its day. On count one, April Ashley was a man.

That just left the delicate question of 'had they or hadn't they and, if they had, did it count?' Seldom can the High Court have listened to more graphic debate. The transcripts are instructional and at times unintentionally close to farce. During a debate as to what the difference would be between 'entering Miss Ashley's artificial opening and that, let's say, of the back passage of a male', Judge Ormrod was moved to observe: 'For the purposes of our analysis, no difference save half an inch or so. In my opinion *vera copula* has not occurred. Miss Ashley was incapable of "normal relations" and her grounds of nonconsummation cannot be upheld.'

If anyone looked around the courtroom for Vera Copula, she wasn't in that day. His Lordship had another final unwitting stab at something approaching a music-hall act when he announced to the court that 'as far as the matter of sex with his wife was concerned, I have formulated the opinion that Mr Corbett simply didn't press it'.

The marriage was declared void solely on the grounds that April Ashley had been declared by Judge Ormrod to be a man and although she went some way towards an appeal she dropped the case on 18 September 1970 and the decree nisi of nullity was declared absolute.

There ends one of the strangest affairs in legal history, illustrative too of how the law relating to gender cases, now much more common, has had to move with the times. By today's standards it may be tame but it was surely an eye-opener for Justice Ormrod.

A QUESTION OF ENTRY

COLCHESTER, 1971

As any law student would heartily testify, *The All England Law Reports* are hardly the most entertaining reading. Yet they have their moments and one of the most celebrated case reports is that under the apparently workaday heading *The Crown v. Collins*.

Yet here is a case that a senior judge of many years' standing described at appeal as 'about as extraordinary a case as I have ever heard. Were the facts put into a novel or portrayed on the stage they would be regarded as so improbable as to be unworthy of serious consideration and as verging on farce.'

The subject matter of *The Crown v. Collins* is of the most serious kind, for a question of rape is involved, but the acquittal of Collins on appeal and the nature of the facts and legal interpretations involved have in time made the case oddly legendary on a level close to music-hall-joke status.

This is a heady mix of *Romeo and Juliet, Confessions of a Window Cleaner* and the best tradition of Whitehall farce with enough double entendres and tacky innuendo thrown in for several remakes of *Carry on Dick*.

The Law Reports relate the tale very much in the style of 'P G Wodehouse meets Jilly Cooper' and strangely it is one of the few cases that most legal professionals will remember almost verbatim from their days as law students.

The basic facts are that, on 29 October 1971 at Essex

166

Assizes, nineteen-year-old Stephen William George Collins was convicted of forcibly entering a house in Colchester in the early hours of 24 July 1971 with intent to rape. He was given a 21-month prison sentence against which he appealed and the conviction was subsequently quashed by Edmund Davies in the Court of Appeal on 5 May 1972.

The All England Law Reports rather quaintly relate that 'one evening the appellant had had a good deal to drink and was desirous of having sexual intercourse'. The narrative they then regale us with is a very lengthy one but the essence was that Collins, on spotting an open window to a first-floor room, which he knew to be the bedroom of an eighteen-year-old girl he was acquainted but not intimate with, decided he would chance his luck.

The girl shared the house with her mother, so clandestine entry was paramount. With this in mind he secured a step-ladder, climbed it and peeped in to see the girl naked and asleep on her bed immediately beneath the window. He descended the ladder again and removed all his clothes with the exception, mindful of preserving the finest tradition of British manhood, of his socks. He later told the court that this was better to facilitate his escape should the girl's mother seek to interrupt the amorous proceedings.

Collins's version of events was that he then ascended the ladder again and before any part of his body crossed the threshold of the open window the girl beckoned him in and then pulled him down on to the bed, where 'full intimate relations' ensued.

The girl's version of events was that after having spent the evening consuming a not inconsiderable amount of alcohol with her boyfriend she had gone to bed and later awoken to see a blond man in a state of 'obvious arousal' looking into her bedroom. She had indeed beckoned him in and she did undeniably 'willingly engage in intimacy'. It was only after the event that she realised Collins wasn't the man she believed him to be.

The Law Reports take up the tale:

When she saw the naked male form in the moonlight she jumped to the conclusion that it was her boyfriend, with whom she was on terms of regular and frequent sexual intimacy, coming to pay her an ardent nocturnal visit. It was only after the lapse of some time that the length of his hair and tone of voice suggested to her that there was something 'different' about him, so she switched on the bedside light whereupon she realised it was Collins rather than her boyfriend. She slapped him on the face and then told him to leave, which he did, via the ladder, and the girl strongly asserted that she would never have agreed to full intimacy had she known the man was not her boyfriend.

It's all very tricky, there's no doubt about it, for Collins's claim was that he simply thought he'd 'got lucky'. Among many issues debated at great length at the appeal hearing, the question of 'entry' became central and the five-inch-wide threshold of the window became the focus of the whole case. If any part of Collins's body had crossed the threshold 'before' he was beckoned in then his entry was deemed to be uninvited and his intention one of rape. If the beckoning occurred before he had begun to cross the threshold then his entry was deemed to be an invitation and the entirely unresisted act that followed a legitimate consequence of that invitation.

The debate about whether 'any' part of Collins's body had entered the building 'uninvited' was a curious one and I can confirm from personal research that if one shares a bottle of wine with a member of the legal profession the rampant embellishment of this and other explicit aspects of this case can become most enlightening. The two-bottle account is even more outrageous and the three-bottle version has Collins also entering the 'wrong' house, believing it to be that of 'his' girlfriend, and the window slamming shut to cut short his ardour rather painfully.

I seem also to recall hazily a version in which the girl's mother and a mousetrap become embroiled in the action, but that only goes to show that embellished yarns are not entirely confined to fishermen – solicitors, in particular, are equally quick to display piscatorial licence given half the chance.

The true facts are that the Appeal Court found that Stephen Collins was not deemed to have forced entry and his place in the annals of law's strangest cases remains that of an innocent, if a little red-faced, Romeo.

A SOUND (ASLEEP?) VERDICT

LEWES ASSIZES, 1971

When two young brothers were convicted of murder at Lewes Assizes in November 1971 their future looked undeniably grim, but they were to launch an appeal of unprecedented novelty (for a murder case), which put the validity of their conviction under far closer scrutiny than the trial judge, Mr Justice Crichton, had ever bargained for.

The evidence against Alan and Keith Langham had been particularly strong. It seems they had entered the home of an elderly Hastings resident, Charles Levett, intent on burglary and ended up stabbing him. Twice in the back and twelve times in the chest was the count, and they broke three knives in the frenzy of the vicious murder.

The brothers' defence that the gentleman had made 'indecent advances' towards them was entirely rejected by the jury and Judge Crichton found them both guilty of murder and sentenced them to life.

But the brothers had a solicitor who kept a close eye on cases of the strange variety and he was aware of the unusual facts surrounding the 1961 case of *The Crown v. Edworthy*. On that occasion Ernest Edworthy, a Royal Army Pay Corps officer, had been court-martialled at Ashton-under-Lyne, Lancashire, for fraudulent financial dealings while serving in Sierra Leone, but the decision was overturned at appeal after Edworthy's legal advisers claimed that the judge, Mr Acland-Hood, had been asleep during important passages of the trial.

170

A close scrutiny of the judge's summing up revealed significant omissions and errors and this was taken as sufficient evidence that he had indeed nodded off during proceedings.

The Langham brothers had complained several times to their solicitor during their trial that Judge Crichton 'was asleep' and those complaints resulted in an unusual affidavit from their solicitors, which looked likely, in the light of the Edworthy precedent, to get them off: 'When the evidence was coming to an end and counsel's speeches were beginning,' it read, 'the judge at about 12 noon was sitting with his head resting on his hands, his eyes shut and his head nodding, and for approximately the next 15 minutes he was manifestly asleep from time to time.'

Such a vehement sworn statement presented Lord Widgery and his colleagues with a tricky problem indeed when the case came to the Court of Appeal in April 1972. Were they to be forced by precedent to sanction the unconditional release of two brutal murderers on such an embarrassing technicality? The newspaper headlines just didn't bear thinking about: DOZY JUDGE GIVES MURDERERS' RELEASE THE NOD.

It is not for me to suggest that their Lordships closed ranks, nor would I advocate that the release of the murderers would have been any sort of justice in the real sense, but I have to report that, faced with an undoubted dilemma, they came up with a corker of a decision. After the most detailed scrutiny of Judge Crichton's summing up, their findings were that he had simply been 'thinking with his eyes shut'.

Judge Crichton's summing up, it appeared, included definite reference to evidence given during the period he was accused of being in the land of Nod. That was sufficient for the appeal panel to find that he only 'appeared to be asleep'.

The Langhams' advisers were hugely put out by what they saw as an abject whitewash and they forcibly suggested that even 'appearing' to be asleep was at best exceptionally rude and at worst a 'reverse' contempt of court.

Lord Widgery, the Lord Chief Justice, listened intently to the argument, with his eyes open it should be said, but remained unmoved: 'The judge was not asleep,' he asserted,

171

'and if he appeared to be, however unfortunate and however much to be deplored that might be, it was not a ground for saying that justice was not seen to be done.'

As a result of that unequivocal statement, and despite a long letter of complaint from the Langham boys' mother, the brothers were detained at Her Majesty's pleasure for some considerable time.

Few would disagree that the decision was 'right' in a moral sense but there is an important legal precept to be learnt here. Whenever you see a judge asleep it would be wise not to insult him, take his name in vain or even pull a face at him because, being all-seeing and not at all like us ordinary mortals, he will merely be 'thinking with his eyes shut'.

CAREERS ADVICE

YORK CROWN COURT, 1971

Burglary may not appear in the careers books but that hasn't stopped thousands of young hopefuls joining the ranks since time immemorial to see if they can make it pay.

Much to the cost of their victims, there are some burglars who have done 'very well, thank you' from this unusual job, but it is heartening to know that there have also been spectacular failures. And they don't come more spectacular than Philip McCutcheon.

Having been arrested for the twentieth time, on this occasion after driving his getaway car into two parked vans, Mr McCutcheon appeared at York Crown Court in 1971. It was an appearance that might have touched even the most hard-hearted of the anti-burglar lobby, for McCutcheon, it has to be said, just didn't look the part.

The judge was certainly affected for, in giving McCutcheon a conditional discharge, Recorder Rodney Percy gave what must be the most heartfelt and brutally honest advice ever delivered from the bench:

'May I advise that I really think you should give burglary up,' he said. 'You have a withered hand, an artificial leg and only one eye. You have been caught in Otley, Leeds, Harrogate, Norwich, Beverley, Hull and York. How can you hope to succeed? You are a rotten burglar. You are always being caught.'

Well said, that man. Sounder careers advice has seldom been given.

It is tempting to suggest that Philip McCutcheon is the worst burglar of all time but in fairness to him, and as this is *The Law's Strangest Cases*, it would be remiss of me not to mention a number of other candidates for the title.

Strong contender from Europe is the Parisian burglar who, on 4 November 1933, attempted to rob the home of an antique dealer. By way of disguise, lest he should be disturbed, he dressed in a fifteenth-century suit of armour. If only he'd stuck to the more traditional black-and-white hooped shirt, mask and bag marked SWAG (strangely seldom seen these days), he might have fared better, for the clanking of the suit of armour awoke the owner, who pushed the burglar off balance, dropped a small sideboard across his breastplate and called the police.

The burglar was cross-examined while still in his suit, and confessed all: 'Yes, I am a thief,' said a muffled voice through the visor. 'I thought I would frighten the owner in this.'

As if that weren't sufficient embarrassment, there was still more to come. It was 24 hours before the hapless thief could be prised from his badly dented metal suit, during which time he was fed breakfast through the visor.

Could anyone possibly top our Frenchman? Well, if everything really *is* bigger and better in the USA, that must include cock-ups. Take a bow, Charles A Meriweather, who in Baltimore in 1978 broke into a house, confronted the woman occupant and demanded money. Although she said she had only loose change, Meriweather's acutely sharp brain was at work in an instant: 'Write me a cheque,' he barked. 'Who shall I make it out to?' asked the woman. 'Charles A Meriweather,' came the immediate reply.

He was arrested a few hours later.

So that's Britain, Europe and the USA all in the running for the worst burglar of all time. Not wishing to be accused of geographical bias, I'll finish in the East.

In January 1998 a thief pulled off a sensational coup when he fled from the Yanmonoki Museum in central Japan clutching a 600-year-old Chinese platter dating from the Ming dynasty and worth an estimated £260,000. It was just like a scene from a movie.

A Laurel and Hardy movie, that is, for the thief dropped the platter in the road as he made his escape and saw it shatter into fragments.

Still tempted to think that crime might pay? Then you will probably ignore the sensible careers advice of Rodney Percy and listen instead to that given by Woody Allen in the film *Take the Money and Run* (1969). As the eager criminal Virgil Starkwell, he justifies his job in a classic one-liner: 'I think crime pays. The hours are good. You travel a lot.'

WHAT A DIFFERENCE A DAY MAKES

GLASGOW, SCOTLAND, 1972

When Joseph Beltrami started his business as a young lawyer from modest offices in Glasgow's Buchanan Street in 1958, there was no guarantee he would make a name for himself.

Yet by 1972 he had become Glasgow's leading criminal lawyer and the favourite of that city's notorious underworld. 'If you want to get off, get Joe Beltrami' was the word on the street, for he was known not to miss a trick.

Yet some cases look pretty hopeless from the start. One such arose from an armed robbery early in 1972 at the Stepps Hotel on the Edinburgh Road. Sawn-off shotguns were used and around £2,000 was stolen.

It was only a matter of days before James H Steele and another youth were arrested. Substantial amounts of money were recovered from both men and witnesses made positive identifications. The police, moreover, claimed to have full confessions. All the prisoners had was a good lawyer. They had indeed 'got Beltrami'.

That was the gloomy scenario facing Joseph Beltrami as he applied unsuccessfully for bail for his new clients. They were duly committed for trial at Glasgow High Court but various delays meant the trial date had to be fixed for some months ahead.

It was just a few days before the Monday on which the trial was due to start that Beltrami first saw a chink of light when he mused over the terms of the Criminal Procedure (Scotland)

Act 1887, which limited the time the accused could be held in custody if refused bail. Although the act has now been amended, it stated clearly in 1975 that 'the accused must be brought to trial, and the trial concluded, within 110 days of their initial committal for the offence'.

Beltrami consulted his diary, counted carefully and calculated that the 110th day would expire at midnight on the Tuesday, the second day of the scheduled trial. He reasoned that the Crown had just two days to complete a complicated trial involving more than fifty witnesses. He knew they were fully au fait with the 110-day rule but he was sure they would struggle to meet it. Their task had been made even harder by the arrest of a third suspect six weeks after the first two, who, even though well within the time limit himself, was still part of the same trial. It was all going to take time.

The Crown, however, seemed quite relaxed, and on the first day proceedings were adjourned at 4.30 p.m. Burning the midnight oil, it seemed, was not necessary. Beltrami and his team kept their heads down – they didn't even tell the prisoners that the clock was ticking, so they thought, in their favour.

Tuesday's proceedings began unflurried and again the Crown prosecution team seemed ultra-cool. This time the court adjourned at 4.15 p.m. Beltrami went home fully expecting a frantic phone call that night from a Crown representative seeking the formal grant of an extension, but none came.

Only on the way into court on Wednesday did Beltrami hear two of the opposition speaking with some resolve: 'We've got to finish today and we will do, even if we sit until midnight,' they said. By their diaries, it seemed, the 110th day was the Wednesday.

Again Beltrami counted meticulously before taking the plunge and ordering his counsel to make a bold statement: 'The first and second accused have now been detained in custody for a greater period than the maximum permitted by law. They are now entitled to be liberated and declared free for all time for the crime with which they are charged.'

Crown prosecution officials looked flustered. Judge Lord Leecham raised a quizzical eyebrow, sent the jury out and took advice. When he called the jury back in he explained that 'owing to some mistake I must ask you to return formal verdicts of not guilty on the two men'.

The stunned prisoners were duly liberated and even the third accused had cause for celebration when the court returned on him later the same day that peculiarly Scottish 'halfway-house' verdict of 'not proven'.

Beltrami had triumphed against all odds. That the case has since become known as 'the Leap Year Case' is the key to his victory, for 1972 *was* a leap year and two armed robbers had been saved by Beltrami's diligence in including the interloping but triumphal day of 29 February in his calculations.

Not surprisingly, a somewhat embarrassed Crown Office ordered an immediate enquiry the next day and the same mistake has never occurred again. The freed prisoners, meanwhile, celebrated their strange path to freedom with wild celebrations.

A final word of warning, though, to those 'getting off' in the face of seemingly hopeless odds against. It pays to celebrate out of court rather than in it.

On 2 July 1981 at Durham Crown Court the jury acquitted a nineteen-year-old Liverpudlian, Tony Mullen, on two theft charges. After five unpleasant months in custody he let his relief get the better of him and as he left court after the verdict he threw up both his arms in triumph. The judge, Angus Stroyan, described this as 'an insolent contempt of court' and, despite an apology from the accused on the next day, he promptly sentenced him to two days in jail!

AN UNCOMMONLY VIOLENT PROTEST

IPSWICH MAGISTRATES' COURT, 1972

Violence in court is by no means common but nor would it be strictly accurate to say it was uncommon, for throughout legal history parties who have felt sufficiently wronged have from time to time sought on-the-spot vengeance of the nonpeaceful variety.

Not surprisingly it is generally the accused who goes for the judge, but victims or their relatives seeking vengeance on the accused undoubtedly run attempted 'judgicide' a close second. On a rather more novel front, solicitors have been known to engage in open combat in court, jurors failing to agree with each other have reached the daggers-drawn stage, and judges, too, have occasionally sought to exercise their powers, especially in the USA, by rather more physical means than their jurisdiction strictly entitled them to.

But scarcely can such examples of uncourtly behaviour have been more bizarre than that witnessed at Ipswich Magistrates' Court on Thursday, 27 April 1972.

In the dock that day was 23-year-old Anthony Francis Joseph Judge, charged with two blackmail offences. The sums of £5 and £10 to which the charges related suggest that his 'information' was more of the tepid than red-hot variety, but the magistrates ruled that he had a definite case to answer and ordered that he should be remanded in custody pending a later trial at Ipswich Crown Court.

Judge certainly didn't fancy the prospect of a spell inside and as the blood rushed to his head his immediate thoughts turned to violence. But there the similarity between Judge and many others ends, for his choice of target was a peculiar one.

With an impassioned cry of 'I do not want to go to prison,' he whipped a razor blade out of his pocket and slashed at his own throat. Death, evidently, was a better option than life inside. Maybe he'd heard bad reports about the food.

Only the prompt action of his solicitor Alan Barker saved the day as he jumped on his client in an attempt to wrest the razor blade from him. The life of the accused was duly saved by this heroic defence but both men left court in an ambulance, the prisoner with a slashed neck and his solicitor with a badly cut hand.

As acts of vengeance go, the behaviour of Anthony Judge was certainly uncommon and there are a couple of strange taglines to this case, too, which can't be allowed to pass unrecorded.

Amazingly, not one of the newspapers reporting the case saw fit to use the headline of the century: JUDGE SLASHES THROAT IN COURT – now there *was* an opportunity missed.

And finally, while we're on the subject of offensive weapons in court, it would be unforgivable not to mention the Frenchman who caused something of a stir during his divorce hearing in Cologne in 1995. Evidently intent on topping Anthony Judge's razor-blade performance in some spectacular fashion, he was discovered to have a Japanese ceremonial sword, with a three-foot blade, concealed in his trouser leg. When he was asked to explain himself, his reasoning was ingenious if not a little improbable.

Not even the German court's knowledge that the French bake bread of an entirely unnecessary length could add credence to the defendant's classic answer: 'It was in case there was a long delay before my case came up. I was planning to use it to make my sandwiches.'

STRAIGHT TALK AT LAST

THE HIGH COURT, LONDON, 1972

Several centuries ago it was by no means unusual to hear the language of the street in court. Judges, lawyers, witnesses and prisoners felt little shame in calling a spade a spade.

But, somewhere along the way, the language of the law became ever more respectable and tortuous. The legal euphemism came to reign supreme and by the time Queen Victoria came to the throne a spade seemingly had every chance of being described in court as a soil-conveyancing implement.

And so it went on. Generations of judges came to talk of a man 'passing water in the street' without a riverside walkway in sight and couples were habitually said to have had 'carnal knowledge' even if they were committed vegetarians. In a 1976 case Lord Denning was at pains to tell the jury in his summing up that the accused, on being apprehended, had 'delivered an emphatic version of "you be off" to the officer concerned'. And again in 1976 Lord Russell could not quite bring himself to quote verbatim as he told the court that 'when the police arrived, the defendant called them adjectival pigs'.

All very discreet and unlikely to offend, but once in a while such delicacy is shown to be entirely inadequate for the circumstances of a trial, which is why the otherwise routine 1972 case of *Evans v. Ewells* hit the headlines when an appeal judge was for once moved to some good straight talking.

Anthony Charles Evans, a farmer from Knighton, Radnorshire, had been convicted by Ludlow justices of 'openly, lewdly and obscenely exposing his person with intent to insult a female under Section 4 of the Vagrancy Act 1824'.

The court at Ludlow heard how he had 'walked past Miss Ewells with his trousers unfastened at the front, exposing a V-shaped patch of bare skin low down on his stomach'.

It was established quite clearly that Mr Evans had exposed nothing more and he claimed unequivocally that his trousers had been left open entirely accidentally. With the benefit of hindsight the alleged offence seemed to amount to little more than a frontal version of the now ubiquitous instances of 'builder's bum', which assail innocent bystanders at every turn.

But Miss Ewells was a sensitive soul and the Ludlow court interpreted the 1824 Act literally. Evans had exposed his 'person' within what the court construed to be the meaning of the Act and he was duly found guilty.

When Evans appealed he was treated no more leniently by Shropshire Quarter Sessions. They, too, took the nineteenth-century wording entirely at face value and upheld the conviction. Evans, it seems, was labelled a 'flasher' and that was more than he could stand. He duly took his case to the High Court, where on Tuesday, 22 February 1972 Mr Justice Ashworth transcended 150 years of judicial bashfulness to get straight to the point: 'The only question to consider,' he said, 'is the meaning of "person" in the 1824 Act. The prosecution insist that "person" means any part of the body. The appellant contends that it only means penis.'

This was the moment when 'euphemism' effectively stood in the dock and Justice Ashworth found it wanting. Having emboldened himself to utter the P-word once, he became a man seemingly possessed as, rather like the small boy who prepares himself for years to utter the word 'bottom' in front of his maiden aunt, he positively let rip once he'd found the courage:

'By 1824,' he proceeded, 'the word "person" in connection with sexual matters had undoubtedly acquired a meaning of its own synonymous with penis. It may be that it was a forerunner of the Victorian gentility which prevented people from calling a penis a penis and I have no doubt that the words "exposing his person" meant someone exposing his penis.'

And, with that hitherto unprecedented five-in-a-row P-word frenzy, Justice Ashworth allowed the appeal of Anthony Evans and quashed his conviction.

It was a turning point in legal history of sorts for gradually thereafter the courts have become less coy on the question of anatomical terminology. So much so, in fact, that during the blockbusting 1998 action concerning Monica Lewinsky and President Bill Clinton, certain alleged unusual characteristics of the presidential person were discussed at some considerable length under the full spotlight of the world's media. It could never have happened in 1824 or even 1972, as Robert Bennett, counsel to the world's most powerful man, solemnly announced that 'in terms of size, shape, direction, whatever the devious mind wants to concoct, the President is a normal man'.

But while the grand old age of euphemism may sadly be a casualty of the modern age, lawyers will still argue about the precise meaning of words just as they have done since time immemorial. So consider as we close this wordy ramble the following hat-trick of all-time corkers.

In the 1916 High Court case of *Slater v. Evans* three of the sharpest judicial brains in the country reached the momentous conclusion only after prolonged debate that 'within the meaning of Section 3 of the Sunday Observance Act 1677, ice-cream is not meat'.

And what about the following summary of the wording of Section 72 of the 1980 Housing Act?

Subsection 72 (1) provides that 'rent tribunals are hereby abolished'.

Subsection 72 (2) adds that 'the functions previously conferred on rent tribunals shall be carried out by rent assessment committees'.

Subsection 72 (3) then rather spoils it all by announcing that 'a rent assessment committee shall henceforth be known as a rent tribunal'.

But it's back to Bill Clinton for first prize. When questioned by the Grand Jury in 1998 about the accuracy of one of his earlier statements, the President surpassed even his prodigious talent for double-speak with the memorable reply: 'It depends on what the meaning of the word "is" is.'

WHAT IS THE VERDICT?

KNUTSFORD CROWN COURT, 1973

The American author Mark Twain (1835–1910) delivered a speech in London on 4 July 1872 in which he expounded some rather cynical views on the system of trial by jury:

'We have a criminal jury system which is superior to any in the world,' he asserted, 'and its efficiency is only marred by the difficulty of finding twelve men every day who don't know anything and can't read.'

It may be true that jury members aren't always blessed with the keenest of intellects. But no matter – as long as they understand English, can follow the basics of a case and have a foreman who can marshal their views and present a coherent decision, there's seldom a problem.

But there's the rub, and if there were any of the Mark Twain school of thought at Knutsford Crown Court, Cheshire, a century later on 7 March 1973 they might well have been justified in delivering a resounding 'told you so' as chaos reigned and a prisoner who thought he was going down for three years escaped scot-free.

In the dock was a 29-year-old Bradford factory worker, Mohammed Rafiq, accused of drug dealing. When he was stopped at Manchester's Ringway Airport with a stash of drugs hidden in the false bottom of his suitcase his prospects didn't look good.

After he'd told the jury that he had no idea what was in the case he'd scarcely improved his chances of getting off: 'I was given it by a man called Ishmael to give to his brother in a restaurant in Bradford,' he explained.

It was the oldest and most unoriginal explanation in the book, of which Lord Justice Lawton was later to observe in the Court of Appeal: 'It was an improbable story that most juries would quickly have rejected.'

But things hadn't been so simple at Knutsford Crown Court. Despite a crystal-clear presentation from prosecuting counsel and a very lucid summing up from Judge David on the bench, the jury dithered. They retired for a full three and a half hours to debate what was apparently an open-and-shut case before their Indian foreman stepped forward to say his piece:

'Do I have to say "verdict"?' he asked, before proceeding to pose a series of basic questions that suggested he had not quite followed the narrative of the case to the clarity level expected of a jury foreman.

After a prolonged exchange with the judge that would have done justice to the Marx Brothers at their anarchic best a verdict of guilty was eventually delivered and a three-year jail sentence passed, but counsel for the defendant raised a vigorous objection:

'The case should have been presented with the lowest common denominator in mind,' said Mr I Wadsworth for Rafiq. 'If one juror has the mind of a five-year-old then everything should be explained as if to a five-year-old.'

An appeal was duly lodged and heard before Lord Justice Lawton on 25 September 1973. Although he made it clear that he considered the verdict of guilty was absolutely correct he was equally sure that he had to free Rafiq without further charge because of the manner in which the decision was given:

'I believe the foreman of the jury was confused and unable to understand simple English,' he explained. 'He did not, in my opinion, know the difference between the words "verdict" and "guilty".'

Although Mohammed Rafiq walked free as a result of this most fundamental blip in the communication chain, proceedings at Knutsford Crown Court in 1973 do not take the prize as the worst ever in the befuddled jury stakes, for five years later they were to be spectacularly outdone by their Canadian counterparts.

A 1978 murder trial in Manitoba had been under way for two days when one juror made it clear that he was completely deaf and had no idea what was going on. The judge, Mr Justice Solomon, asked him if he had heard any evidence at all and, following a telling silence, the juror was dismissed.

This led the judge to enquire whether everyone else was following proceedings. They were, apart from a second juror who said he was a fluent French speaker but admitted to not understanding a word of English. He expressed great surprise when he was told he was at a murder trial and he too was relieved of his duties.

Judge Solomon maintained his judicial cool in the face of these two hiccups but finally abandoned proceedings altogether and ordered a retrial, when a third juror confirmed that he too spoke no English and, for good measure, was also very hard of hearing.

The Manitoba jury must take the prize as the worst of all time but at least one story emerges from the courts every year to suggest that Mark Twain's unsubtle pop at the system wasn't too far off the mark.

Such shenanigans proved all too much for England's senior legal luminary Lord Denning, who used *The Times* of 1 August 1982 to make a telling point for the old guard by having his own pop at the increasingly 'catch-all' jury system:

'It's how a jury is selected that's the problem. It used to be said that they were entirely composed of middle-aged, middle-class men. That was true, but they came to some very reliable decisions.'

A FRUITLESS WAIT

THE HIGH COURT, LONDON, 1974

The question of assessing damages as a result of alleged libel or breach of contract is a tricky one indeed, and the somewhat subjective system has produced triumphant winners and disgruntled losers in equal measure.

It is not unusual for very substantial damages to be awarded after a lengthy and complicated court case; nor is it uncommon for a derisory award to be made after only a short hearing. Somewhat rarer would be the award of a large cheque after only a brief court case, but the oddity of them all must be the award of only nominal damages after a marathon hearing.

And the daddy of that particular field must surely be the 1974 classic of *Evans Marshall & Co. Ltd. v. Bertola*.

Evans Marshall, a Regent Street wine merchant, had signed a sole agency distribution agreement with the Spanish sherry producer, Bertola. Bertola's sherry was the really good stuff, for they were based in Jerez itself, the town from which the distinctive fortified wine gets its very name. The London wine merchants were justifiably pleased that they alone would be dictating which of Britain's 'just-one-more-small-glass' brigade of maiden aunts would be tippling the precious liquid.

But, alas, the agreement was broken when Bertola started supplying Evans Marshall's rivals. The wine merchants duly sued for substantial damages and thus began one of the longest commercial law actions ever heard in England. The case reached its climax in the High Court on Thursday, 17 January 1974.

Two QCs, six barristers, nearly a dozen solicitors and Judge Justice Ackland had studied both the solid facts and alleged fictions long and hard. They had pored over 31 bundles of associated documents and Judge Ackland's final summation lasted four and a half hours. The total costs of the hearing ran well into six figures.

As Judge Ackland neared the end it became clear he was about to uphold the wine merchants' claim and as he finally reached the important bit involving the pound signs the Evans Marshall hierarchy held their breath.

Only two questions concerned them. What figure would follow the pound sign? And how many noughts would follow that?

The answer to the first was 2; the answer to the second might have been 000,000 or 00,000 or even a disappointing 0,000. In the event it wasn't even 000, or 00 or even 0. In fact there were no zeros whatsoever – Judge Ackland had upheld their claim and awarded them £2 damages, explaining that 'the "damages" in this case are only nominal because Evans Marshall had not suffered any damage'.

It was a blow, certainly, although being dealt the 'nominal award' card is always a possibility in this gambling area of the law. But what the unsuccessful litigants really found hard to swallow was that it had taken precisely 72 days to reach that conclusion.

This remarkable case set a new record for length–damages ratios in commercial actions: for each day in court Evans Marshall had accrued precisely 2.77 (recurring) pence.

Whether they spent the £2 on a couple of glasses of sherry to drown their sorrows remains unrecorded. If they did, it seems unlikely it would have been one of Bertola's – nor did a glass of QC seem entirely appropriate in the circumstances.

DIVORCE AT THE DOUBLE

THE HIGH COURT, LONDON, 1975

Even as far back as 1975 statistics suggested that the average man or woman in the street would be more likely to become embroiled in the business of the courts as a result of divorce proceedings than any other matter.

Nowadays, with one in every three marriages in the UK (and rising), failing to run its course entertaining tales of long, drawn-out, acrimonious battles are legion, but just as many parties opt for the 'quickie' – maybe that was what a Nigerian immigrant, Alhaji Mohamed, had in mind when he set a remarkable precedent in the High Court one day in July 1975, for that was the day he settled for divorce at the double and left a very senior judge ruefully pondering the legal consequences.

Under Muslim law a husband is entitled to take up to four wives and Mr Mohamed adopted a pick-and-mix approach that might give him the best of both worlds. First up was the 'mature' Adiza, in her late twenties when he took her as his bride. Second in line was young Rabi, who married Mr Mohamed as a child bride of just thirteen in 1967 and moved to England from Nigeria to start a new life. Here was a man who was spreading his bets.

But Alhaji Mohamed proved that two wives are not necessarily better than one, as both relationships foundered. The women wanted out and Alhaji, a security officer in Walworth, London, wasn't too fussed about stopping their escape.

190

But English law failed to recognise polygamous marriage until 1972, so it was only then that Adiza and Rabi could commence proceedings and their faith in the judicial system was duly rewarded on 17 July 1975, when Sir George Baker, President of the Family Division, granted both wives decrees in the High Court.

First to taste freedom was 41-year-old Adiza, rapidly followed just minutes later by 21-year-old Rabi. Ruefully shaking his head, Sir George later remarked: 'This must be the very first time in these courts that two ladies have been able to divorce the same gentleman in one afternoon.' Then he added with a hint of concern, 'A curious feature of this case is that under English law the three children of the first Mrs Mohamed become children of both wives. It is all potentially very complicated.'

Although Alhaji Mohamed undoubtedly set a record in being divorced by two wives in less than fifteen minutes, the stories of others who have experienced unusual divorces cannot escape a passing inclusion in *The Law's Strangest Cases*.

One must concede that Wilhelm Schulz of Stuttgart probably had a point when he demanded a divorce from his 37-year-old wife on the grounds that she insisted her male psychoanalyst should share their marital bed. The marriage had been going through difficulty and Mrs Schulz explained that her unusual request was 'only so he can interpret what Wilhelm says in his sleep'.

That probably wouldn't have worried a 71-year-old American, Glynn de Moss, who in 1978 made plans to marry for the 22nd time after a life of serial divorce: 'Divorce don't upset me: it's just another racoon skin on the wall,' said the one-time marriage-guidance counsellor.

The USA was also home to multiple divorce of another kind. Dorothy and David King Funk were first married in December 1950 but divorced in 1957. Having patched things up, they remarried but were divorced again in 1962 – and 1964 and 1965. In January 1970 they obtained their fifth divorce from each other after a seven-month marriage – the grounds, as ever, were cited as 'irreparable breakdown'.

It's comforting to know that in the UK most divorces are far more sensible. What man wouldn't have divorced Pauline Turner? The only mystery is that it took 62-year-old John Turner 38 years to do it. In December 2000, Middlesbrough County Court heard from the desperate John that 'she moved the furniture around every day for 38 years; she had a particular mania for blocking up doors. We moved to a mobile home where most of the furniture was more or less nailed to the floor but she still found a way – now I'm moving . . . and I'm going a long long way away.'

I'll finish this sorry saga with arguably the unluckiest divorcee of all time. Monday, 27 September 1971 was a long-awaited day of freedom for Beatrice Sharp of St John's Wood, as she was granted a decree nisi from her husband Leslie at London's Law Courts.

Unfortunately for her (and one supposes for Leslie too) any sense of satisfaction she hoped to derive from the final split was dramatically denied her by her husband – five minutes before the decree was granted he died of a heart attack in the waiting room. And that breakdown *was* irretrievable.

THE TRUTH, PARTLY THE TRUTH
AND EVERYTHING BUT THE TRUTH

THE HIGH COURT, LONDON, 1975

WOMAN WINS LIBEL ACTION AGAINST SON, read the eye-catching headline in *The Times* of 17 July 1975. That was a rarity indeed, for mother-versus-son court cases are far from common.

Yet Mrs Ada Hill of Stourbridge had no reason to be anything but proud of her son Archibald when he first announced to her that he was writing his autobiography, which would contain many reminiscences of his childhood.

Mrs Hill probably had visions of the sort of idyllic world recounted by Laurie Lee in his 1959 classic *Cider with Rosie*. She looked forward to reading her son's work and might well have mused on the title he would choose – *Days of Sunshine* would be nice, or perhaps something deeper such as *The Hills of Plenty*; *Mother Knew Best* had a nice ring to it, too, and she could even cope with *Tizer with Roger*, for these were, after all, enlightened times.

When *Cage of Shadows* was published by Hutchinson and Co. there might have been a fleeting moment in which Mrs Hill would like to have believed that her dear Archie had written the account through the eyes of his pet budgerigar, but, when she read the book and remembered they had never had a budgerigar, she was in for a most unpleasant surprise.

Cage of Shadows was Archibald Hill's account of 'the poverty-ridden years of his childhood' and 'a stirring protest

193

against the abject suffering of the 1930s depression era'. Oh, dear!

Ada was not best pleased. Hadn't she scrimped and scraped to do her best for little Archie all those years ago? Was this all the thanks she got for her years of sacrifice? She took the only reasonable course open to a wronged mother – Ada Hill sued.

Hill v. Hutchinson and Co. and Hill was heard at the High Court in London on 16 July 1975 and it was a triumph for Ada. Mr Justice Eveleigh heard that the publishers had already withdrawn the book temporarily and removed the passages that criticised Mrs Hill for the way she brought up young Archie, now aged 48.

The issue of monetary damages was discussed but all Mrs Hill really wanted was a public apology. Archibald was dutifully repentant: 'I now see that my mother was as much a victim of that era as myself,' he announced, 'and some of my allegations based on childhood recollections were misconceived. I apologise to mother unreservedly.'

Unlike *Cider with Rosie*, *Cage of Shadows* hardly took the literary world by storm. But lest anyone should labour under the misconception that all in the golden-tinged Cotswolds world of Laurie Lee was perpetual sunshine, I'm afraid I have to refocus the image, for *Cider with Rosie* also landed its author in the High Court in the most acrimonious circumstances.

The offending passage on page 272 of Lee's world-renowned 'evocation of a Cotswold childhood' seemed harmless enough:

> I remember very clearly how it started. It was summer, and we boys were sitting on the bank watching a great cloud of smoke in the sky. A man jumped off his bike and cried, 'It's the piano-works!' and we ran the four miles to see it. There was a fire at the piano-works almost every year, it seemed to be a way of balancing the books.

But Lee's short note in the front of his book proved prophetic: 'The book is a recollection of early boyhood, and some of the facts may be distorted by time.'

Lee on that count was spot-on, for the piano-factory episode was pure fabrication and both the long-established firm in Stroud and their insurance company were much put out by the defamatory (and inflammatory) comments.

That the book was withdrawn within a fortnight of their complaint and that in subsequent editions the piano factory became a 'boiler-factory' was not sufficient for the firm. Lee had struck a wrong note and they wanted a personal apology and damages. On 18 July 1960 *Stroud Piano Company Limited v. Lee* was heard in the High Court and the suitably cowed author was ordered to pay £5,000 compensation.

The postscript to this particular case was that the veracity of *all* Lee's writing subsequently came under scrutiny: 'If we know that one episode in the book is untrue, can we have any confidence in other episodes?' wrote a correspondent in *John O'London's Weekly,* and much of Lee's later writing was dogged by similar doubts.

Laurie Lee didn't suffer too badly from this curious episode and he had a novel theory on the essence of truth that, if it was ever accepted by the courts of law, would change the course of legal history forever:

'Memory can be more real than events,' he wrote in his notebook. And in his essay on 'Writing Autobiography' he asserted: 'In writing autobiography, especially one that looks back at childhood, the only truth is what you remember.'

With that in mind, the time I scored 300 before lunch for England against the Australians at Lord's is a story I must write down sometime. Quite an achievement, especially for a nine-year-old who scored a hat-trick in the FA Cup final in the same year.

WHERE THERE'S A WILL THERE'S A WAY

SAN ANTONIO, TEXAS, UNITED STATES, 1977

Resolving to follow the oft-given advice of those not in the law to 'steer clear of lawyers' may seem like a wise move for the average man in the street, but there is one area of the law in which the general public is positively encouraged to participate.

'Have you made your will?' ask the advertisements, in a manner that might suggest the coded translation, 'Are you a brainless moron with no consideration for others?'

The finger-pointing copy then generally proceeds to explain that your dying intestate can make life awfully complicated for those left behind. Which suggests by implication that, if there *is* a will, then all will be plain sailing. Just try telling that to Sol West.

It was in March 1977 that Sandra West, widow of the Texas oil millionaire Ike West, departed this world prematurely at the tender age of just 37. Sandra was a woman of style, a woman who surely expected to live a long and healthy life to the full. In fact just the sort of woman who wouldn't have bothered making a will. But Sandra also had foresight and a keen business brain. She *had* made her will and the instructions for the disposal of her $2.8 million estate were meticulous in their detail.

Her brother-in-law, Sol West, was understandably delighted when he heard that he was the beneficiary of the lot but his face dropped a mile when he heard the conditions. Not for Sandra a quiet funeral and a standard box. The condition of Sol's inheritance was that Sandra should be dressed in her favourite lace negligée and then seated in her beloved 1964 blue Ferrari – 'with the seat slanted comfortably', she added.

But the bizarre instructions didn't end there. As a deterrent to would-be grave robbers the Ferrari was then to be packed into a steel-reinforced wooden container, which was in turn to be encased completely in concrete.

The will then spelt out the penalty for not carrying out this last grand request – Mr West would inherit just a measly $10,000. Faced with the daunting prospect of organising the grandest burial since that of the boy king Tutankhamun, not to mention the possibility of losing over $2 million, he understandably quailed somewhat and contested the terms in court.

It was left to a judge in Los Angeles, a city not exactly noted for its wholesale condemnation of excess, to decide whether Sol West was compelled to comply. Frivolous the request may have been, but strictly on a point of law the court famously allowed Sandra West her exit of a lifetime:

'The average person has a right,' declared the judge, 'to dispose of his or her own remains as he or she sees fit, if it does not violate the law.'

Mrs West was duly buried in her family grave at San Antonio, Texas, on 19 May 1977: 'She got the idea from reading about the tombs of the Pharoahs,' said her nurse, while the undertaker added, 'It was a discreet and dignified ceremony.' Sol West did receive his $2.8 million bequest but it is a macabre thought indeed that in San Antonio to this day his benefactor is a reclining skeleton dressed in what's left of a see-through negligée doing a spot of posing in a 1964 classic blue Ferrari.

Sandra West is by no means alone in her desire to have her dying wish fulfilled, although most requests are rather more modest. That's why, in the UK, sundry cricket fields, football pitches and beaches are routinely scattered with the gritty furnace leftovers that euphemistically pass as ashes.

Among those who could give Sandra West a reasonable run

for her money, though, is the thirteenth-century French aristocrat who evidently saw himself as a pillar of the community, literally. The Comte de Chatelet ordered that he should be buried upright in a hollowed-out pillar in the church at Neufchateau 'in order that the vulgar may not walk upon me'.

That request was in stark contrast to that of Duke Richard the Fearless of Normandy, in 996, who insisted in his will: 'I wish to be buried in front of the church door so that I may be trodden under foot by all those entering the church.'

In the matter of sartorial elegance, many corpses have been buried dressed to the nines but perhaps none more symbolically than the late-nineteenth-century Derbyshire county cricketer Harry Bagshaw. After retiring from playing he became an umpire and when his innings finally came to an end in 1927 he gave himself 'out' in emphatic but fine style by being buried in his umpire's white coat and clutching a cricket ball. His headstone depicted broken stumps, dislodged bails and an umpire's hand with raised index finger pointing skyward.

It proves that when it comes to that final exit it's a case of 'you've either got or you haven't got style', although some choose a deliberately modest final resting place because they just don't want the fuss – or to run the risk of experiencing life after death by appearing in books like this.

So let's finish with a modern-day case of just such a man. Anything for a quiet life was certainly the wish of Dennis Carberry. With typical English reserve his sole wish was that his 64-year-old widow Jean should keep his ashes at their home. Being in the newspapers just wasn't Dennis's style.

Unfortunately, though, he *was* in the newspapers on more counts than one after Jean accidentally put him out for the binmen with a stack of last week's tabloids and the potato peelings.

She was later allowed to visit the municipal tip to search for her husband among hundreds of tons of rubbish. It's to be hoped the publicity-shy Dennis wasn't looking on from above as the newspapers reported Jean's heartfelt comments from down at the dump: 'Dennis was a bloke in a million. I'd recognise him straight away . . . he was in a green Barnardo's plastic bag.'

A NOTE OF CAUTION

CROYDON CROWN COURT, 1978

Drugs trials are not generally noted for their entertainment value. The offences involved are invariably of the most serious kind and, unlike murder trials, they lack the macabre edge and the flavour of detective fiction that strangely makes 'murder most foul' such an appealing subject.

That's why I have kicked the seedier side of the drugs trade right into touch and offer instead, by way of something softer, the cautionary tale of the juror who struck entirely the wrong note with the judge at a drugs trial in Croydon in November 1978.

Although the defence barrister was fighting his client's corner for all he was worth on Tuesday, 7 November, 69-year-old Judge Jean Hall seemed intent on giving him a particularly hard time from the bench. Being rather of the old school, she exchanged sharp words with him on a number of occasions and this evidently aroused the sympathy of a male member of the jury, who communicated this to the defence barrister by passing him a note.

While it is perfectly in order for the jury to communicate with the judge in such a way, it is irregular for a juror to send notes, on whatever subject, to the defence. Who knows what message they might convey? A threat, a bribe, vital evidence?

It was typical of Judge Hall that she didn't miss a trick and sure enough she spotted the note being passed and duly asked to read it. If the juror seemed a little uneasy it was no surprise, as the note of sympathy asked, 'How would you like that as a mother in law?'

Retribution was swift and despite an apology from the juror he was summarily dismissed, one of only a few jurors sent off for their conduct in all legal history.

On the subject of notes and jurors it would be impossible to let pass the opportunity to retell an incident said to have occurred in a rape trial at a Northern crown court in the late 1970s.

According to the account of the local newspaper reporter, when the young woman victim was asked to repeat, for the benefit of the jury, the words said to her by her attacker prior to the incident she was somewhat embarrassed to do so in open court. She was therefore allowed to write the extremely coarse phrase down for it to be passed along the row of jurors. The sanitised translation of the words she wrote on the note would be something along the lines of 'I'm going to give you the most thorough going over you've ever had.'

It proved significant that the male juror on the end of the row had nodded off during this passage of the trial and he had to be nudged awake by the attractive woman juror next to him as she passed him the folded note, which he read before giving her a wink and hastily pocketing the evidence. When the judge asked for the piece of paper back the juror replied, 'I'd rather not, it's a personal matter.'

The name of the poor chap escapes me but there is little doubt that later that day he duly became the most disappointed juror of all time. Or at least I assume he did.

JUNGLE JUICE

JONESTOWN, GUYANA, 1978

In a San Francisco courtroom on 23 September 1981 a 35-year-old former Quaker, Larry Layton, stood trial for conspiracy to kill and complicity in a massacre during November 1978.

The jury was unable to agree on a verdict and Judge Robert Peckham declared a mistrial. That in itself is not particularly strange, for Layton was a bit-part player who had not killed anyone, nor could the level of his involvement in what was known as the Jonestown Massacre be proven, for there were no surviving witnesses and Jim Jones, the man behind the bizarre events, had died with the rest.

But what *is* undeniably odd about this court case is the number of deaths involved and their manner. Never can a courtroom have heard stranger evidence, for 913 persons died in Guyana in just a few minutes of a single day – and, on top of that, all were suicides and it was a minister of the church who was the sole motivator of the act.

James Warren Jones was born in the Indiana town of Lynn in 1931. Even as a child he began to cultivate an obsessive interest in religion, holding mock funeral services for dead animals and delivering his first sermon at the age of fourteen.

When he was eighteen he married his childhood sweetheart, Marceline Baldwin, dropped out of Indiana University and moved with his wife to Indianapolis, where they started a Methodist mission. He was expelled by the church fathers in

1954 because they found his religious views objectionable, and he subsequently travelled, founded an organisation called the People's Temple in 1957 and was ordained a minister in 1964.

His behaviour first began to take an overtly odd turn when, anticipating the end of the world, he led a migration of a hundred of his followers from Indiana to Redwood Valley in Mendocino County, California. Amazingly the world did not end, so the Reverend Jim Jones purchased a synagogue in a run-down area of San Francisco and provided day-care facilities for the black inner-city residents who accounted for 80 per cent of his People's Temple congregation. These were undeniably good works and, despite his kooky behaviour, Jones received the backing of the San Francisco authorities, served as a local government official, became a citizen of some renown and began to attract a cult following.

In 1974 he purchased 27,000 acres (10,930 hectares) of rainforest in Guyana on the northern coast of South America with the idea of turning it into a socialist utopia for himself and his followers. By 1976 Jones's concept of the 'ultimate escape' from the troubles of life and government persecution had extended into a notion of 'mass ritual suicide'. His groups held rehearsal sessions.

Despite this odd element of his religious manifesto, membership of the People's Temple swelled to 20,000 (this was California, don't forget) and Jones began to call himself God as his services became increasingly strange affairs.

In 1977 he began clearing large sections of his jungle and founded the religious colony of Jonestown with almost a thousand members, who duly made their exodus from San Francisco to the promised land.

Reports of odd goings-on were leaked to the press, and the US State Department sent a party of delegates to investigate and visit Jonestown on 14 November 1978. Jones welcomed the party warmly and put on a good show, and when they were leaving the next day the delegation were reasonably satisfied that all was well.

How wrong they were. As they prepared to board their

plane at Port Kaituma airfield the party of congressmen and television reporters were shot at by Jones's henchmen, Larry Layton among them. Five persons died and several more were injured.

Jones knew that that murderous attack spelt the end of his dream, but before the US Marines could be sent in he gave the signal that all present at his rehearsals knew this time was for real.

All of his brainwashed followers gathered in Jonestown's main pavilion and were given a paper cup containing a purple Kool-Aid drink laced with cyanide. Mothers used syringes to squirt the deadly juice into their babies' mouths and parents actively encouraged their older children to take their final drink. Then, as Jones intoned over a loudspeaker that 'We're going to meet again in another place' and screamed 'Die with dignity', the adults downed the fatal potion.

The 913 victims soon lay dead, most lasting no more than five minutes. No witnesses survived – Jones himself died from a single bullet to the head, thought to have been self-inflicted.

The United States Air Force sent planes to retrieve the remains while experts in human behaviour tried to analyse how this extraordinary event could have occurred in a civilised twentieth-century society.

Will a court ever hear more unusual evidence than this? Perhaps even stranger than the Jonestown Massacre itself is the answer to that question: one day it almost certainly will.

SPELLING IT OUT

CALIFORNIA COURT OF APPEAL,
UNITED STATES, 1979

Much as judges derive an inner sense of satisfaction when a decision goes the way they thought it should, their sense of professional ethics dictates that it just isn't on to go shouting the odds if the decision goes the other way.

Nor is it the done thing for one judge to attack another if they disagree with each other. At least, that is, in Britain.

Yet in the United States, where judicial freedom of expression is rather more advanced, having one's say is by no means rare. And in California, surprise, surprise, the mode of that expression has been known to take unusual form. And never more so than in the 1979 Court of Appeal case when two judges spelt out their anger towards a dissenting colleague in a rather cryptic fashion never used before or since.

The subject matter of *The People v. Arno* was not particularly edifying. A court had convicted the company of possessing obscene films with an intent to distribute them. Arno duly appealed and the California Court of Appeal had to make the casting vote.

One must be charitable and assume the ruling of the judges had nothing whatsoever to do with their personal film-viewing predilections. In the event, Judge Lillie upheld the appellant's claim and Associate Justice Thompson wholeheartedly agreed with him. Associate Justice Hanson equally heartily disagreed.

With the majority of the judges upholding Arno's appeal,

the conviction was promptly reversed and a piqued Justice Hanson duly dissented, posing a number of pointed questions to his colleagues that cast serious aspersions on their judgment.

Lillie and Thompson replied in kind, saying that 'we feel compelled by the nature of the attack in the dissenting opinion to spell out a response', which they did in a seven-point reply:

1. Some answer is required to the dissenter's charge.
2. Certainly we do not endorse 'victimless crime'.
3. How that question is involved escapes us.
4. Moreover, the constitutional issue is significant.
5. Ultimately it must be addressed in light of precedent.
6. Certainly the course of precedent is clear.
7. Knowing that, our result is compelled.

This seemed, in the circumstances, a rather restrained response to Justice Hanson's invective. Perhaps Lillie and Thompson were, after all, showing due respect to the sanctity of the law. But the PS that they appended to their formal reply made it clear to Hanson exactly where they were coming from, for it suggested he might like to consult a dictionary.

He probably didn't need it, for SCHMUCK, the initial letters of the seven-point reply, is a popular term of abuse in the States, a derivative from the Yiddish for 'penis'. Americans use it to signify 'a contemptible or objectionable person'. 'Dickhead' is probably the best British counterpart.

In this novel way, without any bawling or brawling, the badly stung Lillie and Thompson gave Hanson his most public comeuppance, which is indelibly preserved in the official US legal records for all time.

Lest any further evidence is needed to suggest that California blazes the trail when it comes to legal oddities, another case in which spelling came to the fore occurred eight years later.

When the Ventura County *Star Free Press* sponsored a junior spelling-bee contest they got rather more exposure than they had bargained for, as the father of the beaten finalist decided to sue. The contest had been badly run, he said, and in losing the final, he asserted, his son had suffered undue mental distress for which he was claiming a cool $2 million.

Although the American courts have sanctioned some of the weirdest litigation victories of all time, this was too much even for California, although it took the dismissal decisions of both a senior state court judge and a state court of appeals before the youngster's father was finally forced to accept that his kid was indeed the weakest link.

In one of the most gratifying judgments ever to come out of California, the Appeals Court explained that the whingeing boy (his name escapes me but we'll settle for 'brat-features') had lost the contest 'not because the spelling bee was badly run but because he had misspelled "iridescent".'

A PICTURE PAINTS A
THOUSAND WORDS

NEW YORK, UNITED STATES, 1980

They say 'a picture paints a thousand words' and a New York jury seemed intent on proving the accuracy of that old chestnut when they delivered a verdict in December 1980 that made US legal history.

Central to their deliberations was the unusual question of whether a person could be libelled by a painting, for a New York artist, Paul Georges, had allegedly been rather more expressive with his brush strokes than two of his arty rivals would have liked.

This being New York, there was only one course of action for Jacob Silberman and Anthony Siani when they saw Georges's *The Mugging of the Muse*: they sued.

The large-scale allegorical work showed three men with knives about to attack a partly nude young woman, the 'muse of art', in a dark alleyway. What incensed the two artists was that the masks on two of the faces were clearly 'theirs' and they subsequently told the court that they were 'being ridiculed not only as violent criminals but as artists intent on murdering art'.

Both the supposedly vilified artists had first asked Georges to change the faces so that they could not be recognised, but he refused to compromise: 'The role of an artist is to find a pictorial truth and this is not the same as literary or photographic truth,' he pleaded.

But the jury disagreed, finding Georges guilty of libelling

his two rivals, who received $30,000 each in damages. It was a landmark decision in US legal history, which served as a warning to all artists of the future that using 'dirty brushes' might cost them dear, but it was by no means the first legal sparring in the artistic community.

Back in 1877 the Massachusetts-born painter James McNeill Whistler, then living and working in England, sued the distinguished art critic John Ruskin for libel after Ruskin had conducted not so much a smear campaign as a 'splatter' campaign against Whistler's modern Impressionist style. On viewing Whistler's *Nocturne in Black and Gold*, which somewhat vaguely depicted a firework display over the Thames, Ruskin was moved to write, 'I never expected to hear a coxcomb ask two hundred guineas for flinging a pot of paint in the public's face.'

Appearing before Judge Sir John Huddleston at London's Courts of Justice in November 1878, Whistler, who had sued for a massive 1,000 guineas, gave a good account of himself as examples of his art were paraded before the court. Asked by Ruskin's defence counsel, 'Did you really ask two hundred guineas for the work of just two days?', Whistler responded instantly: 'No. It was for the knowledge gained through a lifetime.' Maybe he'd been taking lessons from young Oscar Wilde, master of the clever riposte and in time himself to be a tragic victim of a famously unsuccessful libel action.

At any rate Whistler triumphed in his own action as the jury found that he had indeed been libelled, but his joy was quickly quelled when he heard the amount of damages: a paltry farthing! On top of that indignity the judge pronounced a judgment of 'no costs', so Whistler had to foot his own legal bill for nearly £500. The only compensation was that Ruskin, too, had to find £386 to defray his own expenses.

The report in *The Examiner* got it about right when they described the outcome of the case as 'A victory which bears a very striking resemblance to a defeat'.

A salutary lesson to paint merchants of all eras and styles, perhaps. Whether it's twentieth-century New York or nineteenth-century London, it doesn't always pay to be too 'precious' for one's art.

DISPOSING OF THE EVIDENCE

THE OLD BAILEY, LONDON, 1980

It isn't always the most macabre crimes that law-abiding sectors of society find most unsavoury or troubling. Acid-bath murders and their like are all very sensational but how would they compare, for example, with a policeman conning a trusting elderly woman out of her life savings?

It's one of those moral debates that are very difficult to call, but there's certainly something about the perceived sanctity of the institution that is the 'great British bobby' that sends a shudder down the spine whenever an officer of the law steps out of line.

Crimes involving policemen are by no means uncommon, for members of the force are, after all, mere human beings subject to all the temptations, stresses and weaknesses that assail the rest of us. But there was one policeman in particular who seemed intent on blighting the image of his breed in the most spectacular and gruesome way possible.

PC George Swindell's story was not only unsavoury and macabre to a shocking degree, but it also raised legal technicalities and led to a successful appeal, which seemed to suggest that his erstwhile uniform might well have influenced the Law Lords in exercising undue leniency.

If there is an image that seems to epitomise the British bobby at his best it must be the one beloved of all tourists visiting London – the reassuringly stolid but friendly policeman on door duty at 10 Downing Street.

It was while he was on just such a duty at the Prime Ministerial residence that forty-year-old PC George Swindell took to unwinding from his day's toil in a manner that many of London's tourists might well have thought distasteful. On his way home from 10 Downing Street he was in the habit of picking up prostitutes and engaging, with their consent, in what were later described in court as 'bondage sessions' at his terraced house in Walthamstow. His bedroom was chock-full of handcuffs, leg irons and other instruments of torture – mock crucifixion of his lady friends was a particular favourite.

If that was how PC Swindell got his kicks, who are we to condemn him? He might have known, though, that there were risks involved, and the unthinkable happened one evening when he was in the company of Patricia Marina Berkeley, otherwise known as Patricia Marina Malone, otherwise euphemistically known by the court as 'a lady of the street'.

During a session with Swindell in which she wore a mask over her face she died of asphyxiation and the case duly went to the Old Bailey in March 1981, where the jury needed to decide whether Swindell was guilty of manslaughter or whether the death was simply the result of a game that went tragically wrong. The factual outcome of the case was that George Swindell was found not guilty of the manslaughter charge and on that count alone he was a free, if somewhat shamed, 'former policeman'.

All of Swindell's sordid habits were fully aired in court and the *London Evening Standard* squeezed great mileage out of the affair, relating elements of high farce never before witnessed at the Old Bailey:

'The pathologist Dr Alan Grant said one of the exhibited masks was lethal,' they wrote, 'and it was suggested by the judge, Mr Justice Pain, that a policeman should put it on and demonstrate to the jury.'

When the chosen young constable refused, Mr Michael Worsley, prosecuting, came up with an even more novel suggestion: 'I have an inflatable rubber doll amongst the exhibits,' he said. 'Can we put the mask on her?'

With Justice Pain's assent the doll was duly carried to the

witness box, fitted with the mask and supported by a Detective Inspector Rushworth. 'Keep the mask exactly in place,' requested Henry Pownall QC, defending.

But DI Rushworth was forced to address the judge in a state of some anxiety, much to the amusement of onlookers: 'I'm afraid the doll has a puncture My Lord. It's starting to go down.' Who says television sitcoms are far-fetched?

And there the story might end but for the other charge against Swindell, that of 'preventing the burial of a dead body'.

He knew that was an obstructive crime of a serious kind, for in an important legal sense it disposed of possible evidence that could be cited or examined to bring an accused party to justice.

So here's the really awful bit. When he realised Patricia was dead he used all his police experience to decide on the 'best' course of action. In Swindell's case, that was to conceal the possible 'crime' by putting the body in a bath and keeping it there for two and a half weeks. When it began to smell he again exercised his acute sense of initiative by dismembering it, popping the various parts into plastic bags and disposing of them in Epping Forest.

It was a triumph for British justice that he didn't get away with it and he subsequently pleaded guilty to the somewhat sanitised-sounding charge of 'preventing the burial of a dead body'. On that count Mr Justice Pain sentenced him to five years in prison.

A lenient sentence? Some would say so but there the matter should have ended, and would have ended, but for George Swindell's effrontery in launching an appeal. Five years was too long, he argued. Thus it was that on 8 October 1981 the Lord Chief Justice addressed himself to the serious task of reviewing the extraordinary facts of *The Crown v. Swindell* once again.

And what an extraordinary result ensued, for Swindell's appeal was successful and his sentence was reduced to just three years. In announcing the verdict the Lord Chief Justice cited as his reasons that 'the offence was unlikely to be repeated and was not the sort of offence from which it was necessary to deter others'.

Lest any of the public should still have been a little concerned over the outcome, he added a final reassurance by saying that 'the appellant presents very little, if any, danger to the public'.

Has whitewash ever been whiter?

Not only as an individual with a healthy respect for the law but also as someone scarcely able to take the giblets out of the Christmas turkey without wearing rubber gloves, I have to say that I find the case of PC George Swindell one of the most unsavoury I have encountered.

A final word of comfort, though. Next time you see a group of tourists snapping those precious 'bobby' shots at 10 Downing Street, say nothing, for you can be assured that my researches confirm beyond all reasonable doubt that PC George Swindell was the exception rather than the rule.

AN EDUCATIONAL VISIT

LÜBECK, WEST GERMANY, 1981

The party of German schoolgirls were so looking forward to their educational visit to the courtroom in Lübeck, near Hamburg, on 6 March 1981.

They had a vague idea the courts were there to dispense justice but beyond that the procedures were something of a mystery to them. By the time their visit had finished they had certainly been given an education, but the scene they witnessed was one of the most unusual in all legal history.

In truth the trial they attended wasn't altogether suitable for a party of young ladies. It was day four of the trial of Klaus Grabowski, a murderer with a record in perverted child molestation, and the details of the case were most unsavoury.

In 1975, six years before this court appearance, the 35-year-old butcher had already submitted himself to the supreme sacrifice that public outrage so often demands in such cases but seldom gets. He had been voluntarily castrated. Astonishingly, though, his old urges had returned with a vengeance after a course of hormone treatment, and a girlfriend stood up in court to describe graphically how she knew that to be the case despite the missing bits.

The details of his latest atrocity were of the most unsettling kind, not at all suitable for schoolchildren's ears. Seven-year-old Anna Bachmeier had gone out to play on the morning of 5 May 1980 and not returned home. Police called on Grabowski, who lived only a block away, to carry out routine questioning.

213

They got more out of him than they could have hoped, for he made a full confession to murder and led them to a piece of waste ground where Anna's body was found. She had been strangled with her own tights. Although Grabowski had admitted the killing, his counsel approached the court case with one view in mind, to limit the damage by getting the charge reduced to one of manslaughter.

Grabowski duly explained that there had been no sexual motive in his attack. He had invited Anna Bachmeier to his apartment only because he loved children and had killed her in a blind panic when she threatened to tell: 'She tried to blackmail me,' he pleaded.

It was the sort of spurious defence guaranteed to engender strong reaction from the public and particularly from those close to the murdered child. But Anna's mother, Marianne, looked on for three whole days in court maintaining a dignity and self-control that many would surely have found beyond them as judge and jury began to show ominously lenient signs of understanding towards Grabowski.

The crime must have been a particularly painful one for Frau Bachmeier, bearing in mind her own tragic past. The daughter of a former Nazi SS officer, she too had been sexually assaulted, at the age of nine had been and thrown out of home when she became pregnant at sixteen. Two years later she was raped while pregnant for a second time. Life had hardly been a bed of roses for Marianne Bachmeier.

Who knows at what exact point that acutely painful past conspired with her equally appalling present to produce a flashpoint, but on day four of the trial Frau Bachmeier acted as many mothers before and since have threatened but seldom carried through.

On 6 March 1981 she suddenly crossed the courtroom, pulled out a 5.6mm Beretta pistol and fired several bullets into the prisoner, who was killed instantly. As the schoolgirls on their educational visit cried hysterically, she simply lowered the gun to her side and awaited her inevitable arrest. Later the same day the public prosecutor announced that Marianne Bachmeier, having taken the law into her own hands in front of judge and jury in the most dramatic way possible, was to be charged with murder.

There were still more twists in this unusual affair. Despite the atrocity of her own crime, public opinion mobilised in her favour and large sums of money were donated to a defence fund started on behalf of the 'Avenging Mother', as the press quickly dubbed her.

Some presented the other side of the coin, though. Her fellow prisoners with whom she was held in custody told of her arrogant and uncaring attitude.

Her trial began in November 1982 amid intense press and public interest, for it seemed to be a test case that encapsulated one of the most pivotal tenets of perceived justice. The Book of Exodus gave us the biblical phrase that has passed into common usage: 'An eye for an eye, a tooth for a tooth, a life for a life'. Lawyers prefer to call it *lex talionis*, the law of retaliation. Could the principle be upheld to justify Frau Bachmeier's graphic act of revenge?

Not entirely. Despite her suffering, the consequences had to be faced, but, when judgment was finally given on 2 March 1983, the judge displayed clemency in his hour-long summing up. Marianne Bachmeier was convicted of manslaughter, not murder, and sentenced to six years' imprisonment. She was released on parole in June 1985.

In truth few lasting lessons can be learnt from this shocking case; that abuse or murder of children is an emotive issue is hardly a groundbreaking conclusion.

Only one thing is certain. The party of schoolgirls present in court on 6 March 1981 had a lesson in life they would never ever forget.

A PROPER CHARLIE

KNIGHTSBRIDGE CROWN COURT, LONDON, 1981

It might be considered unfair to pick on Judge Sir Harold Cassel as the leading exponent of the art of verbal judicial gaffery, but then again he did put his foot in it in rather a spectacular fashion, for the 'Proper Charlie' epithet that became his in 1981 was one entirely of his own making. All the press did was report the facts.

In the interests of lightening the burden of embarrassment, though, let him share this bench of mirth and shame with other master exponents of the 'I wish I hadn't said that' breed.

First up, though, is the man himself. The scene was Knightsbridge Crown Court on Wednesday, 19 August 1981. Sir Harold was presiding over the trial of 27-year-old Alexander Steel from Balham, who was facing three charges of burglary.

Judge Cassel must have been full of bonhomie that day, because as the court adjourned for lunch he did a remarkable thing. Despite a warning by the police that it might be unwise, he granted the prisoner an hour's bail to go and have some lunch. Conscious that there was a vital element of trust implicit in this temporary grant of freedom, Judge Cassel looked Steel straight in the eye and uttered those famous last words: 'Be sure to come back. If you don't turn up you will make me look a proper Charlie.'

The next day's *Times* could barely disguise their delight in reporting in deadpan fashion: 'Last night police were still

216

looking for Mr Steel.' There have been plenty of jailbreaks for freedom but this unique lunchbreak for freedom dogged Sir Harold Cassel, the self-christened 'Proper Charlie', from that day on.

Mercifully, he can take comfort that he is not alone. From across the Atlantic comes the booming voice of a New York judge who in 1985 was formally admonished for commenting, as a female advocate entered his courtroom, 'What a set of knockers!'

Again from the States, but rather more sinister, was the response of the judge in a 1970s trial to the request of a lawyer of Japanese extraction that he be given more time to prepare his case: 'How much time did you give us at Pearl Harbor?' wasn't exactly a polite rebuff.

Nor do the Americans have a monopoly on such non-humorous indiscretions. On 30 September 1992 at Hereford Crown Court, 65-year-old Judge John Lee incurred the not inconsiderable wrath of British womanhood during the trial of twenty-year-old Robert Ward.

Ward's crime was a hold-up at a solicitor's office, and he explained to the court that he wanted to be arrested to escape from troubles with his girlfriend.

Judge Lee, in passing a lenient sentence of two years' probation, told the defendant, 'So you've had problems with women. Who do you think hasn't? It's part of a woman's function in life to upset men.' When asked later by a female reporter to explain his remarks, the judge further fanned the flames by barking the riposte: 'Which lesbian group are you from?'

In fairness to such exponents of bench buffoonery it ought to be said that some of their most publicised boobs are born entirely from ignorance rather than malice. During the famous *Oz* obscenity trial in 1971, Judge Argyle needed to ask, 'What is *Hair*?' at a time when the famous nude rock musical was plastered all over the papers. And in 1979 Mr Justice Cantley heard a case relating to the ban imposed on a former England football manager by the Football Association. Midway through hearing the testimony of various players he turned to a barrister and asked, 'Kevin Keegan, does he play for England or Scotland?'

Popular music runs sport a close second in the list of subjects inclined to befuddle the judiciary: 'Who is Bruce Springsteen?' from Mr Justice Harman in 1985 might almost seem credible, but 'Who are the Rolling Stones?' from a Canadian judge trying Keith Richards for possession of heroin in 1977 must be regarded as a corker by any standards.

Yet where would we be without such classics? The legal world is certainly more entertaining for these occasional gaffes, some of which have survived many years after their originators have experienced their own final judgment.

Let's give the last word to the Manchester judge presiding in the 1920s at a case in which two young offenders had committed mutual indecency in one of the city's WCs. He told the court in passing sentence, 'The public lavatories of Manchester have got to be cleaned up and I propose to make a start.' Not content with that he finished by saying, 'You two men both have to take yourselves in hand and pull yourselves together.'

And how would our learned judges respond if asked to comment on such classic bloopers?

That's an easy one – 'What is a blooper?'

GOOD OLD GRANDAD

THE OLD BAILEY, LONDON, 1981

Writing in *The Times* on 18 July 1991, Bernard Levin proffered the following checklist of judges' failings:

> Amongst many others they have been accused of naïveté,
> obstinacy, unworldliness, bias, inflexibility, self-esteem,
> ignorance, volubility, interruption, gossiping, pomposity,
> laziness, hectoring, impatience, irritability, deafness, falling
> asleep on the bench immediately after lunch, and haemorr-
> hoids.

Harsh though the observation may sound, a perusal of the
record books would suggest that Levin's attack was based on
cast-iron evidence rather than prejudice, although it has to be
said that his classification of piles as 'a failing' must be hard
for any genuine sufferer to take sitting down.

But why didn't Levin also talk about judges' virtues?
Where is their generosity, kindness, leniency and under-
standing? Is it because these qualities don't exist on the bench?
Well, they may not proliferate, it is true, but in the world of
The Law's Strangest Cases anything can happen. Step
forward, Judge Michael Argyle QC.

The scene is the Central Criminal Court, that place from
which so many notorious wrongdoers have been sent down,
cursing the judge as they are dragged away to their doom. The
date is Monday, 17 August 1981, and Mrs Eileen El-Tarouty

stands before 65-year-old Judge Argyle accused of forging a divorce certificate and remarrying bigamously.

Not the worst crime in the world, but one for which others had done time. Eileen El-Tarouty was worried.

The court heard that Mrs El-Tarouty had married her Egyptian husband illegally at Westminster Register Office in 1978 while still legally married to the man she had wed in Accrington in 1974. She had well and truly duped the Home Office along the way. Pleading for clemency, the accused then went on to say that she had now made the marriage legal and was expecting a child.

It was almost certainly the baby that did it. Maybe the fact that England had retained the Ashes against Australia that very day also softened Judge Argyle's heart. Either way, he uttered the words that no court had ever witnessed before as he put the defendant on probation for two years: 'In another court you might well have gone to prison, but you have caught me on a good day. I became a grandfather this morning.'

As Mrs El-Tarouty patted her bump and thanked him profusely, Judge Argyle warmed to his new-found mood of generosity by treating the next defendant, a Paddington bricklayer named Michael Price, rather more leniently than the villain had expected. As Price thanked him gushingly for being 'perfectly fair and a much less harsh judge than people have said', Judge Argyle waved him cheerio with an avuncular 'Off you go – and best of luck!'

It is heartening to report that Michael Argyle is not the only member of the 'judges are human after all' club, some of whose membership is entirely at odds with their reputations. Take John Toler, later Lord Norbury (1745–1831), generally regarded as Ireland's most notorious judge with a penchant for hanging that ran even the infamous Judge Jeffreys close. Norbury often dispensed sentences with scarcely disguised glee and was famous for once sentencing 97 men to death in a single day.

That made his act of clemency towards an alleged murderer, against whom there was overwhelming evidence, even more remarkable. There was a gasp of astonishment around the courtroom when Norbury recommended the jury bring in an acquittal. When the Crown Prosecutor interrupted to point out that the man was surely guilty, Norbury replied in a loud stage whisper, 'I know all that, my good fellow. But I hanged six men at last Tipperary Assizes who were innocent so I'll let this poor devil off now to square matters.'

Irish judges, it seems, are more prone than many to these aberrations of generosity. Mickie Morris, later Lord Killanin, once passed sentence on a boy found guilty of abducting his sweetheart: 'The father was not averse, the mother was not opposed, the girl was willing and you, my boy, were convenient. I sentence you to imprisonment until the court rises.' At which Judge Morris promptly rose!

A word of warning, though. There is sometimes a hidden agenda in these acts of leniency. The Americans, in particular, are not inclined to give something for nothing. In 1980 an Ohio judge got his comeuppance when he was jailed for corruption in dispensing lenient sentences to women defendants in return for sexual favours; and in 1992 the Pennsylvanian judge Charles Guyer was sacked after a hidden video camera recorded him offering a novel form of plea-bargaining: he offered convicted men lighter sentences if they allowed him to shampoo their hair – a 'conditional' discharge of sorts, one supposes.

Lest anyone should still think that a lenient judge is an easy touch, let's close the case with a return to the Old Bailey. Mr Justice Graham presides, a judge who back in the 1820s enjoyed a particular reputation for his unwavering courtesy. Yet he surely proved that even a judge who gets out of the right side of bed can be damaging to one's health.

When he read out a list of sixteen names of people to be executed he was effusively apologetic when informed he had missed out the name of John Robins. The prisoner must have thought it was his lucky day as the judge appeared utterly mortified by his error:

'Oh, bring John Robins back,' Graham said, 'by all means let John Robins step forward. I am obliged to you, John Robins. I find I have accidentally omitted your name in my list of prisoners doomed to execution. It was quite accidental, I assure you, and I ask your pardon for my mistake.'

So far, so good, but Judge Graham finished with an ingratiating smile: 'I am very sorry, and can only add that you will be hanged with the rest.'

MORE QUESTIONS THAN ANSWERS

THE LAW SOCIETY, 1981

Any student who has ever sat even the most rudimentary law exam will be aware that some of the law's strangest cases are the hypothetical ones that make the heart sink no sooner then those dreaded words 'you may now turn over your papers' have left the invigilator's lips.

They generally start along the lines of 'Farmer Brown owns Blackacre and Farmer White owns Greenacre' and they invariably follow a tried and tested pattern. Farmer Brown's unusually unruly dog, Red, has been making his escape year after year to worry Farmer White's wimpishly timid sheep and it's generally via a broken gate that should have been repaired the week before by Farmer Grey that Red gains his illicit access. There is normally a drainage pipeline negligently laid by a former owner just inches under someone's land and it is only a matter of time before someone like an itinerant Aussie labourer comes along, naturally known to his mates as 'Blue', and plants his pickaxe right through its middle.

The question that follows this scenario, which unbeknown to us city dwellers occurs every day in rural areas, is usually something akin to 'Does Farmer Brown's daughter, Scarlet, have a right to walk Red over the driveway to Blue's tied cottage?' Much as any student worth their salt as a potential lawyer would be tempted to answer this oddly colourful poser with 'who cares?' the desire to enter the legal profession has proved strong enough for many to make at least a brave stab at

223

the answer the most sensible option.

Alas, for many, their efforts have proved fruitless, but the odd affair that I now take pleasure in reporting should give heart to all who have dismally failed in an exam, for here is a story that proves that even the examiners can get it wrong in spectacular fashion once in a while.

This is the celebrated Law Society exam cock-up case and I can do no better than quote verbatim from the Law Society press release which appeared in *The Times* of Friday, 20 November 1981, a day when apparent wretched failure was turned into glorious triumph for 123 hard-working law students:

> The Law Society has apologised to 123 students over errors in the marking of their papers. Three students who had been failed have now been referred in one subject, 18 have to take two papers again and 16 have now been passed. Fifty-three students who had failed only one paper have now passed. Twenty-five students who failed two of the papers have been told they have passed and eight have been referred on one subject.

It's comforting to know that it was all made so clear. Shouldn't there also be a mention of how long it takes two men to dig a hole six feet deep and three feet wide using a stolen shovel and a bucket with a hole in it?

There is only one conclusive message to be garnered from this, the greatest marking error since Maradona's second goal against England in the 1986 World Cup, and that is a message to all members of the law profession who have successfully passed the requisite exams: however much you're earning, you deserve it.

I'VE GOT YOUR FACE!

LEEDS CROWN COURT, 1981

There have always been occupational hazards to being a judge. The threat of being killed is one of them and a select number of cases throughout history have proved that the threat can become reality. In the Peasants' Revolt of 1381 the Lord Chancellor no less, Simon de Sudbury, was chased by an angry mob up in London from Kent and beheaded. And the very next year Lord Chief Justice Cavendish was killed by a baying crowd after being subjected to a mock trial.

Three centuries later, in 1689, the infamous 'hanging judge', Judge Jeffreys, of Monmouth Rebellion 'Bloody Assize' fame, also met his end, aged only 41, as a consequence of being placed in the Tower of London after being recognised while on the run, disguised as a sailor, by a disgruntled former litigant. Even in the unreal fictional world, too, the judges are seldom safe: 'The first thing we'll do, let's kill all the lawyers,' said Dick in Shakespeare's *Henry VI Part 2*.

In modern times the most cold-blooded example must surely be the murder of Judge Gentile while he sat on the bench of Cook County Circuit Court, Chicago, in October 1983. He was shot and killed by an irate husband in a divorce case.

Shocking though that is, for a rather more sinister and menacing example we should look much closer to home at the story that unfolded in Leeds Crown Court in November 1981. It is a story that only the most nerveless of judges would read

225

without looking over his shoulder.

Maybe it was because John Smith was blessed with such an ordinary name that he felt compelled to propel himself into the limelight by fair means or foul. As it was, he chose foul and began his criminal career in 1968 with a spot of thieving, which landed him an eighteen-month stay in borstal on the decision of Judge William Openshaw.

Seventeen-year-old Smith vowed never to forget that incident and he wrote Judge Openshaw's name down as the first on his revenge-fuelled hit list. It was when Smith was 31, all of thirteen years later, that he finally caught up with Openshaw again.

At Smith's trial at Leeds Crown Court in November 1981, Mr Justice Lawson might well have listened with some discomfort as he and the jury heard how Smith had gone to Judge Openshaw's home in Broughton, near Preston, in May of that year, and had hidden in the rafters of his garage at night, full of hate and hell-bent on settling an old score. When the judge came to his car the next morning Smith dropped down and fatally stabbed him twelve times in the head, neck and chest.

Smith was then disturbed by Judge Openshaw's wife and fled the scene, flagging down an innocent passing motorist, Walter Hide, and forcing him at knifepoint to take an unscheduled day trip to Hawick in Scotland. Poor Mr Hide was left tied to a tree in a deserted wood (he'd only nipped out for a morning paper) as Smith took his car and went on the run.

When the police did catch up with him, Detective Chief Inspector Meadows asked the proverbial silly question, 'Why did you do it, John?'

If he expected the sort of in-depth psychological explanation the criminologists would have us believe motivates the Smiths of this world, he was sadly mistaken: 'Because he was a bastard,' said Smith.

It goes without saying that John Smith, whose vengeful thirteen-year judge hunt ended in such a bloodbath, was convicted of murder despite his plea of not guilty. He was duly sentenced by Justice Lawson to a minimum of 25-years in jail.

The end of a remarkable story? Not quite, for Smith railed at the 68-year-old judge after the verdict: 'I am not sorry for what I have done.'

Justice Lawson knew he would need to live to be at least 93 to come face to face with Smith again but, even so, a shiver must have run down his spine as the man who never forgot a face delivered his snarling parting shot as he was dragged from the dock: 'I'll cut your throat when I get out.'

EIGHT OUT OF TEN CATS PREFER HILDA

STONEHAM, MASSACHUSETTS, UNITED STATES, 1982

Many barbarous acts have been discovered by the police in the line of routine duty. Even the vilest sights have to be met with a dispassionate heart and sound stomach. Yet once in a while even the most hardened officer is shocked by how a victim has been treated by an attacker. Such was a nasty-tasting case that comes from the USA.

Hilda Diggdon was one of those delightfully eccentric old ladies who like to take in stray cats. No one knew exactly how many she had but it was certainly more than a few. If there was an abandoned moggy in need of a home she simply couldn't resist it.

Nor could the cats resist Hilda. Maybe they used their psychic powers to spread the word, for the Diggdon home became a magnet for fallen felines from miles around.

Alas, her guests may have had nine lives but Hilda enjoyed only one. Late in 1982 her remains were discovered on the floor of her home. She was 84. 'The body was in a semi-skeletal state,' a police officer confirmed. 'It was one of the roughest things I've ever seen.'

The work of a homicidal maniac on a particularly imaginative day? In fact not, for the autopsy revealed that Hilda had died of natural causes.

Yet even in death she had remained irresistible to her feline friends: not being adept at opening the tins of food that remained in the kitchen cupboard, they had bitten the hand that had fed them – and the foot, and the leg and the neck, until very little remained of Hilda at all.

'They were feeding off her and when we tried to recover the body they attacked us,' said one of the officers who made the gruesome find.

Time was, strangely, when animals committing misdemeanours could face trial (see 'The Accused Have Gone to Ground', page 12). In Savigny, France, on 10 January 1457, a sow who had trampled on a five-year-old boy was charged and convicted of 'murder flagrantly committed on the person of Jehan Martin' and sentenced to be 'hanged by the hind feet to a gallows tree'.

But what of the cats? They hadn't murdered. Perhaps their more considered act was even worse. Did they all partake of the tainted morsels or do some cats have a conscience? In the event the authorities took no chances and all the cats were removed and their lives humanely ended.

But just think of the squeals of that poor medieval swine hanging from its gibbet. Some will say, by comparison, that a swift injection was too good an end for the most ghoulish cats in legal history.

A COMMITTED DRINKER

BRISBANE, AUSTRALIA, 1982

Gathering evidence to support the reputation of Australians as 'legendary drinkers' has never been too onerous a task, but really it shouldn't be a task at all. Just look no further than Tommy Johns.

When he appeared in court in Brisbane, Queensland, on 9 September 1982, no one had to show him the ropes. Indeed he seemed curiously at home in surroundings that have daunted many an accused before him and since. He even appeared to be on nodding terms with some of the officials.

The charge was drunkenness. He elected not to cite previous good behaviour in his defence, for there had been, it was true, a similar incident way back in 1957. And 1958. And 1959. And 1960. The rainforests are just too valuable a resource to commit the full list to paper, but suffice to say that Tommy Johns had previous form of the inebriate kind. It may seem strange that his subsequent conviction for such a routine offence is now regarded as a landmark case in world legal history but a staggering landmark it was. For Tommy Johns, that is.

It is surely an astonishing testimony to his capacity that his conviction for drunkenness that day was his two thousandth in 25 years of perpetual imbibing. Then again, shouldn't he have learned to hold his drink after so much practice?

Many a convicted defendant has left court determined to reform. A court appearance should, after all, be a sobering experience. But not for Tommy Johns. Over the next few years he notched up almost a thousand further convictions and by the time he died in 1988 his grand total was just short of three thousand. No one has been arrested more times.

Appropriately enough, his legendary exploits as the world's most committed drinker have been officially recognised by *The Guinness Book of Records*.

HE JUST WOULDN'T STAND FOR IT

CAMBRIDGE COUNTY COURT, 1982

'Contempt of court' is one of those catch-all phrases that most laymen have heard of. It has, we know, something to do with being rude to judges, doing something not quite proper in a court of law or committing an act out of court that might pervert the course of justice.

Rather more precisely, the Contempt of Court Act 1981 stated that conduct may be treated as contemptuous 'where it tends to interfere with the course of justice in legal proceedings, regardless of intent to do so'.

Yet even that is hugely interpretative and in practice the identification of a potentially contemptuous act falls to the presiding judge him. Which side of bed did he get out of that morning? Does he have a sense of humour? Is he a curmudgeonly old fart? Such are the pivotal vagaries of justice in this delicate area of the law.

Many are the occasions when such weighty matters have been put to the test and none more so in recent history than in 1982 when Sardar Tejendrasingh decided to chance his arm all the way to the top of the legal pyramid amid farcical scenes more suited to humorous fiction.

Tejendrasingh claimed he was owed money by James Clarke and Co. Ltd and he was well aware that an action for recovery through the courts was an option afforded to him by the splendid English legal system. He decided to pursue that course of action.

But, when he was called upon to address the Cambridge County Court in support of his claims, his contempt for the system by which he sought his remedy became all too apparent.

'I have no respect for this country or its civilisation or its courts,' he announced, and refused to stand up while stating his case. Despite repeated requests for him to rise, he steadfastly stuck to his guns (and his seat) and tested the patience of the court officials to its limits. In August 1982 the court registrar decided enough was enough and ordered the recovery action to be stayed until Mr Tejendrasingh decided to show due respect.

But that hard line did little more than harden his resolve, so he took the case a step further. Again he met with stern resistance, this time in the unyielding form of His Honour Judge Garfitt, who ruled in September 1983 that the court would not hear the action until Mr Tejendrasingh gave a written undertaking that he would stand up.

Again he refused to do this. He would *not* stand up in court but he decided he *would* stand up to what he perceived as the tyranny of the system. He promptly appealed.

Over three years after his sit-down campaign began, his case finally reached the Court of Appeal. Three of the highest legal authorities in the land, including the Master of the Rolls, Sir John Donaldson, heard Mr Tejendrasingh's impassioned testimony in November 1985. They sensibly got round the thorny 'stand or sit?' issue by allowing him to remain seated during the hearing itself, but only on the basis that to have asked him to stand might have amounted to a prejudgment of the very issue on which they were about to pronounce a verdict.

If there is such a thing as closing ranks in the legal profession, this was one moment when that tactic seemed to operate. They backed up the County Court judge absolutely: 'The decision will stand,' they chorused. 'Even if the appellant won't,' they might have added, but didn't, because Lords of Appeal aren't supposed to make quips.

Apart from explaining that it was customary to stand in court while giving evidence, they added a headmasterly reproach into the bargain: 'If a court orders somebody to stand,' they said, 'that is no different from any other order of the court. It is something which has to be obeyed.'

Legal opinion was split by the decision. Many within the profession said the appellant should have been permitted to sit. It was a fuss over nothing, they said.

Yet the decision ought not to have surprised anybody, for in Canada in 1965 the Supreme Court of British Columbia upheld the decision of a judge who sentenced a man to three months in prison for refusing to stand, and in the United States in 1969 similar judgments were made.

Bizarre as it was, *Tejendrasingh v. James Clarke and Co. Ltd* was simply one of a long line of cases involving acts that showed contempt, punished or not, for those on the other side of the law. As early as 1631 a man who threw a brickbat (solid not verbal) at a judge received no mercy. Records confirm that the poor fellow had his right hand chopped off and was then 'immediately hanged in the presence of the Court'.

Even spectators aren't immune from a judge with a veritable mood on him: in 1893 Lord Chief Justice Coleridge ordered the detention of a youth for the duration of proceedings for applauding from the public gallery. Nor would that be an anachronism in more recent years, for almost a full century later, in 1992, a crown court judge in Newcastle went even further by jailing twelve members of the public gallery for one night after they noisily celebrated a friend's acquittal.

Perhaps there is a lesson here for all those who seek to challenge judicial authority, a lesson that men of lesser resolve than Sardar Tejendrasingh have been receiving since time immemorial.

Unjust it may be, but the American judge Justice Oliver Wendell Holmes Jr (1841–1935) summed up the futility of standing up (or sitting down) for our rights in the unsmiling face of legal authority when he pointedly reminded a young offender: 'This is a court of law, young man, not a court of justice.'

THE LAWS OF CHANCE

NEW YORK, UNITED STATES, 1982

It was the Greek philosopher Socrates (470–399 BC), heralded as one of the wisest men ever to walk this earth, who arguably put into words most succinctly the qualities required of a good judge: 'To hear courteously, to answer wisely, to consider soberly, and to decide impartially.'

Many judges have passed the Socrates test with flying colours but New York's Alan Friess wasn't one of them. His philosophy in one famous but otherwise insignificant case was altogether of a different sort and it ensured he'd be for ever remembered as the judge who flipped.

If it was going to happen anywhere, then Manhattan Criminal Court was as good a bet as any. It was February 1982 when eighteen-year-old Jeffery Jones stood before Judge Friess charged with a pickpocket offence. He pleaded guilty and Judge Friess sentenced him to thirty days' imprisonment.

Instead of accepting this favourably short sentence with good grace, the defendant railed at the judge that it was excessive. The judge, in turn, rather than dismiss the cheeky brat forthwith, rose to the bait: 'So what do you think would be fair?' he asked. 'More like twenty days,' came the prisoner's reply.

Judge Friess then steered the case proceedings down the road to immortality: 'Is your client a gambling man?' he asked Michael Muscato, the defence lawyer. When the reply came back in the affirmative the judge asked John Jordan, the

Assistant District Attorney, for a 25-cent coin and ordered the defendant to toss and call. The pickpocket called tails and won and Judge Friess promptly imposed the reduced twenty-day jail sentence as his prize.

This is the only known modern case where the outcome of a trial has been decided on the flip of a coin and it served as a prelude to Judge Friess being barred from office by the New York State Commission on Judicial Conduct just a year later. In ousting him from office they took into account his somewhat impetuous earlier conduct in 1982, when he released a woman murder suspect without bail and gave her a lift home. Nor did they entirely ignore his 1983 rush of blood to the head when he asked courtroom spectators to vote on which of two conflicting witnesses to believe. Surely there's a germ of a cult TV game show in there somewhere.

Although Friess is undisputed king of the realm of strange decision making, there are a number of other documented cases where outcomes have been subjected to the law of chance.

It might be argued that they knew no better in 1677 when, in *Foster v. Hawden*, it was the jury who cast lots to decide the verdict. Similarly, in 1737, it was the jury again who reduced the law to a game of chance when they decided the outcome of *Langdell v. Sutton* by drawing halfpennies from a hat.

No modern juror, surely, would countenance such methods of chance. Unless he was at the trial of Trevor Lynch for grievous bodily harm at Newcastle upon Tyne Crown Court in July 1998.

On that occasion Judge Esmond Faulks received a note from a young ponytailed juror asking for the defendant's birth date so he could draw up a star chart to help him decide his fate. Needless to say, he was removed from the jury but seemed deeply wounded and genuinely puzzled by this unexpected turn in his own fate, which he had evidently *not* seen in the tea leaves that morning.

Just as bizarre as resorting to gambling or astrology to decide an outcome was the methodology prescribed by a US Court of Appeals judge, Richard Posner, in 1986. In deciding whether to grant preliminary injunctions pending trials of civil actions he used what he maintained was a simple method, albeit one fully understood only by himself. The injunction would be granted only if $P \times Hp$ exceeded $(1 - P) \times Hd$. I forget the precise meanings of the algebraic notations but I think P may have been the price of monkfish on the last Friday in March.

Who's to say, though, that hours of head-scratching, weeks of deliberation and the application of some of the world's best legal intellects are any more effective in making truly 'right' decisions than the fates? Could there yet be a place in the modern legal system for sheep's entrails and the ouija board?

Just what might Socrates have made of all these shenanigans? At the age of seventy he was tried in Athens, under an indictment sworn by Meletus, of 'refusing to recognise the gods the city recognises' and of 'introducing other new divinities', and for 'corrupting the youth', as reported by Plato in his *Apologia*. Despite conducting his own brilliant and witty defence a jury of 500 found him guilty by an estimated majority of 280 to 220 votes and he was condemned to death by drinking a dose of poison hemlock. Socrates never did say 'the law is a lottery' but if he were alive today it's odds on he might.

ONE CASE TOO MANY

RAMSGATE MAGISTRATES' COURT, 1983

Judges, on the whole, are not too fussy about which cases they handle. Large or small, it's all part of the job. But there was one case that 67-year-old Judge Bruce Campbell really shouldn't have touched, for in December 1983 it made legal history to his own personal cost after interesting proceedings in the unlikely setting of Ramsgate Magistrates' Court.

The case he handled was no ordinary case. A large one? A small one? A quick one? It might have been any, for this was a case of whisky. In fact several cases. And some cigarettes. Oh, dear. The crime of smuggling may be redolent of long-ago moonlit nights on which gnarled old sailor types rowed silently into secluded coves, but Judge Campbell seemed intent on carrying the tradition into the modern era.

His frequent journeys to Guernsey in his motor cruiser *Papyrus* aroused the interest of the vigilant men and women from HM Customs after a tip-off from a public-spirited citizen of Ramsgate. When officers raided the vessel they found the small matter of 125 litres (28 gallons) of whisky and 9,000 cigarettes which Campbell had brought over from the Channel Islands with his friend Alan Foreman, a market trader and second-hand-car dealer.

Imagine the conversation: 'Have you come to a decision, Mr Foreman?' 'Yes, I'll do it.'

Even a well-practised judge couldn't explain away those amounts of booze and fags on the basis of 'personal use' and at Ramsgate Magistrates' Court in September 1982 Judge Bruce Campbell QC was convicted and fined £2,000.

There was bound to be fallout from such an unusual case and it was Campbell who fell and Campbell who was out as on Monday, 5 December 1983 he received a punishment never before meted out to an English judge in modern times when he was unceremoniously removed from office by the Lord Chancellor, Lord Hailsham, under the Courts Act of 1971.

It was, of course, scandalous, and ex-Judge Campbell retreated with his tail between his legs to his country home in Thames Ditton pondering the loss of his £29,750 salary, his pension rights and the nice little flat in the Temple.

All exceptionally bad news for Mr Campbell, but there is a spot of better news for any straw-clutchers rightly mortified that a bastion of the English judiciary could behave in such a manner. Bruce Campbell, it is my duty to report, was born in New Zealand. Critics of the judiciary are forever calling for judges to 'show their human face' and it seems Mr Campbell took it all rather too literally.

There are few real words of comfort to offer anyone disillusioned by this regrettable affair but I'll have a stab at damage limitation by mentioning a couple of cases from across the Atlantic that suggest that Stateside judges are always apt to go one better.

In 1999 the Supreme Court of Mississippi removed Howard 'Buster' Spencer from his position as a judge in Prentiss County for a string of inappropriate acts including swearing at witnesses and lawyers and continually sucking lollipops in court.

But Judge Spencer's behaviour was exemplary compared with that of Richard Deacon Jones of Omaha, Nebraska. He was dismissed in 1998, again for displaying a variety of unusual behaviour patterns, not least signing important court papers 'Adolf Hitler', setting bail bonds for 'a zillion dollars', and throwing lighted fireworks into a rival colleague's office before urinating on the carpet. His fate was ultimately sealed after he promised the authorities that the Hitler business would stop – it did, but he started signing court papers 'Snow White' instead.

Surely a spot of 'gentleman' smuggling is almost admirable after that. So when it comes to the strange world of judges behaving badly, perhaps raising a glass to Bruce Campbell might not, after all, be altogether inappropriate.

CARRY ON ON THE BUSES

LONDON, 1984

No one doubted that Mr Hussain was good at his job as a bus and coach cleaner for London Country Bus Services. As a key team member of the early-evening shift he would hose, scrub, sweep and polish with a vengeance to get those grubby buses out on the road again at breakneck speed and as good as new.

So why did he end up being dismissed? He was, it seems, just too 'orthodox'. But that's not to say his employers wanted him cleaning buses in fancy dress or sporting a red nose. This was a case where religious orthodoxy took centre stage, for Mr Hussain was a dedicated follower of Islam.

Saying obligatory daily prayers five times a day can certainly make life complicated for Muslims. There's *fajr* at dawn, *zuhr* in the early afternoon, *asr* in the late afternoon, *maghrib* at sunset and *isha* last thing at night. Not surprisingly, though, while congregational prayers at mosques adhere rigidly to that timetable, room for 'flexibility' has developed for those who work.

That's fine except for those so orthodox in their beliefs that a departure from that timetable is unthinkable. And Mr Hussain *was* ultra-orthodox. Working that twilight shift played havoc with *maghrib*, there was no two ways about it.

Asr and *isha* he could fit in before and after his stint, but when it came to *maghrib* there was only one thing for it. The ace bus cleaner swapped his squeegee for a prayer mat and left his colleagues to it.

241

Although Mr Hussain was faultless while he was there, the turnaround time for the buses duly suffered by his unscheduled breaks and his colleagues variously simmered quietly, chuntered incessantly or simply went plain ballistic.

Yet Mr Hussain understood their feelings, for he was, after all, a very conscientious man; he even did extra work later in the evening to make up for his absence. But that was all to no avail. After prolonged discussion the company eventually decided it must dispense with his services. Devoted employees they wanted. Devout ones evidently not. The resulting claim for unfair dismissal and compensation led to the landmark case of *Hussain v. London Country Bus Services Ltd*, decided by an industrial tribunal in 1984.

It ruled that the dismissal was not unfair. If Mr Hussain intended to insist on rigid observance of sunset prayers regardless of the pressures of work, they said, he should have made this clear from the start of his employment.

So a devout Muslim suffered for his faith and it was a disillusioned Mr Hussain who entered the legal record books as the only bus company employee ever sacked for strict adherence to the timetable.

INNOCENT OF AN
IMPOSSIBLE CRIME

THE HOUSE OF LORDS, LONDON, 1985

One of the great things about the British justice system is the right of appeal to a higher authority. Some cases go all the way, and that means being heard by selected representatives of the House of Lords.

But naturally, because they are extremely busy fellows, the Lords will only consent to pass final judgment on the really 'big' cases and there is a rigorous prescreening process to check that only the most important ones get through.

Thus it was that on Thursday, 9 May 1985, a pivotal day for the future of British justice, five Law Lords exercised their razor-sharp intellects to decide the fate of Mrs Bernadette Ryan of Manchester in the case of the nicked video recorder.

I feel an explanation, dear reader, is required.

Having paid £110 for the video recorder, Mrs Ryan was not at all happy when it was stolen in a burglary from her home. She duly reported the incident to the police but during the course of questioning the plot began to thicken: 'I might as well be honest,' she told the police, 'it was a stolen one I bought.' A strange brand of honesty, that one.

That admission was Mrs Ryan's first 'mistake', but as it was later to prove it was a mistake in more ways than one.

Under the Theft Act 1968 and the Criminal Attempt Act 1981 she was promptly charged with 'dishonestly handling a video recorder contrary to the 1968 Act knowing or believing it to be stolen and dishonestly attempting to handle that recorder contrary to section 1 (1) of the 1981 Act'.

In a prosecution by James Anderton, Chief Constable of Greater Manchester, Mrs Ryan pleaded not guilty to both charges. It was when the court heard details of her second 'mistake' that things got more interesting, for it turned out that her belief that her video was a stolen one was erroneous. Or at least the prosecution couldn't prove it was stolen. This presented something of a conundrum and as a consequence Greater Manchester Police dropped the first charge of dishonest handling of stolen goods but invited magistrates instead simply to convict her of dishonest 'attempted' handling under the 1981 Act.

Now this was where the 1981 Act should have done its job, for the government had brought it in largely to secure convictions against criminals who cited the age-old so-called 'pickpocket's defence': 'All right, officer, you caught me with my hand in his pocket but the pocket was empty so how can you accuse me of attempted theft?' The 1981 Act quashed the validity of such spurious defences by making provision for convictions against those attempting a 'hypothetically impossible crime'.

Bernadette Ryan was undoubtedly guilty of 'attempted handling of stolen goods' under that interpretation of the Act even though she only 'believed' the goods to be stolen. She had tried to commit the 'impossible crime' but the court in Manchester perversely found her innocent.

This potentially gave leave to all manner of strange acquittal scenarios. Consider a man brutally stabbing his wife while she lies 'asleep' in bed. But a doctor later testifies she had already died some hours earlier from a heart attack. Under *Ryan v. Anderton* the husband must duly be acquitted of 'attempted' murder. Consider another scenario – a jealous wife plunges a carving knife deep into her husband's chest as he lies in bed under the covers. It turns out he has nipped out to see his lover and left only a bolster in his place. The wife is guilty of nothing more than stabbing a pillow and again walks free.

Conscious of the can of worms the *Anderton v. Ryan* case might open up, the Divisional Court subsequently ordered the Manchester court that they must convict Mrs Ryan, but the handler of the sham stolen goods had by this time become truly convinced of her own innocence. She went all the way to the top.

It was entirely to be expected that the Law Lords would back up the government's 1981 legislation and find Bernadette Ryan guilty. But this is *The Law's Strangest Cases* and the only thing to expect with any certainty is the unexpected. They found Mrs Ryan innocent of the charge on a vote of four to one and therefore allowed her appeal.

The Times somewhat incredulously wrote of the decision that 'on 9 May 1985 the Law Lords drove a coach and horses through the Government's 1981 Criminal Attempt Act'.

This strange affair really set the philosophers of the legal world buzzing with what-ifs: 'What if a man steals a briefcase full of waste paper when he really believes it to contain £20,000?' poses one. 'Under the 1981 Act he ought to be guilty of attempted theft of £20,000,' says the second. 'But after the Ryan acquittal all he can be found guilty of is stealing the waste paper,' chips in a third. 'And the suitcase,' pipes a pedantic but quite correct fourth.

So there is the odd affair of *Anderton v. Ryan*, which goes to show that sometimes the smallest cases can become the biggest. It doesn't pay, though, to spend too much time pondering the mind-boggling implications and permutations of this one, as an exploding brain is not a pleasant experience.

One final thought, though. A facet of this case that is surely truly astonishing is that Bernadette Ryan should have had the bare-faced cheek to report the 'burglary' of goods she believed she had dishonestly acquired in the first place.

Would *you* invite the boys and girls in blue into your home in those circumstances? Now *that* really is strange.

IT'S UNCLE NORRIS!

THE HIGH COURT, LONDON, 1986

Libel is a strange business. The traditional test for spotting one is whether the words written or spoken bring a person into hatred, ridicule or contempt. That's a difficult one to call and more recent thinking has suggested that an approach better suited to modern life would be 'to determine whether the words lower a person in the estimation of right-thinking people'.

Could anything be simpler? Differential calculus or the translation of Serbo-Croat into Japanese come to mind, for the history of libel cases shows that a person can be libelled not only by the written and spoken word but also by image, theme and juxtaposition. The possibilities are simply endless and in truth it's all a bit of a minefield, but one that any legal strangeologist is more than happy to negotiate because oddities are guaranteed.

Take the 1975 case of *Cosmos Air Holidays v. BBC*. For the BBC to tell their *Holiday Programme* viewers that some hotels used by Cosmos weren't up to scratch might just have been bearable to the tour company's bosses but it was the accompanying music that really got their goat. They settled for several thousand pounds in out of court damages – after all, how else could the viewers interpret the opening music of the *Colditz* television series? There was no escape for the BBC at any rate – it was libel by theme, literally.

As for libel by juxtaposition, look no further than Mr

Monson, who, even as far back as 1894, was sufficiently litigation-aware to get himself all worked up about the waxwork of himself that Madame Tussaud's placed in the anteroom of their Chamber of Horrors. Monson *had* been tried for murder in a Scottish court, it was true, but he had equally certainly been acquitted by that peculiar Scottish verdict of 'not proven'. To place his likeness next to those of convicted murderers just wasn't on, he argued, and he won the princely sum of one farthing's damages for having his reputation sullied in such a way.

And then there's image. Here we come to the star of the show. I give you Norris McWhirter, well-known editor of *The Guinness Book of Records*, no less.

Perhaps he was trying to get into his own book for the shortest and most tenuous incidence of libel of all time. Or maybe he'd just lost his sense of humour. Or just 'lost it' full stop.

It all started with the television broadcast of a 1984 episode of *Spitting Image*, the series whose excursions into latex lampoonery through the medium of cruelly parodic puppetry has caused many a celebrity to fume.

The good news for Norris was that he wasn't on it. Or was he? For thereby hangs the tale.

The Times subsequently reported that Mr McWhirter, aged 59, had taken out an action for libel against the Independent Broadcasting Authority at Horseferry Road Magistrates' Court. McWhirter was clear that he had seen 'a grotesque and ridiculing image of my face superimposed on the top of a body of a naked woman'. It really doesn't bear thinking about. He asserted that the broadcasting of the image was a criminal offence under the Broadcasting Act 1981, but not because of 'what' it was – it was how long it lasted that was the real bone of contention.

'And how long did it last?' asked the judge with due concern. Norris McWhirter's reply was brief but not nearly as brief as the offending image: 'A quarter of a second,' was his stunning reply.

McWhirter's contention was that the image had been

broadcast subliminally, using the sort of technique that unscrupulous advertisers or political régimes are said to employ to implant subconscious images and messages into the addled brains of the world's couch potatoes.

This wasn't the sort of case to be decided in the blink of an eye, and so to the High Court on Thursday, 30 January 1986, where Lord Justice Lloyd, sitting in the Queen's Bench Divisional Court with Mr Justice Skinner, held Norris McWhirter's reputation in his hands.

Lord Justice Lloyd asked the question that any person in the street would have asked: 'If the image was only on screen for a quarter of a second how did you see it?'

That was where the evidence of Mr McWhirter's fifteen-year-old nephew came into its own: 'He was watching the programme on video using the slow-motion,' said McWhirter, 'and when he used the freeze-frame button he suddenly shouted "Look, there's Uncle Norris!" '

Unconcerned as to why the teenager should have been using the freeze-frame in the first place (looking for naked women?), Lord Justice Lloyd remained singularly unimpressed, promptly quashing the summons and prohibiting further proceedings.

Thus it was that Norris McWhirter failed to get into *The Guinness Book of Records* and he was left to bemoan the verdict, leaving the court with an impassioned parting shot: 'This is a matter of profound constitutional importance,' he said. 'This brainwashing should be suppressed – these subliminal messages are deceitful and I want them stopped.'

Has there ever been an odder libel case? I'm still looking, but there is certainly a lesson we can all learn from Uncle Norris. Now I know why I get those sudden urges to slip away from the television to visit the local. Ban those subliminal messages, I say. My waistline is thickening and I intend to sue.

NOT SO DUMB WITNESS

SOUTHAMPTON, 1987

I have always thought it rather unfortunate that the 'Queen of Crime', Agatha Christie, should have titled her 1937 novel *Dumb Witness*; Bob the dog, who is the witness referred to, was undoubtedly devoid of speech but certainly not stupid in the sense that the American meaning of the word dumb has come to convey. Then again, Dame Agatha did call Chapter 18 of the same book 'A Nigger in the Woodpile', which does show how times change.

The idea of a dog, or indeed any creature, as an articulate witness is an appealing one, though. One imagines it could happen in the world of Kipling's *Jungle Book*, or that of *Doctor Dolittle*. Richard Adams's rabbits, too, in his celebrated *Watership Down*, were pretty cute on the verbals.

And thereby hangs a curious link. Who said contrived? For in Southampton in 1987 that very same Richard Adams did score a major hit for the anthropomorphic lobby when he called his dog Tetter as a witness in an industrial tribunal case involving the unsavoury antics of a gun-toting bunny-sniping gamekeeper.

It was in the late summer of 1985 when Adams and Tetter went walking on a public footpath near Whitchurch, Hampshire, close to the area Adams used as the inspiration for his book.

There he encountered David Hunt, head gamekeeper on an estate at nearby Middleton to Captain Andrew Wills of the

249

famous tobacco family.

There was not a whiff of trouble in the air that day but Gamekeeper Hunt, not known for his sentimentality towards rabbits, or humans for that matter, seemed to be spoiling for a confrontation.

Spotting that Tetter wasn't on a lead, he launched into a fierce verbal tirade, turning the air a shade too deep a blue for Adams's liking. Nor did Hunt altogether endear himself to the multi-award-winning author when he finished off with 'You're the one who wrote that poxy book about rabbits.'

Shots were fired. Tetter was threatened but not hit and Adams had nightmares about the incident for months afterwards. Yet it was entirely by coincidence that he was able to gain a measure of redress and clear Tetter's name from Hunt's scandalous accusation that he had been 'out of control and scattered my pheasants'.

It seems Hunt's volatile temper also affected his fellow employees, for his assistant David Claridge was so unnerved by the unpredictability of the outbursts that he quit his job. It was a job he otherwise enjoyed and as a result he sued his employer Andrew Wills for constructive dismissal and the case went to an industrial tribunal in January 1987.

Adams was called as a witness to testify to the ferocity of Hunt's temper and he told the hearing how the gamekeeper used language that was 'a celebration of filth' before firing his shotgun in Tetter's direction: 'I thought he had shot my dog dead,' said Adams.

Hunt's defence was that Tetter was uncontrollable, but Adams assured the tribunal that Tetter would obey his every command, even in strange surroundings. There was only one thing for it. 'Call Tetter.'

The dog's big moment was on 27 January 1987 and this rare canine witness even made the pages of *The Times*: 'The dog bounded into the tribunal room,' the reporter wrote. It didn't look good. 'But when Mr Adams commanded it to sit, it did so instantly.' In a scene reminiscent of the best *Lassie* episodes, Tetter had won the day. His reputation remained unsullied and Andrew Wills agreed to pay Claridge the gamekeeper £2,000.

It is to be hoped that Tetter was rewarded with a tasty morsel or two.

Lest I should be accused of canine bias I must continue the theme with the 1983 case of 'Blackie the Talking Cat'. Blackie was a variation on the age-old music hall acts of animals that give responses to certain questions posed by their owners, but it seems Blackie's business status had got his keepers into a spot of bother regarding the imposition of a business-licence tax.

Their desire not to pay it led the case to go all the way to the US Court of Appeals and there was much talk of 'animal rights' and 'free speech'. The result for Blackie, though, was something of a humiliation, as the court asserted that 'even if an animal could enjoy such rights we see no reason for the appellants to assert them for him as Blackie can clearly speak for himself'. Touché for Blackie, regrettably, who dismally failed to respond.

That begs the final question of how animals might really assert themselves in this law business.

The special 'dog court' set up in 1979 in Multnomah County Court, Portland, Oregon, sounds like a good start and it created enough canine-related business to keep a judge occupied for one day a week.

Heartening, too, is another US case, this one involving Bimbo the performing elephant. In 1972 a Los Angeles judge, Justice Title, awarded Bimbo's owners $4,500 as a result of injuries received by the elephant in a road accident. It was accepted, Justice Title asserted, that 'as a result Bimbo has completely lost interest in dancing and water skiing'.

It is to England, though, that we should look for action of a more direct and graphic kind. The teenagers who attacked a woman in Dalton, near Huddersfield, and snatched her plastic bag got nothing but soiled goods – the poop-scoop contents left by her pet terrier. No doubt specimen charges were later preferred.

The final word, though, must go to the feline world and a symbolic act which struck at the very heart of English justice.

On 22 March 1979, an unnamed cat made its views on

matters legal all too clear, as the *Daily Telegraph* reported in admirably deadpan style: 'Court proceedings at the Old Bailey were delayed for 15 minutes while the court was disinfected owing to a cat's misdemeanour.'

THE ICING ON THE CAKE

BELFAST, NORTHERN IRELAND, 1988

As strange libel cases go, this one certainly takes the biscuit. Nineteen eighty-eight may have been a year of much more important cases than *Boal and McCartney v. The Sunday World* but as far as the legal community of Belfast was concerned it was the tastiest morsel to come their way for many a long year.

For once, the public gallery at Belfast's High Court was patronised not by a handful of curious onlookers but tightly packed instead by an audience of barristers, solicitors and court officials relishing the prospect of the bun fight of the year as the case opened in October 1988.

Bringing the action, as plaintiffs, not lawyers, were the two best-known QCs in Northern Ireland, the leading criminal barrister Desmond Boal and the top civil QC and Unionist politician Robert McCartney.

The action centred not on some complex legal ruling but on the much simpler and far more entertaining matter of chocolate eclairs, or rather alleged chocolate eclairs, for the plaintiffs were to claim in the strongest possible terms that said cream-filled confections were entirely illusory.

It was a freelance journalist writing in the Dublin-based *Sunday World* newspaper who started it all. In 1987 the paper ran his piece headed WHO NEARLY HAD A BUN-FIGHT? which informed its undoubtedly amused readers that the two eminent QCs had entered a bakery shop both intent on buying chocolate eclairs.

253

'Unfortunately,' said the piece, 'there were very few left and some other shoppers were amazed as the two "had words" about who saw them first.'

Boal and McCartney were not at all amused by the story and Boal's QC, Michael Lavery, was at pains to tell the court that the report was 'pure garbage' and that 'my client has been held to ridicule'. If the evidence of the universally smirking ranks of Belfast's legal community was anything to go by it seems he may have had a point. The courtroom abounded with much undisguised mirth.

Mr McCartney's evidence was no less forgiving: 'When you have put as much effort as I have into achieving a position as a respected, I hope, and respectable QC, then to be portrayed in a totally pernicious and lying article as some form of contemptible and senseless clown who would make an exhibition of himself in a bakery shop made me very distressed and very angry.'

Those strong denials were all very well but the question that all in court must undoubtedly have been asking themselves was why a journalist should choose two legal heavyweights as his comic characters in a fabricated tale. How, too, could he possibly have had the imagination to create the chocolate-eclair affair? Surely there's no smoke without fire?

The answers duly came when the evidence for *The Sunday World* was presented. When pressed on the point they readily admitted that the incident had never occurred. There was no shop, no encounter between the two QCs and no chocolate eclairs. The freelance journalist responsible for the entire confection said from the witness box, 'I thought it was true at the time and it was only a trivial humorous item.'

Trivial and humorous it may have been to him but the two QCs sought substantial damages. It seems *The Sunday World* had made an unwise editorial decision in picking on the legal bigwigs, for damages were duly awarded. And this was no 1p-each case.

Blessedly Boal and McCartney received exactly equal shares in the rather mouth-watering award, as *The Sunday World* paid out for the most expensive eclairs, or alleged eclairs, in history. The two QCs received £50,000 each.

THE MOST DESPERATE APPEAL EVER

SONORA, CALIFORNIA, UNITED STATES, 1988

No lawyer likes losing a case but, unless there are good grounds for an appeal, taking it on the chin is the only truly professional way to handle such hazards of the job.

But meek acceptance just wasn't the way for a US defence attorney, Clarke Head, who ran the risk of being labelled a windy loser as he launched the most spurious appeal in legal history.

Head's client at the trial in Sonora, California, in December 1988, faced a tough prospect. Thirty-seven-year-old Gary Davenport was charged with five counts of felony and one misdemeanour stemming from a break-in at a state highway maintenance yard in September 1986.

The prosecuting lawyer, Assistant District Attorney Ned Lowenbach, presented a forceful case against Davenport. All Clarke Head could do was brace himself for one last effort in defence of his client in his closing speech.

Meanwhile Lowenbach, it seems, was also bracing himself for an effort of a different kind, one he hoped might serve as a silent but deadly sabotage of his opponent's eloquence. But, if Head's subsequent accusations were to be believed, the attack was more in the way of a foul and noisy quickfire.

AN ILL WIND IN COURT BRINGS GALES OF LAUGHTER, said the *Independent*'s headline of 14 December. Gary Davenport had been unsurprisingly convicted on six counts but Clarke

Head announced his intention to appeal on the grounds of 'gross misconduct' on the part of Lowenbach.

'The closing speech is supposed to be sacred,' he complained. 'It's like the defendant's last chance and you aren't supposed to interrupt, especially making the jury laugh like Lowenbach did.' It was a curious statement to make because, according to Mr Head, Ned Lowenbach had spoken only once during the closing speech and that was to mutter a rather sheepish 'sorry' through tightly clenched teeth.

Head further explained: 'During my closing speech Lowenbach farted about a hundred times and made the jury laugh. He claims it was an accident but I don't think it was. He just kept on doing it to show his disrespect for me, my case and my client. He continually moved around and then he would fart again. I've been through fifty jury trials and never heard anything like this. It was impossible to concentrate.'

It is a toss-up which is more astonishing. The utter desperation of the grounds of the appeal itself or the possibility that anyone could really achieve the magic century entirely at will. District Attorney Eric Du Temple immediately defended his assistant: 'We are not going to dignify this with a response,' he sniffed.

The end result of this unseemly spat was that there was no let-off for Davenport but eyebrows were certainly raised on this side of the Atlantic as a senior member of the Bar Council was moved to remark, 'I know of no barristers being accused of similar behaviour in a British court. The difference between acceptable courtroom conduct in Britain and America is quite marked.'

One must wonder what became of the only alleged serial flatulator in legal history, but an alternative career as a novel variety act must surely have been his for the taking in the land where the law and the ass are now for ever inextricably linked.

DUMB WITNESS

CARDIFF CROWN COURT, 1989

The law concerning the right of an accused person to maintain absolute silence when questioned is undeniably complex. That has encouraged rather than deterred generations of suspects to say, 'I am saying nothing', which, despite its being rather a contradiction in terms, has put a spanner in the works on many occasions.

It is at times like this that a persuasive judge or barrister might coax such a silent witness into opening up, but at Cardiff Crown Court on Friday, 19 May 1989, Patricia Morgan was taking no such chances of breaking her silence.

The charges against Ms Morgan were of the all-too-familiar kind, namely defrauding the Department of Social Security by obtaining £9,000 in benefit payments via false claims.

She denied the charges and as her cross-examination was about to begin she made it clear to Judge Michael Evans QC that her lips were sealed. This she achieved by passing a note to him, which read: 'Your Honour, I Patricia Morgan have superglued my mouth to draw the public's attention to the mistrial and injustice of this court.' The note further alleged that a police tape-recorded interview with Ms Morgan had been tampered with.

Not having encountered such a determined silence before, Judge Evans sent out the jury and pondered the next move. Ms Morgan, from Newport, Gwent, was taken to hospital with her lips firmly stuck together and returned to the dock three hours later apparently none the worse for her experience.

Judge Evans announced to the jury, 'Ms Morgan is now back with us and her mouth has been unstopped,' before adjourning the case until the following Monday, when the silent lady finally came unstuck.

Further to the theme of silence in court, it may be the accused who most often favour that stance, but on at least one occasion the tables were well and truly turned when the Judiciary had *their* say – or not, as the case may be.

It was in Paris on 18 February 1971 that all proceedings in the Palace of Justice were suspended for the afternoon when judges responded to recent criticism by leading political figures that they 'lacked courage' by holding a silent vigil. *The Times* reported that 'all the judges held an impressive demonstration, moving impassively through the long corridors of the Palace in complete silence'.

There was on that occasion not even a smidgeon of glue involved, but nor was any needed, for, as everybody knows, judges under criticism are renowned for sticking together.

CUSACK'S LAW

HENDON MAGISTRATES' COURT, 1989

'Anything which could possibly happen in a court of law almost certainly will in the course of time.'

If ever that unwritten maxim was given a name it must without question be called Cusack's Law in honour of the man who on Thursday, 3 August 1989, added yet another strange chapter to the annals of legal oddity by both prosecuting and defending his client in the same case.

When Christopher Bailey turned up at Hendon Magistrates' Court that day he was anxious just to get his case over with, for twice already it had been postponed. He intended to plead guilty to driving at 102 m.p.h. on the M1 while disqualified and without insurance – an extended disqualification or possibly even prison looked likely to follow, despite the able backing of his solicitor Patrick Cusack.

Bailey's prospects took an even worse turn when the Crown Prosecution Service solicitor failed to turn up at Court 3 and the magistrates gave the bad news that a further postponement seemed inevitable. But that was the cue for 'Cusack's Law' to make its glorious debut in the English courts as Patrick Cusack ventured to suggest that he could quite ably and fairly both defend and prosecute his client if the court would permit it, which they duly did.

Cusack proceeded to deliver an accurate and considered account of his client's dreadful driving habits before swapping legal hats to deliver an equally erudite and persuasive speech in mitigation. As a result of this novel dual approach Christopher Bailey was fined £300 and ordered to perform two hundred hours of community service, an outcome with which he expressed the utmost satisfaction. Fresh from his theatrical Jekyll-and-Hyde performance, Patrick Cusack told reporters, 'I know it was an unusual step to take but my client was anxious to have the matter dealt with. Exceptional circumstances require exceptional action. At the end of the day everybody was happy and it saved the public purse – I didn't ask for prosecution costs against myself.'

DEFENCE LAWYER PROSECUTES CLIENT, headlined the *Independent* as the Crown Prosecution Service were left to mutter feeble excuses concerning 'shortage of personnel, a tube strike and a misunderstanding between two members of staff'. They had, they explained, 'only been operating as the prosecuting organ of the police force for three years and there have been teething troubles. Matters will certainly improve in future.'

All of which unmitigated fudge makes it a pity that Patrick Cusack wasn't around at Highbury Corner Magistrates' Court twelve years later on Monday, 7 May 2001, something of a Black Monday for the new improved version of the CPS.

23 FREED AFTER FIASCO IN COURT screamed the *Daily Express* as a Crown Prosecution solicitor again failed to turn up. In the absence of anyone willing to implement Cusack's Law, the presiding magistrate was hustled into discharging the 23 relieved defendants, including a rape suspect, as legal commentators and politicians made capital of the 'scandalous mix-up'. With no prizes for originality the shadow Home Secretary Anne Widdecombe observed, 'This just makes the law look a complete ass,' and the director of the Victims of Crime Trust roared, 'It's an absolute disgrace sending these alleged offenders home because the prosecution doesn't turn up. It's time for the CPS to be disbanded.'

As for the poor Crown Prosecution Service, there was no tube strike for them to fall back on but there was, blessedly, a bank holiday: 'This was a special Bank Holiday Monday hearing of the court set up to deal with the weekend's offenders,' said their spokesperson. 'We only planned to have one prosecutor attending and unfortunately there was a mix-up. Matters will certainly improve in future.'

There are four sure-fire assertions that can be made after these odd goings-on. First, that the universal application of 'Cusack's Law' will never be officially sanctioned; secondly, that there will be at least one sorry tale of an absentee CPS solicitor every year until kingdom come; thirdly, that someone will say with the utmost sincerity that 'matters will certainly improve in future'. And, fourthly, that they just as certainly won't.

THE SHOCKING AFFAIR OF THE ROLLED UMBRELLA

THE OLD BAILEY, LONDON, 1990

Every right-thinking judge and all upright members of the public want justice to be seen to be done. But at any price? Now there's the rub, for trials cost money, and public money at that. That's why judges and the public occasionally raise an eyebrow over cases they consider to be 'a waste of time and money'.

Take Judge Abdela in August 1981: 'Yes, it was true that Anthony Luckie had underpaid his tube fare by eighty-five pence,' he said, as he fined the unemployed 24-year-old £50, 'but why am I hearing this case at the Central Criminal Court over two days at a cost of four thousand pounds when it should have been dealt with routinely at Kingston?'

Judge Abdela was not really interested in the answer, that is that the Old Bailey generally helps to clear the summer backlog from London's crown courts. What he was really demanding was that 'this should never ever happen again'.

He might have known better, for cases of this type habitually occur year after year. Many would qualify for *The Law's Strangest Cases* but selectivity calls and it is my duty to make the pick of the bunch. With that in mind let's drop in at a petrol station in Hackney, east London, in the summer of 1990.

Keith Gonaz, aged 31, was topping up his car with petrol. He had a £10 note in his pocket ready to pay for the £10 worth of fuel he intended to put in, but, like many motorists before and since, he found that self-service can be a little tricky. His nozzle control, in particular, needed some fine tuning and he accidentally overshot the mark by 2p. 'It was a hair-trigger reaction,' he pleaded to the cashier. 'I tried to stop it but it was too late.' Many drivers will sympathise.

Mr Gonaz consequently refused to pay the additional 2p but the cashier, evidently a founder member of the little-known 'Jobsworth Employee Rights Kinship', otherwise known as JERK, remained entirely unmoved and insisted on the 2p payment forthwith.

A momentary impasse and verbal spat ensued but Mr Gonaz was determined not to budge. In a good-humoured but arguably puerile effort to defuse the situation he pointed his rolled umbrella at the cashier, made a machine-gun noise and drove off. 'Jobsworth' promptly pressed the (aptly named in this case) panic button and the police rounded up the dangerous desperado just a few minutes later.

Again, owing to a backlog at the lesser courts, the case came to the Old Bailey, where there was sufficient capacity to hear it. Shouldn't their publicity department have been drumming up some more serious crimes? 'Ever fancied trying your hand at murder? Give it a go. We need the business' has a certain ring to it.

As it was, Friday, 7 December 1990, was a day when Judge Bruce Laughland QC must have wondered what all his years of training were really for as the charges against Gonaz were read out.

That the incident should have given rise to formal charges of 'failure to discharge a debt of 2p, affray, and threatening behaviour' seemed rather over the top, but the real *coup de grâce* was 'possessing an imitation firearm' – to wit, the rolled umbrella.

As the judge ordered not-guilty verdicts to be entered on the firearm and affray charges, and the jury found Gonaz not guilty on the count of threatening behaviour, his mood displayed no sign of fitting his name. 'Laughland'? Not exactly.

'This has been a two-day case,' he concluded at the end of the farcical proceedings, 'and I should point out that each court costs at least £25 a minute to run, not including counsel and solicitors' fees. Pursuing this matter and holding a trial by jury was an unjustified waste of public time and money and will cost the taxpayer at least £13,500.'

He was absolutely right of course, and concluded in the standard manner: 'This must never be allowed to happen again.'

Judge Laughland had spoken and he expected his words to be heeded. That being the case any subsequent reports you may have read about three youths being cleared of stealing two cans of lager costing £1.80 in a trial at the Old Bailey costing the taxpayer an estimated £131,000 must be purely a figment of your imagination. That is your imagination in June 1998 by the way.

Where will it all end? one wonders. With such evil criminals at large there will be no let-up at the Old Bailey, that's for sure.

Why, only the other day I experienced at first hand the terror that now stalks our streets as I was the victim of an attempted gang murder just yards from my home. A party of elderly ladies disgorging from a bus trip bore down on me with indisputably merciless intentions, for without exception they were carrying . . . rolled umbrellas.

A BAD DAY AT THE OFFICE

SUTTON COLDFIELD MAGISTRATES' COURT, 1990

It may be a romantic notion to think of a typical courtroom scene as the Old Bailey or the Royal Courts of Justice, where the country's top barristers and most eminent judges resolve the weightiest matters of the law, but the workaday truth is far more commonplace.

A Birmingham solicitor, Gerald Davies, would have been the first to admit that little out of the ordinary ever happened on his patch. Certainly his visit to Sutton Coldfield Magistrates' Court on 20 December 1990 to defend a client on a minor dishonesty charge promised to be routine fare of the most tedious kind. Gerald's chances of making it into *The Law's Strangest Cases* were remote indeed. But make it he has, for it's not every day a solicitor gets arrested in court, especially for trying to be helpful.

It was while the magistrates were out of the courtroom that Gerald got chatting to the prosecution solicitor and showed him a document, purely as a matter of courtesy, which he felt might have been of value to him in presenting his case had he had knowledge of it.

The opposition was grateful for this helpful pointer and it was the sort of pleasant exchange that might occur in a provincial courtroom to lend heartening credence to the fact that the business of law needn't always be a cutthroat affair.

The prosecution solicitor asked if a police constable might see the document and the ever-affable Gerald duly agreed.

265

But, when the officer cast his eye over it and asked if he could keep it, the conscientious Gerald was aware that it might later be used as evidence in other cases, so although he thought there would be no problem, he kindly suggested to the officer that he felt the correct approach would be a more formal request from one of the officer's superiors. Handing over documents from the defence file willy-nilly wasn't really the done thing, he explained tactfully.

It was a pity for poor Gerald Davies that the constable just happened to be the most pedantic in the entire West Midlands Police Force. He made a second request for the document and when Gerald again displayed a proper and discreet reluctance to hand it over he was promptly arrested on the spot for 'obstructing a police officer in the execution of his duties'.

Instead of returning to his office, Gerald was taken to Sutton Coldfield police station and held in a cell for more than an hour before being released without charge. He was probably not the only solicitor in legal history to be arrested in court but Sutton Coldfield had seen nothing quite like it and Gerald's unscheduled adventure became the talk of the town, causing much mirth among his legal brethren.

Somewhat piqued by the affair, Gerald wrote to Ronald Hadfield, Chief Constable of the West Midlands force, requesting an apology. When the letter remained unanswered he appointed his own solicitor to press for further action: 'It's absolutely outrageous,' said Steven Jonas. 'The whole thing stinks of a police state. It suggests a police officer is unable to distinguish between the hooligan and a solicitor in court. It has caused my client considerable embarrassment.'

The twentieth of December 1990 is a day Gerald Davies would certainly wish to forget but, being conscious of my responsibilities in the field of legal strangeology, I fear I am obliged to report the matter.

I do so, however, with the utmost concern for the feelings of the unfortunate Davies, to whom I offer my sincere apologies for resurrecting his very public 'bad day at the office' so long after it had been forgotten.

AN UNEXPECTED STRETCH

THE OLD BAILEY, LONDON, 1992

Wilfred and Peggy Harte lived a quiet enough life at their maisonette in Walworth, southeast London. With Tweek the budgie they made a cosy threesome, but then Peggy's relatives came calling.

That was Wilf's first bit of bad luck and he was soon to find that he was in for a stretch of it. It was a run of ill-fortune that led the 61-year-old straight to the Old Bailey.

When four of the in-laws arrived for a three-day visit he took a deep breath and determined to smile his way through. When they decided to stay for an extra day his spirits sagged. When that stretched to another day he got a bit twitchy and longed to hear those four little words that all the best-loved relatives time to perfection.

Alas, Peggy's tribe mastered 'What's on the telly?' with ease but seemed to encounter untold difficulty with the much more resonant 'We'll get our coats.' By the time the three days had stretched to three weeks Wilf wondered whether the unwanted guests would ever leave. His wife, though, was loving the company and when three weeks became three months Wilf was near the end of his tether.

At his trial at the Old Bailey in November 1992 he relived the torment for the benefit of the jury: 'I felt they'd taken over my life,' he said. 'They watched television until five in the morning. My electric bill doubled and I paid the rent, poll tax and all the other bills on top. I got the idea they were permanently settled so I decided to do something drastic.'

Wilf's version of drastic was five gallons of petrol poured on the floors while the aliens slept. After he had first made sure that Tweek the budgie was safe, a single match did the rest.

The court heard that it was amazing good fortune that nobody was seriously hurt. Wilf's arrest had swiftly followed and he told police, 'It was a good blaze. I feel euphoric.'

He had little choice but to admit the charge of reckless arson and was inevitably found guilty. No doubt Wilf felt he'd already served a three-month sentence but more was to come as he was jailed for three and a half years.

When asked if he had anything to say his response went unrecorded – but it probably wasn't 'Will I be allowed visitors?'

A KNIFE-AND-FORK JOB

LINCOLN CROWN COURT, 1992

When Allison Johnson arrived at Lincoln Crown Court on 24 August 1992 accused of aggravated burglary, it wasn't his first time. In fact the 47-year-old had already spent a total of 24 years in jail, so getting off this time round didn't look likely.

True to form he was found guilty of breaking into two homes and threatening the residents with a knife. He was promptly sentenced to four years. Yet it wasn't because of his choice of weapon that Johnson was known as 'the cutlery man', for during the trial the open-mouthed court heard evidence of his unique brand of stealing silverware.

The prosecution were at pains to point out that the accused had stolen knives, forks and spoons at countless restaurants – by swallowing them! The loot was invariably washed down with liberal quantities of something strong. He favoured beer over Brasso.

This remarkably strange habit had landed Johnson in the operating theatre even more times than he'd been sent down. At the last count he'd been under the knife no fewer than thirty times to remove pieces of cutlery from his stomach.

Adrian Robinson, for the defence, sought the sympathy vote: 'My client still has eight forks lodged in his stomach and has only been given a year to live,' he said. 'The cutlery-swallowing-and-alcohol habit comes from his lack of self-esteem.'

The jury were evidently neither moved nor amused as they

duly pronounced him guilty. But at least one report of the trial saw the humorous side of this rather tragic case: 'As Johnson was led away he was clearly rattled.'

THE ACCUSED IS FREE TO CROW

BIDEFORD, 1992

Such was the high feeling surrounding a case heard at Bideford, Devon, on 11 May 1992, that almost an entire community turned up in court to back the accused.

The idyllic little village of Stoke only had 27 houses, yet 54 of its residents hired a coach to descend on Bideford to cheer on their local favourite. That unprecedented ratio of support was all the more remarkable for the fact that the dastardly villain of the piece was a cockerel named Corky.

This unusual town-versus-country battle started in November 1991 when a 'townie', John Ritchings, moved to the village and complained about Corky's early-morning crowing. Much to the irritation of the long-standing locals, he successfully obtained a noise-abatement order from Torridge District Council and poor old Corky was forced to move from the cosy home he shared with fourteen hens to a life of solitary confinement in a distant converted conservatory.

Corky's owner, Margery Johns, was outraged. Nor was Corky overly impressed. The village was duly mobilised and an appeal launched. The Sunday before the case came to court even the vicar pleaded clemency for Corky as he addressed the issue in his sermon.

Jeremy Ferguson for Mrs Johns was brief and to the point: 'This is a case of town versus country, pure and simple, and we say Corky is simply doing his natural duty. You shouldn't complain about country noises in the country.'

271

Mr Ritchings, cast in the guise of Public Enemy Number One, was eloquent in his assertion that Corky woke him up far too early and, as a consequence, had caused him to suffer ever-mounting nervous tension.

But Corky knew all about mounting tension too, and Mrs Johns spoke passionately in her cockerel's favour. So passionately that the drama proved all too much for her – she suffered a fainting fit after giving evidence.

Corky himself did not appear but waited anxiously, now henless for fully six months, back in the village.

He might almost have heard the cheers as the magistrate, David Quance, overturned the abatement order, but Mr Ritchings, clutching a file two inches thick on what had become to him a battle royal, vowed to fight on.

Thus it was that a county court judge in Barnstaple was put on the spot a week later to pass final judgment. There was good news and bad news. The bad news for Corky was that he was confined to his second home from 10 p.m. to 8 a.m. on Monday to Thursday and 10 p.m. to 3 p.m. Friday to Sunday. But the long-awaited good news was that he was free to join his hens during the day.

He was soon reported to be enjoying himself immensely, making up for lost time. John Ritchings may have got his lie-in but Corky, the accused with the best court following of all time, was certainly crowing the louder.

A SYMBOLIC CRIME

CARDIFF COUNTY COURT, 1992

Some respected authorities on the folklore of the legal system have asserted that the real authority of a judge or barrister comes not from his mastery of the law, or his pin-sharp mental faculties and incisive use of language, but from his wig.

Some eminent legal commentators have gone to pains to elucidate the vulnerability of a wigless judge, none more pointedly than Judge H C Leon (1902–76), perhaps better known by his writing pen name Henry Cecil: 'A judge complained that he had to share the same lavatory as the litigants and witnesses,' he wrote in 1970. 'But many people who have seen a judge in court do not recognise him without his wig. And it is highly undesirable, in my view, that the judge standing next to a man in the lavatory should have the opportunity of hearing himself described as a "cock-eyed old so-and-so".'

Over a century before, in 1841, Charles Dickens had one of his characters in *The Old Curiosity Shop* voice a similar opinion from the punter's point of view: 'Would you care a ha'penny for the Lord Chancellor if you know'd him in private and without his wig? Certainly not.'

It seems the case *for* pantomimic fancy dress is clear. Not only does it identify the legal luminaries but it also lends dignity and formality to the grave business of the law itself.

Yet the case *against* is equally strong, for the paraphernalia of court dress isolates litigants from legal professionals, suggests a certain pomposity and imbues the law with mystical qualities beyond the grasp of the common man or woman.

Quite a conundrum, this wig business, which is why rather a stir was caused in 1992 when certain dissident voices within the profession suggested they be cast aside as part of a sweeping modernisation of the legal system. There was even talk of name badges for court officials, not to mention piped music and potted plants in the waiting areas. Where would it all end? 'Would the accused care for a massage before he enters the dock?'

It was all put to the test in November 1992 when a survey conducted by the Criminal Bar Association found that a resounding 72 per cent of its members were in favour of retaining their wigs for crown court cases.

The traditionalists rejoiced, none more so than Judge Hugh Jones, a county court judge since 1988 who took pride in his rather 'distressed' hairpiece. But on 10 November at Cardiff County Court it was Judge Jones who was distressed as the unthinkable happened. *The Times* gravely reported the heinous crime: 'A thief sneaked into the chambers of Judge Hugh Jones and stole his horsehair wig valued at £500, along with its box.'

Court officials were said to be hugely embarrassed by this supremely symbolic theft and a lawyer said, 'To say the judge was displeased is an understatement. A well-used wig shows authority and experience, so it's no good just going out to get a new one.'

Judge Jones was not available for comment and the culprit remained undetected.

This unsavoury but perversely delicious incident did nothing to stem the wig debate as those for and against continued to address the prickly subject from time to time. But as the century came to a close the lower echelons of the legal hierarchy were still sticking to their guns, insisting on donning the horsehair even though the Law Lords, the highest authority in the land, had long since ceased to do so.

Judicial rugs continued to make the news stories, including that under the deliciously intriguing headline RECORDER'S

WIG FOUND IN ELECTRIC KETTLE, but perhaps the last word on the absurdity of the debate should go to one of the wiggy fraternity themselves.

In a letter to *The Times* of 2 February 1999 Lord Millett mused somewhat quizzically: 'English judges are an eccentric lot. When I had a full head of hair I wore a wig. Now I have no hair, I have dispensed with my wig.'

Judge Hugh Jones might have smiled at that. But probably not.

CAUGHT IN THE ACT

GREAT YARMOUTH MAGISTRATES' COURT, 1992

Some of the strangest cases in legal history are fictional, for on the written page or in film liberties can be taken that no court of law could possibly countenance:

> 'Give your evidence,' said the King, 'and don't be nervous, or I'll have you executed on the spot.'

It could surely only happen in Lewis Carroll's *Alice's Adventures in Wonderland* (1865). And would Spike Milligan really have dared to utter in court his delicious 1972 line from *The Last Goon Show of All*: 'Policemen are only numbered in case they get lost'?

Even in *The Law's Strangest Cases* those two would have difficulty passing muster as the authentic article, but in Norfolk on 9 July 1992 the lines of delineation between fact and fiction did become rather blurred. The result was that a habitual burglar serving two years at Norwich jail stood wrongfully accused of committing a crime that even he found too shameful to contemplate.

The prelude to Norman Douglass's unthinkably foul act was the 1989 survey by Norfolk Police that revealed that the costs of transporting remand prisoners from Norwich jail to Great Yarmouth Magistrates' Court were becoming prohibitive:

'The equivalent of twenty-eight police officers are engaged full-time in escort duties each day,' said Inspector Phil Jones from his eerily deserted office. Might it be an idea, posed the powers that be, to introduce a live audio-visual link between the prison and the court? That way the prisoners could 'appear in court' without leaving jail. Inspector Jones had apparently seen the system used to great effect in Dade County, Florida, and in Toronto. Might Inspector Jones also have seen rather too many episodes of *Kojak*, *Ironside* and *Starsky and Hutch*? one wonders.

It was decided to run a four-week pilot scheme and four convicted prisoners at Norwich jail were press-ganged into adopting the roles of criminals. Little rehearsal was needed, although a couple of the prisoners did complain they might become typecast.

First up was Eben Gordon, in his twelfth year of a life sentence, asked to play the role of a juvenile burglar: 'You are Dan Shifty?' the prisoner was asked, showing his best side to the cameras as magistrates, a court clerk and two solicitors back in court in Great Yarmouth got into the swing of things amid all the paraphernalia of a real trial.

Shifty's sentence remains unrecorded although his alter ego Gordon did wish the court to know his feelings: 'Many remand prisoners like to travel from prison to court and back,' he pleaded. 'It's a day out, a break from prison routine.'

Next in the virtual dock was Jack Thumper, accused, you may not be amazed to learn, of serious assault. He was followed by Fred Biggs whose surname strangely belies the fact that he was actually charged with reckless driving. One would have imagined train robbery at the very least, bearing in mind the brilliant ingenuity of the prison scriptwriters. Or even indecent exposure if they'd opted for the 'Carry On' brand of comedic subtlety.

Again the sentences of these two desperadoes remain unrecorded. That just left Norman Douglass, serving two years for burglary. I have no idea what poor Mr Douglass had done to upset the prison authorities but being asked to look straight into the camera in front of all his live-studio-audience colleagues to confirm that he was indeed 'Dick Rumpole, an alcoholic shoplifter' didn't seem altogether fair.

But it wasn't that which really upset the hapless Norman, as he told a reporter from *The Times* sent to review his performance: 'The name and the drink problem didn't really worry me. What I find really embarrassing is the crime. I've been accused of stealing knickers from Marks and Spencer.'

Thus suitably shamed, Dick Rumpole, this depraved monster of the East Anglian under(wear)world, provided an instant answer to all those who seek to bring in stronger sentences or reintroduce the death penalty.

Forget it. Make 'em play charades or walk around the prison corridors dressed as Andy Pandy. A good dose of squirming embarrassment could yet be the solution reformers have spent centuries looking for.

WHEN IS A BEACH NOT A BEACH?

EUROPEAN COURT OF JUSTICE, LUXEMBOURG,
1993

When the European Court of Justice sat in Luxembourg on 15 July 1993 it came to a simple enough verdict: 'Three beaches at Blackpool and the bathing coastline at Southport fall short of EC cleanliness standards.'

As a bald statement it vindicated the action of the European Commission in bringing the case against the British government. But beyond the high-handed bureaucracy lay a long-running saga of raw sewage, paddling grannies, and British 'bangers', which made this one of the more surreal cases in recent history, not least for the strange defence put up by the British government that Blackpool, the British holiday resort with a capital 'B', didn't really have a beach at all!

It was 1987 when European Commission representatives in Brussels first objected to the raw sewage being pumped into the sea off the coast near Blackpool. For good measure they threw in 'dog dirt on the beach' as a double-whammy. At least the case was clear even if the sea wasn't. Blackpool beach fell short of EC standards.

Faced with such a charge the British government might well have denied the accusation but, it had to be admitted, the famous Golden Mile *had* become a little less golden than it used to be. Like it or not, the Euro thumbs-down certainly wasn't good for the tourist trade, so the simple solution would have been a major clean-up operation to meet the standard.

Maybe it was too simple, or perhaps just too expensive, for the British government then appears to have had what can only be described as one of those Laurel-and-Hardy brainwave moments that invariably lead to mayhem. You know the sort of thing:

LAUREL (British government): If we want to meet the EC standard for beaches we could say Blackpool beach wasn't really a beach so in any case we wouldn't have to meet the standard anyway. See?

HARDY (highly paid government lawyer): Just tell me that again.

Five years they had to prepare the case, for the preliminary hearing didn't take place until October 1992. Millions of contented British holidaymakers had continued to enjoy Blackpool's famous sandy-type thing in the meantime.

John Collins, counsel for Whitehall, opened with a stunner: 'Blackpool was not a bathing area prior to 1987. To be a recognised beach under EC law it needs to have over five hundred people in the sea at one time or more than fifteen hundred people per mile congregated on the foreshore. Our survey proves that the coast at Blackpool falls short on both counts and therefore Blackpool does not have a beach.'

Who knows when the survey was done? November, perhaps? By this stunning piece of logic the government further showed that there were only 27 beaches in the whole of Britain. In Scotland and Northern Ireland, moreover, there were none at all.

The counsel for Europe, Xavier Lewis, was not impressed: 'May I ask the court to consider why my grandmother and millions of others have happily bathed at Blackpool since the turn of the century?' he said. Then, sensing that the granny card had struck a chord, he warmed to the theme: 'She would have told you that Blackpool was the first place she ever went to the seaside at the turn of the century and she bathed there many times . . . almost until the end.'

No doubt checking to see if there were any moist eyes, he

then hit the court with the most incontrovertible evidence of all: 'Do you know,' he began earnestly, 'that it is one of the most popular resorts in Europe? Why, there are more than forty-three point five miles of sausage consumed there every summer.'

Faced with the great British banger in such mind-boggling profusion, the entire courtroom was won over. The EC Advocate General, Otto Lenz, swiftly confirmed that Blackpool *did* have a beach and it was no longer fit for a respectable granny to bathe on. Although his decision was not legally binding, it was finally ratified in Luxembourg on 15 July 1993.

As this momentous judgment was delivered at great public expense, the seafront at Blackpool was awash only with carefree holidaymakers having a great time, not giving a stuff about Europe or the British government, making their way, hot dogs in hand, to *the beach*.

ACTING IN SELF-DEFENCE

NEW YORK, UNITED STATES, 1993

It is uncommon, but by no means unheard of, for an accused party to conduct his or her own defence, occasionally with celebrated success. But it is rare indeed for a murder suspect to take on such a daunting challenge, least of all someone accused of multiple killings. But perhaps no one gave Colin Ferguson the statistics, for he was to try, with the oddest of consequences, where most would have feared to tread.

Despite a good middle-class upbringing in Jamaica, Colin Ferguson grew up convinced the world was against him and this paranoid state of mind had been frequently fuelled by disappointment at all stages of his life.

He became convinced he was a victim of white conspiracy and his confused world all began to pile in on him on the evening of Tuesday, 7 December 1993. Sitting in the corner of car number three on the packed 5.33 p.m. commuter train from New York's Penn Station to Hicksville, he looked around at the mostly white well-paid commuters heading for their comfortable Long Island homes and something inside him flipped.

Minutes later he had coldly and calmly unloaded round after round of ammunition from his semi-automatic pistol. In a scene straight out of the worst nightmare movies, he left 25 seriously wounded and six dead. The toll would have been far higher but for three have-a-go heroes who overpowered him.

Even the greatest legal team in the world would have struggled with this one. There were scores of witnesses and

Ferguson confessed on tape to the police. All his defence team could think of was damage limitation, so they pondered a plea of insanity, citing the unusual defence of 'black rage' by which they suggested that the existence of 'white racism' had rendered Ferguson temporarily crazy. Psychiatric experts were called in and it looked odds on that Colin Ferguson would be declared unfit to stand trial.

In the dire circumstances it was a good tactic but not good enough for Ferguson, who, after twice vehemently rejecting a plea of insanity, finally convinced himself that he was innocent after all and promptly sacked his entire legal team. He announced he would now plead not guilty and would conduct his own defence.

It might have been a futile gesture for his sacked defence team to present him with a copy of *Fundamentals of Trial Technique* but it was all they could think of. Ferguson read this and other books in the prison library while awaiting trial; he also watched old episodes of *Perry Mason* – the prospects of an unusual court performance grew greater by the day.

Sure enough, when Ferguson's hour finally came his defence and conduct in court stunned all those present: 'Colin Ferguson is not the Long Island Railroad Killer,' he said. 'All the evidence will show that Colin Ferguson was a well-meaning passenger carrying the gun to a place of safety, but like all passengers he dozed off and the gun was taken from him by a mysterious white man who proceeded to shoot.'

As imaginative defences go, it certainly took the biscuit and Ferguson's constant use of the third person to refer to himself suggested he was mentally distancing himself from all sense of reality. Too many late-night reruns of *Perry Mason* episodes perhaps?

Nor was his procedural sense too clever. First of all he objected to the jury because it contained whites, then he demanded a retrial after Judge Donald Belfi (sensible fellow) refused to allow him to handle the pistol shown to the court as evidence.

It got worse. The reason he was charged on 93 counts, claimed Ferguson, was because the year was 1993: 'It's just a random figure,' he ranted. 'If it had been 1925 it would have been a twenty-five-count indictment.'

He prowled the court using legalesque language and mannerisms picked up from his books and television, and periodically, often at entirely inappropriate moments, he barked 'objection'. At one point he demanded that President Clinton take the stand to give evidence and when the request was refused he began his cross-examination of the prosecution witnesses, including some of the survivors and relatives of the dead.

All that had gone before seemed almost normal by comparison as Ferguson constantly sought to elicit the response that none of the witnesses had ever seen him before. Tears of grief and rage were openly shed as relatives gave evidence and one of the men who had been severely wounded lunged at Ferguson in sheer desperate frustration at his brazen denials.

But Ferguson had even more up his sleeve. He called a secret witness who didn't take the stand but gave a press conference outside the court in which he told stunned reporters that the CIA had implanted a computer chip inside Ferguson's brain, which programmed his behaviour. No doubt he had moon cheese in his sandwiches that day, too.

Ferguson's three-hour closing speech was a shambolic, incoherent outrage during which many of the witnesses stormed out in protest. Anybody and everybody was accused of victimising that cruelly wronged innocent man, Colin Ferguson.

The jury prepared to give their verdict. I would ask you to remember, before hearing it, that this is the world of *The Law's Strangest Cases*. But not *that* strange. Colin Ferguson was, of course, found guilty (what did you really expect?) and sentenced by Judge Belfi to a cumulative term of over three hundred years in prison.

Even then, Colin Ferguson, the man who had conducted the worst defence of all time, wasn't quite finished. In a last perverse act he reappointed his sacked lawyers and asked them to prepare an appeal on the grounds that he had never been mentally fit to stand trial.

Now haven't we been there before?

DAVID V. GOLIATH

BOLTON, 1997

Parallels between the worlds of sport and the law, where there are two directly opposed sides but only one ultimate winner, are legion.

And just as in football, where there is always the possibility that the might of Manchester United could meet a lower-league minnow in the cup, the legal world once in a while throws up its own unlikely David-versus-Goliath clashes, which hit the headlines. But the law goes a step further than even football in some cases. It seems unlikely that a team of international renown could ever meet a set of local lads from Bolton, but that was exactly what happened when Swedish car giants Saab decided to flex their muscles against a manufacturer of Indian condiments in one of the oddest legal challenges of all time.

How could the House of Raja Indian food company, diligently peddling their exotic wares in the Lancashire heartlands, home to tripe, pigs' trotters and meat pies to die for, possibly anticipate getting a snotty letter from the Saab car company's legal department?

Only the ultra-sensitive Saab executives know the answer to that one, for it seems the supercool Swedes got themselves unduly worked up when, in 1995, Sital Raja decided to name her new range of flavoursome spices and chutneys 'Memsaab'.

It was, of course, nothing but a more easily pronounceable and less clumsy variation of the word 'memsahib', an Indian

285

term of respect for a European married woman.

There was no earthly reason why she should want to name her pickles after a car – both might well be products of the highest quality coming in a variety of colours and arguably sharing a go-faster effect, but there the link surely ended.

Yet this did not appeal to the Swedish sense of humour: 'People will get confused,' they said. 'They will think it is part of our range. The company is taking advantage and exploiting our name.'

Not surprisingly, House of Raja disagreed with that ridiculous accusation but Saab pressed ahead with litigation: CAR FIRM IN A PICKLE OVER SPICE NAME headlined *The Times* on 2 April 1997, but it wasn't the result of an April Fools' Day press release.

Only after a two-year battle in which House of Raja spent £12,000 in legal fees pointing out the obvious differences between cars and pickles amid considerable tongue-in-cheek press coverage did Saab begin to think better of their action. SAAB BACKS OFF finally announced *The Times* in December 1997, as the car company wrote to House of Raja withdrawing their objection after the Trade Marks Registry ruled in the food firm's favour.

Saab's reluctant climbdown must certainly have come as a great relief to others who feared their products might be the subject of a vehicular identity crisis – a dog-food company was said to be highly relieved that their tins of *Rover* could remain on the shelves, while manufacturers of chocolate mini-rolls, understandably fearing law suits from both extremes of the car market, were thought to be celebrating wildly.

In fairness to Saab, they are by no means the only members of the ludicrous litigation league, although most such cases are brought *against* rather than *by* the more powerful party, often as a point of principle.

Typical of that have-a-go spirit was the case of a Norfolk pensioner who embarked on an eight-month legal battle costing him £745 simply because he was convinced his gas bill was 1p too high. Even when British Gas agreed to waive the bill and offered him £10 compensation, Philip Flinders, a retired bus driver, pushed ahead with his court action.

It was an action he lost when a county court judge ruled that British Gas had no case to answer, but Mr Flinders left court expressing satisfaction that 'at least I got an explanation'.

Few abortive actions have exceeded that one in the strangeness stakes, but America, as ever, offers good competition. In 1978 an accountant, Tom Horsley, filed a suit against a waitress, Alyn Chesselet, after she had stood him up on a date: 'I had a one-hundred-mile wasted journey,' moaned Horsley, as he sued his nondate for 'breaking an oral contract to have dinner and see the musical *The Wiz*' and claimed abortive travel expenses totalling the equivalent of £21. Again the action failed as Ms Chesselet told the court, 'He's nuts.'

Such misguided prosecutions look set to contribute to the world of legal oddity for many years to come as long as lawyers are prepared to take the fees, but once in a while even the courts are prepared to use their guile to nip things in the bud.

Full marks on that score go to the Canadian judge who in 1999 dismissed the case of René Joly, a 34-year-old sales manager, who claimed that a bank, the Canadian defence minister and several drugstore chains were all conspiring to kill him because he was a Martian.

Faced with this novel circumstance for the first time in his career, the judge rose magnificently to the occasion, resisting the obvious temptation to deny Mr Joly his Martian citizenship. Instead he merely told him, 'Your case is dismissed because, as a Martian, I'm afraid you have no status in the Canadian courts.'

A COMEDY OF ERRORS

LEWES CROWN COURT, 1998

No aspect of the law ought really to be a laughing matter, but the records show time and again that many court cases have a humorous side. All too often, however, that moment is a fleeting one and a swift reminder from the judge that 'this is no place for levity' is generally sufficient to restore a suitably sombre atmosphere in which the serious business of the courts can proceed.

Thank goodness, then, for the historic first at Lewes Crown Court on 4 September 1998, when a judge decided to halt a trial and declare the prisoner innocent because the entire court, including the police prosecution, was helpless with laughter.

Impersonating a police officer is a potentially serious crime. When the offence is coupled with damaging and stealing police property it's even worse. Breaking in to do the deed doesn't help the cause, and when the entire act is perpetrated at a police station itself, then it has to be said that the prospects for the offender don't look good.

But that was precisely the scenario facing 29-year-old Simon Davey after a night out that took a surprising turn.

The jury looked on with suitably intense concentration as Davey's story began. He had been to the Eastbourne Darts Open and, as darts spectators are wont to do, had got into the spirit of things with a spot of drinking: 'eight or ten pints', according to his evidence.

Having sensibly decided to have a taxi home, he realised halfway through the journey that he hadn't got any money to pay the fare. After alerting the driver to the impecunious state of his affairs, he was understandably turfed out without due ceremony.

It was probably the fresh air that then caused the effects of the beer to kick in. It seems that a well-meaning but equally half-baked logic and sense of fair play began to drive Davey's brain cells. What he obviously needed to do, he told himself, was report himself to the police so that they wouldn't pursue him for his terrible crime when the taxi driver spilt the beans.

In consequence of that honourable train of thought he dutifully made his way to Hailsham Police Station, East Sussex, in the dead of night to make his confession, but on his arrival there the station was locked and there was no one around. Again the solution was obvious – he would break in and leave his confession on an answering machine.

Now it has to be said at this stage that Simon Davey had a nice turn of phrase and a jaunty laddishness in his demeanour that made him rather a likeable soul, and if he'd been a professional comedian his catchphrase would certainly have been 'It's the way I tell 'em.'

Members of the jury began to smirk. They knew they shouldn't but they did and, rather like the taboo of getting the giggles in church, this only made matters worse. Shoulders began to move up and down, noses were blown, eye contact was avoided and cheeks were sucked in as Davey's yarn proceeded.

After he had climbed into the deserted station through a toilet window, they heard, his noble effort to leave a message failed dismally when he broke the machine. It was then that he saw the inspector's hat and sergeant's jacket hanging on a peg. Overcome by a sense of indignation that there was no one on the enquiry desk he donned the uniform and remedied the situation by manning the front office himself. 'And why did you do that?' asked the prosecution: 'Just in case there was another idiot like me that night. Someone needed to be on duty,' was the matter-of-fact reply. For good measure he went on to describe how he had then started filling out a statement form which he had found in a desk.

Bottoms shuffled uneasily in the jury box. Lips began to twitch uncontrollably. At least one handkerchief was now stuffed permanently into its owner's mouth and several jurors appeared to be in severe danger of wetting themselves as the story progressed.

When a passing special constable knocked on the door of the station in the early hours he was let in by Davey who, anxious to appear as authentic a policeman as possible, rocked back on his heels, flexed his knees and greeted the visitor with a cheery 'Evenin', all.'

The masquerade was unlikely to fool even a bobby of the hobby variety and reinforcements soon arrived. It was then that the taped interview was made, and Davey's explanation while he was still under the influence of eight to ten pints (did he spill the ninth or what?) was always going to make for interesting listening.

It was when the police prosecution insisted on playing the tape in court that all the laughter-stifling techniques of the jury and court officials finally gave way. As the court heard the hilarious story of Davey's night out 'as it happened' the corpsing of the jury began in earnest, quickly spreading to the lawyers and even the police officers present.

For the first time in its illustrious history *The Times* was moved to report: 'Judge Richard Brown had to stifle a chuckle as jurors wiped away tears.' It was then that Judge Richard Brown attained the state of mind that few judges before or since have managed to emulate – he saw the funny side. Ordering the tape to be stopped with Davey still in mid-babble he consulted lawyers for the defence and prosecution and duly directed the jury to deliver a verdict of not guilty.

They say laughter is the best medicine and it was certainly a tonic for Simon Davey as he walked free from court bound over to keep the peace for two years.

One man who would certainly have appreciated that uplifting end was a solicitor's clerk, Stephen Balogh, because his own attempts to lighten up court proceedings in 1974 ended in a jail sentence. When caught lurking on the roof of St Albans Crown Court he explained to police that he intended to release laughing gas into the ventilation system 'to liven up long-winded and boring court proceedings'.

That he failed in his mission was evidenced by the stern face of Mr Justice Melford Stevenson as he gave him six months. Nor was Balogh amused – as he left the mirth-free zone of Stevenson's court he shouted, 'You are a humourless automaton.'

SILENCE IN COURT

WINCHESTER CROWN COURT, 1999

JUDGE DELAYS TRIAL IN FAVOUR OF COURT, said *The Times*'s headline of 29 June 1999. That curious eye-catcher was echoed in every domestic newspaper in some form or another on the same day. The tabloids, in particular, had great fun at the expense of Judge Patrick Hooton, the unfortunate gentleman concerned. But he'd have been perfectly all right if only he'd kept his mouth shut.

The trial of David Hunter, from Basildon, Essex, charged with indecent assault, was estimated to last four days. It was routine fare for 47-year-old Judge Hooton, called to the Bar in 1973 and a circuit judge since 1994. Nothing suggested the trial would become front-page news.

Proceedings were due to commence at Winchester Crown Court at midday on Monday, 28 June, but, as a start was made, the prosecution and defence told the judge that they'd probably need five or six days to see the trial through.

Judge Hooton's heart sank, for he knew he had a prior engagement on the Friday and was then off on holiday for four weeks after that. Being a diligent sort of fellow keen to see that the course of justice was properly run, he was concerned that the case might have to be rushed, so he made up his mind to ask the parties for an adjournment there and then. That was by no means a strange occurrence. It happens all the time.

He duly addressed the assembled lawyers: 'Unless I can send the jury out first thing on Thursday morning I can't start this trial. It would not be right to make everyone feel they have got to rush it.'

Lawyers acting on the case saw no problem and the trial was put back for six months until December. If only Judge Hooton had left it there – but no, he'd pulled off something of a coup that year and just couldn't contain himself. He had to tell someone his wonderful news. Thus he proceeded:

'Some months ago I arranged to take this Friday off. I won't be doing anything this Friday apart from sitting at Wimbledon watching the tennis. Normally I would take the time for this case out of my holiday. Everybody knows my devotion to my duty but it's the tickets to Wimbledon, you see. I'm never likely to get them again.'

Robert Conway, agreeing to the adjournment for the defence, understood completely: 'Wimbledon is on my doorstep,' he lamented ruefully, 'but I can't get tickets.' Judge Hooton replied with a smile: 'They are only given to the deserving.'

With that pleasant exchange the affair should have ended but the local press were present and made the most of their scoop. Soon the story of the judge who put the prospect of a men's semifinal before a case of indecent assault was national news: JUDGE POSTPONES ASSAULT TRIAL TO WATCH WIMBLEDON, bawled the *Guardian*.

Either you'll feel sorry for Judge Hooton or you won't. So often seen as aloof, placed on a pedestal of their own making, judges are, after all, human. Why shouldn't they enjoy themselves? But they are also well paid and have a responsibility to society. Shouldn't Patrick Hooton have missed the tennis for the sake of justice?

The camps will inevitably remain split, but what is certain is that Judge Hooton wasn't the first to let his passion for sport creep into courtroom proceedings. At the end of the nineteenth century there was always silence in court on at least one day a year when Mr Justice Hawkins was presiding. He routinely closed his court on Derby Day and that was that, even if the press did lambast him for it.

And during an important criminal trial in 1977 Judge Alan King-Hamilton famously interrupted proceedings to tell the jury, 'The Australians are four for one wicket.'

Cricket made an even more bizarre unscheduled appearance at a tax fraud trial in 1986. On that occasion Judge Michael Argyle opted to shoot himself in both feet by solemnly telling the jury that the lack of Test Match cricket on television was 'enough to make an Orthodox Jew want to join the Nazi party'.

Eloquent and learned as they can be, perhaps all judges should know the predatory nature of the press well enough to take a leaf from the book of Mr Justice Cassels, one of the twentieth century's most characterful judges. As an aid to making his court a personal gaffe-free zone he invariably placed a large notice in front of himself on the bench, stating in capital letters: KEEP YOUR TRAP SHUT.

WWW.SENDHIMDOWN.CO.UK

SOUTHWARK CROWN COURT, 1999

Wouldn't it be every television drama writer's dream to create a hybrid of *Crown Court* and *A & E*? 'The compelling series in which British law meets hospital gore' – surely it couldn't fail.

Well, all is not lost, and it's thanks to cutting-edge technology and the determination of a resourceful lady judge that *Emergency Court 10* (working title only) could yet go into production. The climax to an extraordinary case came on 30 July 1999, when Judge Valerie Pearlman (62), made legal history by using Internet technology to conclude a six-month fraud trial from her hospital bed.

When Gian Lombardi, his wife Veronica and colleague Gianfranco Udovivich first appeared at Southwark Crown Court charged with deceiving international clients with the offer of cheap finance, Judge Pearlman was in fine fettle. Even when she broke her leg partway through the trial she presided from the bench with little ado, but when complications set in she required urgent treatment at St Bartholomew's Hospital in the City.

Conscious of the huge expense and inconvenience that the likelihood of a retrial looked like causing, Judge Pearlman pulled all the stops out to continue. Early in July, with the trial at an advanced stage, she sought the approval of the Lord Chancellor's Department for a novel remedy.

As Their Lordships gave the nod, surprised jurors, lawyers

and the defendants were given just an hour's notice to decamp from Southwark to the oak-panelled Great Hall at Bart's Hospital. There the jury listened intently as Judge Pearlman spent two days summing up the evidence from the unlikely throne of an NHS wheelchair.

When she had finished, the jury returned to Southwark to spend nearly three weeks considering the case, but neither Judge Pearlman's ordeal nor her ingenuity was at an end.

She was transferred to a hospital near Worthing, West Sussex, for an operation on the troublesome limb. It was from her hospital bed there that she chalked up a legal first by creating a virtual-reality courtroom, using a two-way Internet video link to follow the progress of the trial sixty miles away as Judge George Bathurst Newman kept an eye on things at the Southwark end. Jury questions were sent on-line and the entire court saw Judge Pearlman, without wig and gown, sitting on the end of her bed giving rulings on the issues raised.

By the time the jury found the three defendants guilty of conspiracy to defraud, Judge Pearlman was being credited with saving the taxpayer more than £2.5 million in retrial costs.

It was a judicial triumph indeed, but by no means the first time that justice had been dispensed out of court. In the first half of the nineteenth century the Lord Chancellor, Lord Lyndhurst, once issued a decision while sitting in a theatre box at the opera, and in the 1890s *The Law Times* reported: 'Baron Huddleston, being confined to his bed in Lewes by an attack of gout, charged the grand jury from that comfortable position.'

Early in the twentieth century, too, Sir Samuel Evans, highly respected president of the Probate, Divorce and Admiralty Division, delivered a verdict from his bedroom nattily attired in his nightwear – a dressing down in a dressing gown, perhaps, but no video-conferencing facilities to capture the magic moment.

As for that television drama idea, potential scriptwriters might be heartened by a case from 1996 that could see the medical action switched back to court with elements of *The Bill* thrown in for good measure.

A former police officer accused of growing cannabis spent

his trial on a bed in the courtroom because of his bad back (now there's a rarity). There's surely a humorous episode to be made from that one.

The *South London Press* certainly entered into the right spirit – although the officer was acquitted they couldn't resist the headline from heaven: EX-COPPER LIES IN COURT.

HEARTILY SICK OF THE LAW

EXETER CROWN COURT, 1999

Few civilians would ever really relish the prospect of appearing in court but the prize for the most reluctant of all time must go to a fraudster named Paul Purvis. His repeated failure to attend for trial caused a judge to set arguably the most unusual bail condition in legal history.

Paul Purvis obviously had many fine qualities. When he was appointed chief executive of North Devon District Council in 1975 he was only 32, the youngest chief executive in the country. Evidently a high flier and a young man who would know how to balance the books.

But it subsequently came to light that the only book balance Purvis was really interested in was the one in his own building society account. Amid sundry allegations he was forced to resign after just two years in the job.

In common with many fraudsters, Purvis didn't know when to stop. From his home in Clayhidon, near Honiton, Devon, he planned a number of scams and eventually graduated to mortgage fraud, obtaining a loan of £70,000, despite being an undischarged bankrupt, for a second home in Hayle, Cornwall, under the false name of Paul Warren.

As both Purvis and Warren he also made a series of false insurance claims and thereby lay his undoing. He was unlucky enough to have the same loss adjuster visiting his homes in both Devon and Cornwall and the watchful insurance man, ever alert to strange goings-on, recognised the claimants as one and the same man.

When police investigated they discovered a string of other frauds under the name of Paul Warren. Purvis's explanation was that Warren did exist but was 'a British spy who had had to disappear for reasons of national security'. Strange that he generally appeared for reasons of Purvis's security, sometimes of the social kind.

It was classic 'dreamworld' fabrication. The game was up for Purvis and his trial was set for a date in 1997.

It was at that point that the defendant developed his curious distaste for courtroom interiors, an aversion that was to secure him the title as the country's greatest serial trial-absentee. He didn't attend for his first date, so the trial was promptly cancelled. Purvis, it seemed, had developed a heart condition. He was, he said, 'too ill to stand trial'.

He was still too ill on the second date, and the third, and the thirtieth. His courtroom aversion, though, oddly seemed to apply only when he faced being in the dock himself, for at other times Purvis was well on the way to becoming Britain's most prolific serial litigant. Over a hundred times in twenty years he'd brought civil actions against neighbours, business colleagues and even members of his own family, another tidy little contributor to the Purvis coffers. Those trips to court also affected his heart, but in a gladdening 'I love other people's money' sort of way.

This double standarding somewhat tried the patience of Judge William Taylor, who in 1999 set the oddest bail condition of all time by ordering Purvis to have triple-bypass heart surgery.

Yet, despite the claimed severity of his condition, the master of double-speak quickly added hospitals to his list of institutional phobias. He successfully challenged the ruling and announced he would not be having the surgery because he had 'lost confidence in the surgeon'.

Again, this somewhat racked off the legal powers that be and they resolved to try Purvis once and for all. The trial was duly fixed for the last week of September 1999 at Exeter Crown Court, but with a sense of timing both canny and uncanny Purvis admitted himself to hospital with yet another cardiac flutter.

Judge John Baker was ready for this latest absence, though, and, after asking a cardiologist for a report, he ordered that when Purvis was discharged from hospital he should be immediately arrested and taken straight to court.

In the event, the hospital never did discharge Purvis. Instead he discharged himself and promptly vanished into thin air. As the court found him guilty of mortgage and insurance fraud and Judge Baker passed sentence of three years' imprisonment, police were already hunting the 56-year-old whose heart condition had cost the taxpayer an estimated £100,000 in abortive court time.

While Purvis is undoubtedly the champion when it comes to throwing a legal sickie, a number of other incidents have hit the headlines from time to time.

The year following Purvis's trial a man who claimed he had become a nervous wreck after being assaulted by a police officer was awarded £7,750 damages after he told Nottingham County Court that the ordeal had affected him so badly that 'when I switch on *The Bill* on telly it brings it all back'.

And the year before the Purvis saga a judge at Bristol Crown Court decided that he, the lawyers, clerks and ushers should remove their wigs, gowns and other formal legal paraphernalia as the defendant had 'a phobia about uniforms'.

It goes without saying that our American friends have been somewhat ahead of the game in the rich field of health matters where the sickness phenomenon has extended beyond defendants. At the hugely serious 1993 New York trial of Shaikh Omar Abdel-Rahman, accused of bombing the World Trade Center, a potential juror was excused from service after he explained the mere sight of the Manhattan courthouse always made him feel unwell. In a line that would grace the best of Woody Allen's films the man explained: 'I get the runs, I get a bad headache, I get pains in my chest. I feel terrible.'

And finally, as they say, by way of balance, it ought to be noted that sometimes it's the legal fraternity themselves who don't quite make it.

A hearing at Guildford Crown Court in 1997 looked set to run and run when an afternoon's proceedings had to be stopped after both the prosecution and defence counsel fell ill after eating a lunchtime curry in the court canteen.

At least that one sounds uncontrollable, but I do have my suspicions about the good solicitors of Nottingham who evidently enjoyed Christmas 1972 in the time-honoured fashion. On 29 December 52 cases at Nottingham Magistrates' court had to be adjourned – the defendants were there but 'sickness among the prosecuting solicitors' caused the cancellations. Rather like Paul Purvis, they were obviously heartily sick of the legal treadmill.

TRUST ME, I'M A DOCTOR

PRESTON CROWN COURT, 1999

It isn't everybody who gets into *The Law's Strangest Cases*. Some of the most evil and sensational murderers in history failed to get beyond the first selection stage simply because murder in itself just isn't an unusual enough occurrence to qualify as of right.

So Jack the Ripper (1888) failed to make the cut, as did the Boston Strangler (1964), the Black Panther (1976) and the bodies-in-the-drains murderer Dennis Nilsen (1983). The chillingly cool schoolgirl killer Mary Flora Bell (1968) also missed out, as did the two juvenile killers of two-year-old Jamie Bulger, whose inconceivable act of cruelty caused such outrage in 1993 and beyond. Even the Moors Murderers Myra Hindley and Ian Brady, given life sentences at Chester Assizes in 1966, scored insufficient points on the 'strangeometer' and they were joined by the Yorkshire Ripper Peter Sutcliffe (1981), the 25 Cromwell Street fiends Rose and Fred West (1994), and sundry other celebrity killers from several centuries of material.

That such a gruesome bunch should be upstaged by a mild-mannered 54-year-old bespectacled doctor from the quiet town of Hyde in Cheshire might seem unlikely. But then there was a fair bit that was unlikely about Dr Harold Shipman, whose calculated dispatch of his patients to the other world gives him the title of Britain's worst ever serial killer.

Yet Shipman's catalogue of death might never have been

uncovered but for the watchful tenacity of solicitor Angela Woodruff. When her 81-year-old mother, Kathleen Grundy, died in June 1998 Mrs Woodruff was naturally surprised to find that the bulk of her mother's substantial estate had been left to Harold Shipman, the doctor who had cared for her so ably and been there for her even at the moment of death. It was Mrs Woodruff's own detective work that exposed the will as a forgery, and it was her instinctive feeling that something more was amiss that then led her to persuade police to exhume her mother's body.

When they discovered it contained a lethal dose of morphine, suspicion fell instantly, but incredulously, on Shipman. But when police showed that it was certainly the good doctor who had forged the will, the case against him mounted and they began to investigate other deaths among his patients.

What they discovered horrified the residents of Hyde, for it became apparent that Shipman, under the guise of showing the utmost professional concern, had taken to visiting his women patients in their homes. There, in a firm but gentle tone that his ailing ladies heard as 'Trust me, I'm a doctor', Shipman would suggest an injection to relieve their symptoms. And relieve them it did, for there they would die of the lethal morphine dose as Shipman informed the relatives that he had done 'everything possible' to preserve their lives.

As the case received huge media coverage, more and more relatives came forward to police expressing retrospective concern over the circumstances in which their loved ones had died. Soon the confirmed tally of suspicious deaths had reached the horrifying count of fifteen and Shipman was eventually tried on that indictment at Preston Crown Court in October 1999.

But fifteen proved merely to be a fraction of the true count as more and more bodies were exhumed and coroners found lethal doses of morphine time and again. By the time the trial began, experts suggested that over a hundred deaths might be laid at Shipman's door, spanning his entire medical career.

Such revelations undoubtedly didn't help his cause, but during the 57-day trial Shipman stared impassively in court and protested his innocence throughout. His wife Primrose, married to him for 33 years and mother of their four children, was present in court every day to support her beloved husband.

When the trial closed, the jury deliberated for 34 hours and the foreman took six minutes to deliver the verdict. Dr Harold Shipman, the man with the worst bedside manner in history, was duly found unanimously guilty of murdering fifteen women between the ages of 49 and 81. On Wednesday, 2 February 2000, he was convicted and given fifteen terms of life imprisonment.

Mr Justice Forbes articulated the horror of a nation as he passed sentence: 'I have little doubt each of your victims smiled and thanked you as she submitted to your deadly administrations. None of these ladies realised that yours was not a healing touch.'

The South Manchester Coroner, meanwhile, compounded that horror by confirming that Shipman's likely tally had reached 265 and suggesting that 'the final figure might prove to be as high as a thousand'. The true figure will never be fully ascertained but Harold Shipman proved to a Britain entering the enlightened 21st century that deeds more suited to the most far-fetched Victorian melodrama can still be perpetrated in our very midst.

Could anyone possibly dispute that the man they called 'Doctor Death' and 'The Dr Jekyll of Hyde' deserves his place in *The Law's Strangest Cases*? It is unlikely Britain will ever see his like again – but then that has been said before.

THE SCALES OF JUSTICE

SUNDERLAND MAGISTRATES' COURT, 2000

The connection between the philosophical concept of 'Justice' and the physical act of 'weighing' is as old as civilisation itself. In ancient Egyptian mythology the god Osiris presided in the Hall of Two Truths, where the souls of the dead were weighed in the balance against a feather of truth, which symbolised the just treatment of one's fellow men – those wretched souls who failed the balance test were devoured forthwith by a fearsome monster.

It is the same principle that lies behind the world-famous statue of the goddess Justitia, which stands on the summit of the Old Bailey, holding in her left hand the scales of justice and in her right the double-edged sword to punish the guilty.

All of which symbolic talk is particularly pertinent to the case that follows because many things were weighed in the balance along the way. *Thoburn v. Sunderland City Council* was dubbed variously as Britain v. Europe, David v. Goliath and Common Sense v. Gobbledegook – it earned a 36-year-old greengrocer, Steve Thoburn, the tag of 'Metric Martyr' and put his picture in all the leading newspapers. Steve Thoburn had handled many cases of bananas in his life but never one quite like this.

The date of 1 January 2000 may have been heralded as the start of a new millennium but it was the start of an altogether new era for Britain's greengrocers as a European directive decreed that they must sell all their loose produce using either

305

solely metric scales or ones that had both metric and imperial measures. Such a directive from the European Economic Community was a not entirely unexpected consequence of Britain's willingly joining the Common Market in 1972 and it was issued as a phased control pending full metrication in 2009.

Suffice to say, though, that the person in the street was by and large not impressed and many of the nation's greengrocers ignored the directive and happily continued to weigh and sell a pound of whatever they fancied – it was, they insisted, what their customers preferred.

It was only a matter of time before someone took this weighty issue entirely at face value and in July 2000 it was the trading standards officers of Sunderland City Council who decided to prosecute in what was destined to become a test case of national interest.

Steve Thoburn was the hapless victim as Lynda Hodgson, undercover trading standards officer, went to his shop and bought a bunch of bananas for 34 pence. They were priced at 25 pence a pound and Mr Thoburn weighed them in pounds and ounces on scales not delineated in metric.

Steve Thoburn was duly prosecuted under the Weights and Measures Act 1985, an action that immediately sparked off a silly season for quotes and punny headlines: Vivian Linacre of the British Weights and Measures Society suggested that 'maybe the Brussels bureaucrats would like to change my name to Vivian Linhectare' while fishmonger Neil Herron threw his support firmly behind his greengrocer chum with the splendid 'If Prime Minister Blair's baby Leo can weigh in at six pounds, twelve ounces, then it's good enough for a haddock.' Others asked why the McDonald's burger chain were allowed to sell their famous Quarter Pounders and daftness surely reached new heights when a pensioner, Ernest Riley, phoned his local radio station trying to start a campaign to rid Brussels sprouts of the evil 'B' word: 'They look like small cabbages,' he said, 'so we ought to call them 'mini-cabs'. Sorry, Ernest, next caller, please.

By the time the preliminary hearing was due to start at

Sunderland Magistrates' Court on 15 January 2001 Steve Thoburn had already been dubbed the 'Metric Martyr' and huge numbers of Britain's Euro-sceptics, Ernest included, prepared for battle.

A fine of up to £2,000 or a jail sentence if he refused to pay lay in wait for Steve Thoburn, but it was the principle of British Law v. European Law that became the much bigger issue. With so much at stake a decision was delayed until Monday, 9 April 2001, when the eyes of a nation again turned to Sunderland Magistrates' Court as District Judge Bruce Morgan announced the long-awaited verdict:

'This case revolves around possibly the most famous bunch of bananas in legal history,' he told a packed court. His mystifying use of the word 'possibly' seemed a mite super-fluous as he continued by finding the 'Metric Martyr' guilty and ordering for his illegal scales to be destroyed.

At a stroke a judge in an English court of law had overtly confirmed that European Union directives must take prece-dence over the laws of the British Parliament!

Steve Thoburn escaped with a conditional discharge but he was still accorded hero status by much of the British press for his stand. The *Daily Mail* headline screamed THE DAY SELLING A POUND OF BANANAS BECAME A CRIME LIKE BURGLARY OR RAPE, while trading standards officers all over Britain prepared to pay their 'friendly local greengrocer' a surprise visit.

Where will it all end? ask the sceptics. In an inevitable victory for Europe, of course.

As we go to press, Steve Thoburn is still contemplating an appeal but if he really wants to make a point might I suggest he employ a steeplejack to scale the Old Bailey and place a giant bunch of bananas in Justitia's scales complete with '25p a lb' price tag and a notice on her thrusting sword saying UP THE EUROPEAN UNION.

It might not kill the kilo but what more fruitful way of marking the day the law went bananas?

THE BIRTHDAY SUIT LAWSUIT

SOUTHWARK CROWN COURT, 2001

Vincent Bethell was a man with a mission. Maybe, as a native of Coventry, he was inspired by Lady Godiva, or perhaps he was just an exhibitionist, for Vincent Bethell's mission was to fight for the absolute right to appear naked in public.

Now we're not talking a quick streak across a rugby field or a spot of discreet naturism among the sand dunes. This was the full monty. Any time, any place, anywhere. Quite what possessed Vincent to campaign to show his private parts in the most public of places, no one really knows, but show them he did.

After several years of baring all in high streets and even up lampposts around the country, he started to get really serious in the summer of 2000. And if it was media attention he was after he certainly chose the right place on 15 July. What better spot to cavort in the altogether than outside New Scotland Yard? The press and television loved it. The police weren't so keen and Vincent was duly arrested, warned and released on bail.

But two weeks later he was at it again, this time in St Augustine's Parade in Bristol. Next stop, appropriately, was Exhibition Road in London's Kensington, quickly followed by Euston Station, the Strand and Covent Garden.

'It's bare-faced cheek,' cried the puritans. 'But you can't deny he's got balls,' countered the liberals. 'Then string 'im up by 'em,' ranted the latter-day followers of 'Disgusted of Tunbridge Wells'. It was all a vexing question.

308

As the tawdrier television chat shows clamoured to get the 'Naked Campaigner' into their studios, always *au naturel*, the magistrates he kept appearing before for 'causing a public nuisance and offending public decency' became ever more impatient.

After yet another full-frontal attack on society he was finally remanded in custody and spent five months in Brixton Prison. Despite being detained during a bitterly cold winter he refused to wear clothes at Her Majesty's pleasure. Frostbite, known for attacking the extremities, blessedly showed due respect.

His case came to Southwark's Crown Court on 8 January 2001. Many men and women have professed to feelings of 'standing naked before a court of law' as their misdemeanours are recounted but none in history actually did so prior to Vincent Bethell.

The proceedings were unique indeed. For almost a week he sat in court on a cold plastic seat and, each time he was led into and out of the dock, Judge George Bathurst-Norman insisted the court be cleared lest anyone should get an offensive eyeful.

As Bethell prepared to give evidence, though, his counsel Isabella Forshall argued that to clear the court for his short walk to the witness box might prejudice the jury. The judge agreed but advised the jurors: 'I suggest the ladies among you close your eyes or look away.'

One duly checked that she'd put her shoes on the right feet that morning and the other made a close scrutiny of the splendid ceiling. Or at least they feigned to.

Vincent Bethell gave a persuasive performance: 'I was born naked and twenty-eight years later this is just me and my skin as nature intended, being a human being, going about my existence.'

His naked ambition duly won the day as the jury ruled unanimously and historically that he was 'not a public nuisance'. Punching the air in triumph, he shouted, 'Being human is not a crime,' and strode manfully from the court moments later clutching his clothes in two plastic bags and vowing 'to put this precedent to the test and see if it makes any difference'.

He started his new life as a legitimate public nudist with a vengeance by appearing live on breakfast television next morning. While the unflappable interviewer Fiona Phillips looked him straight in the eye during a revealing performance, only a strategically crossed leg saved millions of viewers from choking on their eggs and bacon.

CALL BRENDAN MICHAEL FORRESTER

DERBY MAGISTRATES' COURT, 2001

When Crown Prosecution solicitor Ian Shaw arrived at Derby Magistrates' Court on Tuesday, 6 March 2001, there was one listed case that took him by surprise because Derbyshire Police had not sent him the case file.

That in itself was by no means a unique occurrence and he hoped for a quick briefing to bring him up to press so that the prosecution on behalf of the force could proceed as if nothing untoward had happened.

But what did happen next *was* a unique occurrence, and it left Derbyshire Police and court staff with very eggy faces and Ian Shaw furious that his time had been wasted.

When he looked at the computer-generated list of cases that morning the list of charges against Brendan Michael Forrester astonished him. Perhaps it was no wonder the file was missing, for such would have been its thickness that a special freight delivery would surely have been needed.

The computer records showed that 28-year-old Forrester, of Kingsway Place, Swadlincote, was charged with eleven offences on 4 January – and what reading they made: six motoring offences including death by dangerous driving, two drugs charges, obstructing a police officer, possessing a rocket launcher and living off immoral earnings.

Ian Shaw was taken aback: 'He must be one of Derbyshire's most wanted men,' he commented. 'Looking at this list of charges it's amazing that a person like this would ever have been granted bail.'

As Shaw girded his loins to prosecute as well as he could without full notes he prepared himself for coming face to face with this evident desperado, but when court staff called Brendan Michael Forrester he was nowhere to be found. Several hours passed and still he failed to turn up.

Court officials became concerned. Should a man with his record really be at large? The rocket launcher sounded particularly ominous. Surely he was a danger to the good people of Derbyshire.

By lunchtime Forrester was still missing and Crown Prosecution Service representatives called Derbyshire Police to establish his possible whereabouts.

Did you ever see the magnificently incompetent Will Hay as Sergeant Dudfoot, ably hindered by Albert and Harbottle, in the 1939 film *Ask a Policeman*? It would be difficult to imagine more farcical antics ever being repeated on celluloid, let alone in real life. But maybe they should have made the sequel, *Ask a Derbyshire Policeman*, which would have taken comedy genius to new heights.

Having looked into this most disturbing matter, a police representative telephoned the Magistrates' Court with his findings: 'We have no record of a fatal road accident on 4 January,' he said, 'nor do we have a record of an arrest of Brendan Michael Forrester.'

It got worse: 'He doesn't appear on the electoral register either, and there is no such address as Kingsway Court, Swadlincote.'

Again it got worse: 'What I'm saying to you is that Brendan Michael Forrester doesn't actually exist. Except on the computer. That's why he's on your court list.'

Initial relief at court that such a supposedly dangerous man wasn't actually on the loose soon gave way to embarrassment and anger amid much finger-pointing. 'The police log the cases on to the system,' claimed court officials. 'But not all of them,' countered the force. 'Some of your people do have access.'

Ian Shaw was not amused. Turning up to prosecute phantoms wasn't his line. The deputy justices clerk Margaret Shanahan was left to face the press, already sharpening their pencils gleefully: 'It appears we have a fictional case on our hands,' she explained. 'A full investigation has been launched.'

As Ian Shaw left the court in a furious temper he gave his own take on this curious affair: 'I'll push for someone to get to the bottom of this. It looks very much like a police training exercise that went too far.'

As we go to press Derbyshire Police looked set to get off the hook as a 23-year-old employee of the Magistrates' Court was suspected of creating the mystery criminal during his lunch break and was charged under the Computer Misuse Act 1990. It must have been a great relief to the people of Derbyshire to be assured that their police force were not the buffoons that this unique case at first suggested.

Latest reports from their headquarters confirm that 'the Phantom' is still at large but no threat to the public. Meanwhile, they are considering calling in Sherlock Holmes, Father Brown, Miss Marple and Inspector Morse to get to the bottom of this most baffling affair.

TWENTY-FIRST CENTURY JUSTICE

GUANGZHOU, CHINA, 2001

Legal history is full of barbaric accounts of justice summarily visited on a helpless victim under full view of a watching public. No proper trial, no right of appeal, a death sentence quickly and brutally carried out – those are the staples, retrospectively fascinating and entertaining, of the law as it used to be.

Thank goodness, in our modern and blessedly civilised age, that accounts of such shameful spectacles are nothing more than grim reminders of ignorant and cruel regimes long since banished to the pages of history.

It just wouldn't be considered 'amusing' if these things were happening now. Imagine, for example, if a country that was home to one-fifth of the entire world's population still resorted to practices more akin to the medieval world than our own.

Imagine no more. Take a journey to China.

There are twenty thousand people crammed into the football stadium in the southern city of Guangzhou. It is April 2001. A smartly dressed young woman stands in the middle of the pitch but she is not about to lead the community singing or draw the club's lottery. She is flanked by two smartly uniformed soldiers in pristine white gloves and immaculate collars and ties but they, too, are not part of the half-time entertainment. At least not in the traditional sense.

The woman is a prisoner with her hands tied behind her

back and a rope around her neck which acts as a restraint as the soldiers hold her firmly. She cries out in anguish as she is found guilty of murder and, next in line just a few yards away, a young man is then found guilty of drug trafficking.

Both prisoners are sentenced to death for their own particular crimes, but there are 66 other offences for which the punishment would have been the same – illegal share-dealing, drink-driving and certain types of burglary are among them.

There are no armies of lawyers lodging appeals and no dignified sense of ceremony to the final fatal act. Both prisoners are led straight out of the stadium to a piece of waste ground and shot in the head. On no account must the soldiers make a messy job of their task because it is likely that the bodies will be quickly stripped of their vital organs for use in transplant operations. Ninety per cent of kidney transplants in China involve the use of organs from prisoners and there is no consent procedure.

Such public trials and executions are commonplace in China and considered 'an education' for the people. In fact the Chinese regime executes more people than the rest of the world put together – almost 20,000 in the last decade of the twentieth century.

'Capital punishment is our way of upholding justice,' explains a senior police official to a Western journalist. 'We need it to control social disorder and the people expect it. There would be great public discontent if we stopped it.'

And is it working? When the Communists came to power in 1949 crime was said to be virtually nonexistent in China. But as the country has 'developed' through economic, political and social reform there has been an explosion in offences.

So there is China and Chinese law. Not in the safe remote world of 'then' but in the very real world of 'now' at a time when China is beginning to stake a serious claim as the world's number-two superpower, second only to the USA, and in July 2001 Beijing won the honour of staging the 2008 Olympic Games, much to the horror of human-rights activists the world over.

There has to be a place for a chastening story like this in *The*

315

Law's Strangest Cases but what is stranger and more troubling than anything is that its place is at entirely the wrong end of the book.

A HAPPY ENDING

GOZO, MALTA, 2001

In autumn 2000 the British judge Lord Justice Ward, sitting in the Court of Appeal, delivered a high-profile and emotive judgment that condemned a three-month-old girl to death. That bald statement suggests a scandalous state of affairs in the British courts, yet it was a landmark decision that was to lead to heart-warming scenes of joyous celebration on the Maltese island of Gozo in June 2001, when the baby girl's twin sister visited her parents' home for the first time.

That homecoming marked the symbolic end of one of the most remarkable affairs in legal history, the case of the Siamese twins Gracie and Rosie Attard, known throughout the legal proceedings as Jodie and Mary.

When building labourer Michaelangelo Attard and his wife Rina heard they were expecting twins they were overjoyed, for Rina's first pregnancy had ended in miscarriage. But when an early scan revealed that the twins were conjoined, arrangements were made for Rina and her husband to travel from Gozo to St Mary's Hospital, Manchester, where experts in that condition would attend to the babies' birth and their subsequent care.

Maltese doctors had advised that the chances of a successful separation were excellent but when the twins were born on 8 August 2000 Manchester doctors had to deliver much more harrowing news.

Gracie and Rosie were joined at the abdomen and spine,

317

sharing an aorta, a bladder and circulatory systems and with their legs splayed at right angles to their single torso. An operation to separate them was indeed possible but, with only one functioning heart and set of lungs between them, the death of one of the babies during the operation was a certainty. It was Rosie, the weaker, who would need to be sacrificed to give the possibility of life to Gracie. Without the operation, both babies would die within a matter of months.

Michaelangelo and Rina Attard were devout Catholics and their beliefs dictated they could not sanction Rosie's death. They decided to let 'God's will' take its course.

St Mary's Hospital, taking a more detached professional view, went to the High Court in an effort to have the operation legally sanctioned and the decision went in their favour despite much-publicised opposition from the parents, the Pro-Life Association and the Catholic Church.

Michaelangelo and Rina Attard decided to challenge the decision and the case duly went to the Court of Appeal, at which Lord Justice Ward, faced with the most difficult legal decision of his career, delivered the historic verdict that permitted the hospital to operate. The ethical, spiritual and medical implications of the decision were immense and Lord Ward described it as 'the greatest dilemma in my life'. Michaelangelo and Rina Attard considered challenging the decision by appeal to the House of Lords but decided, agonisingly for them, to let it stand.

A 22-strong medical team began the twenty-hour operation on Monday, 6 November 2000, and Rosie died on the operating table at 12.20 a.m. on Tuesday. Three-month-old Gracie survived in a critical condition.

That a British court of law should effectively order a baby's death in that way made for unique circumstances, and the Manchester Coroner set aside his established range of verdicts at the inquest: 'Accidental death, misadventure, manslaughter, unlawful killing or an open verdict are all inappropriate to this unique case,' he said. He recorded simply the facts – that 'Rosie Attard died after surgery to separate her from her twin sister'.

Rosie's body was duly taken back to the tiny village of Xaghra in Gozo and buried at the parish church after a service attended by two thousand people, almost ten per cent of the island's population.

Gracie's progress, meanwhile, astonished the medical team at St Mary's and, after ten months in the Manchester hospital, the subject of intense media interest, she flew home to Gozo on Sunday, 17 June 2001, dubbed by the press 'the miracle baby'.

There was a joyous family party and a photo call, which showed a happy and smiling baby girl taking her first visit to the beach with her proud parents: 'Rosie will never be forgotten,' they said, 'but now all our lives will move on.'

The Law's Strangest Cases began with the shameful trial of Jesus Christ, who died on the cross so that others might live. It ends with another controversial case in which an innocent life was sacrificed to give life to another.

Michaelangelo and Rina Attard would surely contend that even with the passage of two thousand years there is an inextricable link between two of the most unusual cases in legal history.

SELECTED BIBLIOGRAPHY

Abbott, Geoffrey. *The Book of Execution.* London, Headline, 1994

Beltrami, Joseph. *The Defender.* East Kilbride, M&A Thomson, 1988

Bingham, Richard. *Modern Cases on Negligence.* London, Sweet & Maxwell, 1978

Bland, James. *True Crime Diary Volume 1.* London, Futura, 1987

Bland, James. *True Crime Diary Volume 2.* London, Macdonald, 1988

Bland, James. *Crime Strange But True.* London, Futura, 1991

Campbell, Lord. *Lives of the Chancellors.* London, Murray, 1856

Comyn, James. *Irish at Law.* London, Secker & Warburg, 1981

Curzon, L B. *Dictionary of Law.* London, Pitman, 1996

Fido, Martin. *The Chronicle of Crime.* London, Little, Brown, 1993

Fido, Martin, & Skinner, Keith. *The Official Encyclopedia of Scotland Yard.* London, Virgin, 1999

Fleming, Justin. *Barbarism to Verdict.* Sydney, Angus & Robertson, 1994

Gaute, J H H, & Odell, Robin. *Murder Whatdunit.* London, Harrap, 1982

Gaute, J H H, & Odell, Robin. *The New Murderers' Who's*

Who, London, Headline, 1989

Griffiths, Major Arthur. *Mysteries of Police and Crime.* London, Cassell, 1898

Hamilton, Dick. *Foul Bills and Dagger Money.* London, Cassell, 1979

Hooper, David. *Public Scandal, Odium and Contempt.* London, Secker & Warburg, 1984

Irving, Ronald. *The Law is a Ass.* London, Gerald Duckworth, 1999

Jones, Elwyn. *On Trial.* London, Macdonald & Jane's, 1978

Lock, Joan. *Tales from Bow Street.* London, Robert Hale, 1982

Lock, Joan. *Blue Murder? Policemen Under Suspicion.* London, Robert Hale, 1986

Lustgarten, Edward. *The Judges and the Judged.* London, Odham's Press, 1961

McLynn, Frank. *Famous Trials: Cases That Made History.* London, Chancellor, 1999

Mortimer, John. *The Oxford Book of Villains.* Oxford, OUP, 1992

Pannick, David. *Judges.* Oxford, OUP, 1987

Pannick, David. *Advocates.* Oxford, OUP, 1992

Pile, Stephen. *The Book of Heroic Failures.* London, Routledge & Kegan Paul, 1979

Shaw, Karl. *The Mammoth Book of Oddballs and Eccentrics.* London, Robinson, 2000

Sparrow, Gerald. *The Great Judges.* London, John Long, 1974

Tibballs, Geoff. *Legal Blunders.* London, Robinson, 2000

Tumim, Stephen. *Great Legal Disasters.* London, Arthur Barker, 1983

Warner, Gerald. *Being of Sound Mind: Book of Eccentric Wills.* London, Elm Tree Books. 1980

Winkworth, Stephen. *More Amazing Times.* London, George Allen & Unwin, 1985